UNDERSTANDING

Irène Némirovsky

Margaret Scanlan

The University of South Carolina Press

Published by the University of South Carolina Press
Columbia, South Carolina 29208

www.sc.edu/uscpress

Manufactured in the United States of America

27 26 25 24 23 22 21 20 19 18
10 9 8 7 6 5 4 3 2 1

Library of Congress Cataloging-in-Publication Data
can be found at http://catalog.loc.gov/.

ISBN 978-1-61117-868-5 (cloth)
ISBN 978-1-61117-869-2 (ebook)

This book was printed on recycled paper with
30 percent postconsumer waste content.

To the new members of our family:

Tracy, Shaun, and Caitlin

and to the newest, Theodore Liam and Benjamin Ian

Contents

Series Editor's Preface

Understanding Modern European and Latin American Literature has been planned as a series of guides for undergraduate and graduate students and nonacademic readers. Like the volumes in its companion series Understanding Contemporary American Literature, these books provide introductions to the lives and writings of prominent modern authors and explicate their most important works.

Modern literature makes special demands, and this is particularly true of foreign literature, in which the reader must contend not only with unfamiliar, often arcane artistic conventions and philosophical concepts, but also with the handicap of reading the literature in translation. It is a truism that the nuances of one language can be rendered in another only imperfectly (and this problem is especially acute in fiction), but the fact that the works of European and Latin American writers are situated in a historical and cultural setting quite different from our own can be as great a hindrance to the understanding of these works as the linguistic barrier. For this reason the UMELL series emphasizes the sociological and historical background of the writers treated. The philosophical and cultural traditions peculiar to a given culture may be particularly important for an understanding of certain authors, and these are taken up in the introductory chapter and also in the discussion of those works to which this information is relevant. Beyond this, the books treat the specifically literary aspects of the author under discussion and attempt to explain the complexities of contemporary literature lucidly. The books are conceived as introductions to the authors covered, not as comprehensive analyses. They do not provide detailed summaries of plot because they are meant to be used in conjunction with the books they treat, not as a substitute for study of the original works. The purpose of the books is to provide information and judicious literary assessment of the major works in the most compact, readable form. It is our hope that the UMELL series will help increase knowledge and understanding of European and Latin American cultures and will serve to make the literature of those cultures more accessible.

J.H.

Acknowledgments

I owe a debt to the libraries and institutions where this book was researched and edited: most notably, L'Institut mémoires de l'édition contemporaine, IMEC, whose excellent archives are located at l'abbeye d'Ardenne on the outskirts of Caen in Basse-Normande, France. I also appreciate the hospitality of the University of Notre Dame's Hesburgh Libraries and of my home institution, Indiana University South Bend. Maureen Kennedy directs the interlibrary loan office there with enviable dispatch and enthusiasm. A writer searching for a long-out-of-print pamphlet of Vichy propaganda could have no better champion.

As always, I am grateful to supportive colleagues and family for their good sense, encouragement, and cheer. I would particularly like to thank my two favorite historians, Roy Schreiber and Micheline Nilsen, for their many lively discussions of topics such as French anti-Semitism and collaboration. My husband, John, has read every draft of every chapter and made incisive comments on them all. A husband who asks questions over breakfast such as "So what really *was* a Vichy novel?" cannot always be assured of a warm reception, as John knows to his sorrow. But in the end he almost always turns out to have been right, as he also knows. He is so much a part of my writing process that I sometimes take him for granted, and I am grateful to him for this and so much more.

A Note on Texts

Anyone who studies Irène Némirovsky is indebted to Olivier Philipponnat. He is coauthor with Patrick Lienhardt of *The Life of Irène Némirovsky* (Knopf, 2010) as well as editor of the two-volume edition of Némirovsky's complete works, published by Livre de poche in 2011. In addition to the annotated French texts of Némirovsky's fiction, the *Oeuvres complètes* is accompanied by a scholarly introduction, a fifty-five-page chronology that includes a literary history and genealogy dating from 1847 to 2010, and a series of "notices" that provide valuable historical context and citations from reviews published in Némirovsky's lifetime, as well as interpretative insights.

Throughout this book, *The Life of Irène Némirovsky* is cited as PL. The complete works are cited as *OC* 1 and *OC* 2. Because this series is intended for the general reader, I have used the recent English translations published by Vintage International, all but one the work of Sandra Smith. Where a published translation is not available, I have used the *Oeuvres complètes* and provided my own. In a very few places, I have identified an alternative to the published translation to support a critical argument. English titles for Némirovsky's novels are used whenever a translation is available; otherwise titles are provided in French.

Chronology

1903	Birth of Irène Némirovsky in Kiev, Ukraine, on FEBRUARY 11. Only child of Leonid Némirovsky and Anna Margoulis. Father is a banker and financier.
1905	OCTOBER 18: Pogroms against Jews in Kiev and Odessa. Irène is hidden behind a bed by the cook, Maria, an Orthodox cross around her neck.
1906	FEBRUARY: Attends carnival in Nice, France. Her oldest memory.
1910–1914	Family lives in prestigious neighborhood in Kiev, with numerous trips to France. Stays in Paris, Côte d'Azur, Côte Basque, and spa towns, including Vichy.
1914	Némirovsky family moves to St. Petersburg. AUGUST 1: Germany declares war on Russia. AUGUST 18: St. Petersburg renamed Petrograd.
1917	FEBRUARY: Uprisings in Petrograd. Czar Nicholas abdicates. Némirovskys move to Moscow. OCTOBER 25: Russian Revolution. Bolsheviks take over government. DECEMBER: Russian banking system nationalized. DECEMBER 15: Russia signs armistice with Central Powers.
1918	JANUARY: Némirovskys flee to Finnish border town, Mustamäki, and move into a boarding house with other refugees from Russia. APRIL: Fleeing Finnish civil war, Némirovskys move to Helsinki. NOVEMBER 11: Armistice between France and Germany.
1919	MARCH: Family moves to Stockholm. JULY: Némirovskys take a furnished apartment in Paris. Irène enrolls at the Sorbonne.
1921	Irène receives undergraduate degree in Russian letters from the Sorbonne.
1922	Maternal grandparents arrive in France. JULY: Irène receives a certificate in Russian language and literature from the Sorbonne. OCTOBER: She enrolls in the new comparative literature program.

1924 Irène receives a "certificate of advanced studies in comparative literature" from the Sorbonne. DECEMBER 31: She meets Michel Epstein, son of an exiled Russian banker.

1926 FEBRUARY: *The Misunderstanding* published by Fayard. JULY 31: Marriage to Michel Epstein in a Jewish religious ceremony followed by a civil ceremony. Begins first draft of *David Golder.*

1927 Fayard publishes "L'Enfant génial" (no English translation, "The Child Prodigy").

1928 Fayard publishes *L'Ennemie* (no English translation, *The Enemy*).

1929 FEBRUARY: Fayard publishes *The Ball*. NOVEMBER 9: Daughter, Denise France Catherine Epstein born. Nurse Cécile Mitaine, native of Issy-l'Évêque, engaged. DECEMBER 7: Bernard Grasset, publisher, accepts *David Golder.*

1930 JANUARY: *David Golder* published to high critical acclaim: André Maurois compares the author to Proust. MAY: Julien Duvivier adapts *David Golder* for film, his first with a soundtrack. SEPTEMBER: Grasset republishes *The Ball*. DECEMBER 26: Premier of dramatic version of *David Golder* in Paris. The play has a short run.

1931 JANUARY 14: Death of Iona Margoulis, maternal grandmother. MARCH 6: Film premier of *David Golder* attended by well-known writers Paul Morand and Colette. Film receives positive reviews. JUNE: Musical version of *The Ball* filmed. Léon Némirovsky suffers massive losses when Swedish magnate Ivar Kreuger refuses to come to his aid. DECEMBER: Grasset publishes *Snow in Autumn*.

1932 MARCH 12: Ivar Kreuger found dead in Paris, an apparent suicide. SEPTEMBER16: Death of Léon Némirovsky.

1933 Hitler comes to power in Germany. Grasset publishes *The Courilof Affair* to discouraging reviews. OCTOBER: Signs a twenty-year contract with Albin Michel.

1934 *Le Pion sur l'èchiquier* (no English translation, *The Pawn on the Chessboard*). JANUARY 8: Suicide of infamous Jewish-Ukrainian financier Alexander Stavisky. FEBRUARY 6: Anti-parliamentary, anti-Semitic riots in Place de la Concorde. Fifteen demonstrators killed by police. Premier Daladier forced to resign. Anti-Semitic forces revive (Action Française, Croix-de-Feu, Jeunesse Patriote). MAY 30: Highly negative review of *Le Pion sur l'échiquier* by right-wing novelist Robert Brasillach, previously favorable to Némirovsky, in *Action française* journal.

1935 *The Wine of Solitude.* JULY 5: Interview with Jewish newspaper in which she says she would have written *David Golder* very differently after Hitler. SEPTEMBER 30: Denise Epstein receives French citizenship; Irène reapplies for naturalization.

1936 MARCH 7: Germans march into the Rhineland, occupied by French under terms of the Treaty of Versailles. No military opposition. JUNE 5: Léon Blum, a socialist, becomes France's first Jewish Prime Minister. MAY: *Jezebel.* René Doumic of the *Revue de deux mondes,* who had supported her application for naturalization, rejects the story "Fraternity" as "anti-Semitic."

1937 MARCH 20: Birth of second daughter, Elisabeth Léone.

1938 SPRING: *La Proie* (no English translation, *The Prey*). MARCH 11: Anschluss (Germans take over Austria). SEPTEMBER 30: England, France, Italy, and Germany sign the Munich Accords, authorizing Germany to take over German-speaking sections of Czechoslovakia. NOVEMBER 9: In Germany, Kristallnacht (brutal pogroms and wide-scale arrests of Jews). In France, a decree-law limits the naturalization of foreign-born inhabitants. DECEMBER 11: Decree-law authorizes the creation of internment camps for undesirable aliens.

1939 *Deux* (no English translation, *Two*). *Le Maître des Âmes* serialized in *Gringoire,* an anti-Semitic journal. FEBRUARY 2: Irène, Michel, and the two Epstein daughters are baptized. MARCH 15: German troops occupy the remaining independent areas of Czechoslovakia. AUGUST 23: Germany and the Soviet Union sign a ten-year mutual nonaggression pact. SEPTEMBER 1: Germany invades Poland. SEPTEMBER 3: France declares war on Germany. Denise and Elisabeth are sent to stay with their nurse's mother in Issy-l'Évêque.

1940 *Dogs and Wolves.* MAY 13: German invasion. Collapse of French Third Republic. Némirovskys in Issy-l'Évêque with their children. Refused permission to return to Paris. JUNE 22: Surrender of France. JULY 10: Parliament votes to give full power to Marshall Philippe Pétain, who establishes capital of État Français (the French State) at Vichy. France dismembered, with Alsace-Lorraine incorporated into Germany; most of the North, including Paris, occupied by Germans; central and southern areas controlled by Pétain's Vichy government. SEPTEMBER 27: Census of Jews. All foreigners "redundant to the economy" subject to internment. OCTOBER 3: Vichy government proclaims Jewish code. Jews are barred from military, civil service, journalism, film, theater, and education. "Surplus Jews" excluded from professions. Publishers and journals banned from publishing Jewish writers. Némirovsky continues to write but can be published only under pseudonyms.

1941 APRIL 26: Jewish bank accounts frozen. JUNE 2: Second Jewish codes establish more rigid definitions of Jewishness; extend ban on Jewish business from Occupied Zone to Vichy Zone. Jewish quotas in universities: 3 percent, professional schools; 2 percent, liberal arts. First general round-ups of Jews begin.

1942 MARCH 27: First deportations of Jews from Drancy internment camp to Auschwitz. JULY 13: French police arrest Irène in Issy-L'Évêque; she is taken first to Pithiviers, then Drancy. JULY 16–17: Eleven thousand Jews rounded up in Paris and detained in the Winter Bicycling Stadium. July 17: Irène deported to Auschwitz. AUGUST 19: Irène dies at Auschwitz, possibly of typhus. She is thirty-nine. OCTOBER 9: Michel Epstein arrested. German officer gives Denise and Elisabeth forty-eight hours to get away. NOVEMBER 6: Michel Epstein deported to Auschwitz, where he is sent to the gas chambers on arrival. Julie Dumot puts Elisabeth and Denise in Catholic boarding school in Bordeaux, using false names. NOVEMBER 10: Germans occupy Vichy Zone.

1944 FEBRUARY: Conditions deteriorate, and Julie Dumot takes the children from school, where they move between temporary shelters and experience bombardments. AUGUST 28: Bordeaux is liberated; Elisabeth and Denise return to school in September.

1945 Guardians, including publisher Albin Michel and Banque du Nord, agree to provide for children's support and education until they are of legal age.

1946 *The Life of Chekhov* published in French by Albin Michel.

1947 Albin Michel publishes *All Our Worldly Goods.*

1957 Albin Michel publishes *The Fires of Autumn.*

1992 Daughter, Elisabeth Gilles, publishes *Le Mirador: Mémoires rêvés.* Translated by Marina Harss as *Le Mirador: Dreamed Memories of Irène Némirovsky by Her Daughter* (New York Review of Books, 2011).

1996 Elisabeth Gilles dies of cancer.

2002 Denise Epstein delivers transcribed manuscript of *Suite Française* to Denoël.

2004 *Suite Française* published. Novel wins Prix Renaudot for 2004, a prize normally reserved for a living author.

2006 Sandra Smith's translation of *Suite Française*. Smith goes on to translate eleven more of Némirovsky's novels.

2013 APRIL 1: Denise Epstein dies.

2014 British film of *Suite Française*, directed by Saul Dibbs.

Introduction

Published in 2004, Irène Némirovsky's *Suite Française* became one of the best-selling novels of the decade. The original French edition won the prestigious Renaudot prize, selling over 640,000 copies ("*Suite* Smell of Success"). Sandra Smith's English translation won the French-American and Florence Gould Translation Prize for 2006 and the PEN/Book-of-the-Month Club Translation Prize in 2007. By January 2014 over 2 million copies of this translation had been sold, and on March 15, 2015, a film adaptation directed by Saul Dibbs was released (Marle; "Fall Festival Preview"). What drew so many people to these stories set in the early 1940s, during the German invasion and occupation of France? Riveting events, surely, including the mass exodus of Parisians who flood the roads in June 1940, blocking the progress of their own army as they run out of gas and food and dodge German bombers. The author's spot-on characterizations, her flashes of sarcastic wit directed at a cast of characters ranging from famous writers and rich industrialists to pious clergy and factory workers, jostling against each other as they seek shelter in the same ditch, surely played a part. And so did a vivid love story featuring a Nazi officer and the wife of a French POW, which is thwarted when the young woman experiences an uncharacteristic surge of patriotism and ends when Hitler orders the Wehrmacht to invade Russia.

The additional knowledge that the author, whose story is briefly recounted in the preface, had been murdered at Auschwitz in 1942 added its own note of poignancy. Every copy of the novel, either in English or French, includes this information, which will seem to some like essential background. On the other hand, one of Némirovsky's harshest critics has accused the publishers of a cynical marketing ploy intended to increase sales, either by creating sympathy for its author or by framing the book, which has no Jewish characters and never strays outside the fictional French village of its setting, as a Holocaust novel.[1] But the history of the *Suite Française*'s manuscript carries its own drama, too.

Irène Némirovsky left the manuscript at home when she was arrested; her husband, who was arrested some three months later, packed it in a small suitcase with instructions to his older daughter, Denise Epstein, to preserve it at all costs. She did so but made no effort to find a publisher for it until 2002. For years she believed that the manuscript, written in almost illegibly small handwriting, was a personal journal; when she first opened it in 1975, she found reading it "too painful." Years later, a flood prompted her to safeguard the manuscript; transcribing it with the aid of a magnifying glass, she discovered that it was a novel. Because the manuscript was unfinished, Epstein hesitated to publish it, thinking that to do so might be a betrayal of her mother. By the time the editor at Denoël "recognized its importance both as a historical document and a literary masterpiece," the once best-selling author had been forgotten by all except her family members and a handful of specialists ("Denise Epstein").[2]

And the question readers immediately asked—"Who was Irène Némirovsky?"—proved to be much more elusive than anyone picking up a copy of *Suite Française* in 2006 could have imagined. Indeed, it will take a whole book to answer this question. Approaching Irène Némirovsky requires us to ask questions about French history and about the identity crises emigration and the experience of bigotry provoke. Certainly it leads us into the problematic process by which fictions filter and shape realities, whether historical or psychological. And we might as well concede at the outset that our answers will never satisfy everyone.

So to begin with the simple facts: Irène Némirovsky was born into a financially successful Jewish family in 1903 in Kiev. When she was two years old, a family maid put a Christian cross around her neck to protect her from a raging pogrom. The family soon moved to St. Petersburg, a city "beyond the Pale," to which Jews were traditionally confined in czarist Russia.[3] As readers of Tolstoy know, upper-class Russian families often spoke French at home; and as a French governess was hired early on, Irène grew up speaking fluent French. Then, too, her family frequently vacationed in Paris or the South of France; France was a living culture with which she could engage directly, not just a place to read about in books.

The Russian Revolution erupted in St. Petersburg when Irène was fourteen years old; her father moved his family to Moscow for safety. But, of course, Moscow was no refuge for a Jewish financier after the Communists won, and in January 1918 the family moved again, this time to Finland. Russia, however, had ruled Finland for over a century (1809–1917), and the revolution was in full swing there as well; some of the worst violence the author saw occurred in Finland. The family moved from the small town of Mustamäki to Helsinki and from there to Stockholm. Shortly after the end of World War I, the Némirovskys resettled in France, where they intended to remain. The news coming from the Russian Civil War, in which at least fifty thousand Jewish people died in pogroms for which Communist Reds as well as czarist Whites were responsible, was enough to discourage any thought of returning home.[4]

So childhood established a pattern that would persist: Irène Némirovsky lived out a mostly privileged, upper-middle-class existence against a background of violent politics. The pogrom from which the Christian maid protected Irène as a small child was one of 657 in Russia during the period October 1905 to January 1906 (Budnitskii 38). When she was ten, Menahem Mendel Beilis, a Jewish resident of Kiev, was indicted for the "ritual murder" of a thirteen-year-old Christian boy. Though Beilis was acquitted, the prosecution's claims shocked many Europeans; clearly, in twentieth-century Russia the old blood libel, the medieval claim that innocent Christian blood is a key ingredient in Passover matzos, was still widely credited (Budnitskii 31).

Anti-Semitism also reached virulent levels in France when in 1894 Alfred Dreyfus, a Jewish army captain, was falsely accused of spying for Germany and sent to Devil's Island. The anti-Semitic Action Française movement, which had helped whip up public hysteria, appeared defeated when Dreyfus was acquitted in 1906. But it remained a force in French politics, reviving from time to time—in 1934, for example, when the Jewish financier Alexandre Stavisky committed suicide just as the police arrived to arrest him for fraud. As Hitler tightened his grip on Germany, Jewish refugees flowed into France, and their numbers, coupled with the continuing economic depression, made the native French more susceptible to Action Française's views. By the time the Germans invaded in 1940, homegrown anti-Semitism was already thriving, promoted in popular daily newspapers and even in influential literary journals.

Family Dynamics

Of equal importance to understanding Irène Némirovsky is her family history. Unlike many Russian émigrés, her father, Léon, quickly recovered his fortune in France. His wife, Fanny, beautiful, fashionable, and luxurious, vacationed for weeks with her lovers on the French Riviera; nothing about her was maternal. Irène, an only child, was largely left to the care of a governess, though occasionally subject to her mother's tirades. One of Fanny's chief concerns was concealing any signs of her own aging; thus she insisted on dressing Irène as a child well into adolescence, discouraged her marriage, and advised abortion on learning that the young couple were expecting their first baby. Openly unfaithful in her youth, the older Fanny took to hiring gigolos, decorating her bedroom as if it were a bordello, and indulging in the tastes of the Hollywood elite of her era. Yes, the narrator of Élisabeth Gille's *Mirador: Dreamed Memories of Irène Némirovsky by her Daughter* would admit to a friend, the stories about her mother bathing in donkey's milk were true (133).

This unhappy family, so crucial to Némirovsky's development, offered nothing of the celebrated warmth of the Jewish home. Irène not only had no religious education, but she was never introduced to the rich cultural legacy of the *shtetl* or to Jewish spirituality, as evoked in Isaac Peretz's Prince of the Ghetto stories, in so many mid-twentieth-century American accounts of Jewish immigrant life on New York's East Side, and even, in musical-theater homage, by *Fiddler on the Roof*.

Léon Némirovsky was a much warmer human being than his wife. But he was a workaholic whose business affairs often required travel, and as he grew older, he also developed a passion for gambling. At both work and play, he took enormous risks with money; the brilliant successes that marked his early career were followed by major losses before his death in 1932. Irène clearly loved him, but he did not oversee her day-to-day life. That role was played by "Zézelle," Irène's gentle French governess, "whom I loved as a mother" (PL 58). One can never entirely separate Irène's love of the French language and culture, her idealization of French civilization as the guarantor of human rights and the guardian of high culture, from this primary attachment of her childhood. Sadly, Zézelle committed suicide in 1917, perhaps because Fanny had dismissed her; the war at home and the unsettled atmosphere of St. Petersburg must have contributed to her despair.

It would be difficult to find someone else who hated her mother with the intensity that Irène demonstrated in her letters, her notebooks, and, repeatedly, her published fiction. This is a nearly pathological emotion, at odds with the well-mannered and charming young women her contemporaries described; it does not jibe easily with her measured writing style, her preference for irony and observation over sensational incident, or even with the many smiling pictures of the author with her two daughters, Denise and Élisabeth. Perhaps as a mother she modeled herself on Zézelle. But something uncharacteristically lurid and disturbing creeps in whenever Fanny Némirovsky emerges in her daughter's comments or when we read about one of her fictional avatars, variously labeled "the enemy," "the monster," or "Jezebel." Irène Némirovsky spoke elegant French and was at home in polite society, but a sense of ruthless drives and violence lurking beneath polished surfaces is never far away.

After the Némirovskys settled in Paris, Irène enrolled at the Sorbonne, where she received degrees in comparative literature and Russian. Before and during her university years, Irène led an active social life, both in Paris and on the Riviera, where the family vacationed. The many scenes in her novels set among the idle rich as they dance, gamble, or drink in seaside resorts reflect her own experience, as well as her observations of her parents. At age twenty-three, in 1926, she married Michel Epstein, the son of another Russian Jewish family that had immigrated to Paris. Michel worked for a bank, but he was not the successful, risk-taking financier her father had been. A respected manager, he used his fluent German in a "French and foreign affairs department" that was created to "prevent another war" (PL 123). His salary was often lower than his wife's income from her writing.

Early Fame

Irène had been writing poems and stories since mid-adolescence, publishing her first magazine story under a pseudonym in 1921; her first short novel, *Le Malentendu (The Misunderstanding)*, appeared in a literary review in 1924 and was published as a book two years later. As a young married woman, she set aside daily periods for writing. Shortly before her daughter Denise was born on November 29, 1929, she completed the manuscript of her first best-seller, *David Golder,* and dispatched it to Bernard Grasset, the publisher of Marcel Proust, among others. She sent the manuscript under the name Epstein, in care of General Delivery, Paris-Lourdes. The story is that the enthusiastic first reader passed the manuscript on to Grasset, who stayed up all night reading it and dispatched a letter to "M. Epstein," inviting him to his office to sign a contract.

David Golder has many autobiographical elements, but what struck its readers initially was its insider's look at the world of finance, of speculation on oil markets, and the sordid machinations of outsiders scheming to accumulate wealth. It was a man's world, and the publisher, or so the legend goes, was astonished to discover that its author, when she turned up in his office, was a young woman apologizing for keeping him waiting three weeks: "I've just had a baby" (PL 151). By December 5 the book was in print, promoted by the astute publisher as "a fictional creation of great merit . . . which recalls *Père Goriot*" (PL 152). As it turned out, Némirovsky had not yet read Balzac's famous masterpiece about a father ruined by his daughters' greed, but the comparison seemed apt to many reviewers. Appearing so soon after Black Friday and the Wall Street crash of 1929, the book had the added merit of being topical. It was adapted into a play that opened in December 1930, with only limited success, and then into one of the new "talking films," premiering on the Champs-Élysées on March 6, 1931. The film, like the translations in languages ranging from English and German to Hungarian and Japanese, was a success. Throughout the 1930s, Némirovsky was a well-known figure on the Parisian literary scene, the subject of admiring reviews from such diverse figures as the Jewish novelist André Maurois and Robert Brasillach, the fascist literary journalist who would be executed in 1946 for his collaboration with the Nazis.

Jewish Readers in the 1930s and the Question of Anti-Semitism

The near-universal acclaim for *David Golder* was not echoed in the Jewish press. Golder is a Russian Jew who has schemed and scraped his way to wealth in France; his first act in the novel is to drive his business partner and old friend to suicide. His equally avaricious wife, Gloria, is an aging social climber with a series of lovers. In other words, the characters and even some of the novel's language draw on stereotypes; one does not easily overlook a description of a character whose nose is "enormous and hooked, like the nose of an old Jewish moneylender" (58). One might counter that David Golder evolves far beyond those initial stereotypes or that the "hooked nose" observation is attributed to Gloria, a character intended to repel. But one cannot erase a history that includes Shylock or a phrase that might have been at home in *Der Stürmer.*

We will explore *David Golder* later, at more length. But let us at least say that the novel introduces a subject that Némirovsky explores almost obsessively, the evolution of ambition in a person born into poverty and exclusion. Némirovsky was fascinated with the question of how people manage to rise in the world, what qualities they need to succeed, and how the single-minded pursuit of money and success damages an individual or society consumed with it. She understood that an economy driven by unregulated ambition will have political and cultural repercussions, and was convinced that her knowledge of the private lives of successful bankers and speculators offered sociological and political insight.

But she was also increasingly distressed that outsiders associated sharp financial practices with Jewish people, as if they sprang from some genetic abnormality rather than from the social conditions she understood so well. So she retold the story of a man ruined by his ambition, in two cases making sure to avoid labeling him as Jewish. In *La Proie* (*The Prey,* 1938) the predator, Jean-Luc Daguerne, is a middle-class Frenchman fallen on hard times, who rises first through a conventionally opportune marriage and then through his association with a minister in the French government. In *Le Maître des âmes* (*Master of Souls,* 1939), the desperate outsider is a society doctor who gets rich playing on the susceptibilities of wealthy neurotics.[5] Dario Asfar is not Jewish but "Mediterranean" or "Levantine," words that unfortunately were often taken as euphemisms for "Jewish." And so close to the old stereotypes does the hero's characterization remain that even Susan Suleiman, Némirovsky's most ardent defender against charges of anti-Semitism, has observed that "although he is not explicitly identified as a Jew, he is clearly portrayed as one" (Suleiman, "Jewish Question" 23).

But turning economic ambition into a universal failing or attributing it to Christians because they were not stereotyped as pushy or scheming did not satisfy Némirovsky. As anti-Semitism grew more politically powerful, she seemed driven to explore Jewish characters, to show how their historical experiences had damaged them, shaped them into survivors who might, whatever their repellant features, be fully understood. In her last novel published during her lifetime, *The Dogs and the Wolves,* which appeared just as the Germans were invading France, she takes the reader back to Ukraine, describing the terror of two Jewish children who survive a pogrom by hiding in an attic. The novel takes us forward into an unspecified future in which one of these children is a Jewish refugee living in central Europe with her newborn son.

In her lifetime, the book received only one review and had limited sales. Vichy newspapers did not review Jewish novelists, and the Vichy regime soon saw to it that they did not publish. Although lacking booming sales, *The Dogs and the Wolves,* like *Suite Française,* was fated to be read outside its own time. Here it will be read attentively to see how this last novel with Jewish characters portrays the persecution of Jews in czarist times but also to see how the expulsion of two of its protagonists from France reflected the politics of the 1930s, as well as the hostility to foreign Jews that preceded the German invasion. Also important are the conflicting responses of present-day readers, some of whom insist on seeing this novel, too, as anti-Semitic, while others see it as offering a new vision of a Jewish future, freed from the compulsive cycle of persecution and revenge.

From Manners to History

Throughout her career, Némirovsky wrote both novels and stories in a genre often referred to as "domestic fiction" or the "novel of manners." In both France and England, its earliest examples appear in the eighteenth century, when the home was a woman's sphere; most were written by women; and they were usually marketed to women. They take place in the private home and center on personal relationships: marriage and courtship, yes, but also domestic crises arising from a sudden loss of income, a serious illness, a death in the family. Even in the late 1930s, when she was well known, Némirovsky occasionally published in *Marie-Claire,* the still-popular French women's magazine. Many of us grew up reading novels set on whaling ships, or in the trenches, or on a bear hunt, stories about men in mostly all-male settings, and were taught to read them for "universal" truths. In the same era, the adjectives "domestic," "women's," or, worse, "sentimental" marked limitation and carried more than a whiff of condescension. Books set in the home, dealing with marriage and children and domestic economic pressures, were about the private lives of women and had no implications for the public worlds of commerce and politics. They were not universal.

Today let us hope that we have more generous ideas about women and their experiences; certainly poststructural theory has urged us to be suspicious of people claiming that their experiences are "universal." Feminist critics such as Susan Gubar and Sandra Gilbert have instructed us that the madwoman in the attic has her own history: the first Mrs. Rochester, raving in the night, occasionally breaking out to set fires, is a Creole. That is, she is a product of British colonialism, of slavery and deceit about racial intermarriage. Thus *Jane Eyre,* although certainly a love story and "domestic," has a political dimension, and once we have opened that attic door, we are free to see orphanages that starve little girls and even the marriage customs of Victorian England as politically and historically conditioned. As Matthew Arnold so aptly pronounced, this "children's classic" is in fact full of "hunger, rebellion, and rage."

Given Irène Némirovsky's highly troubled relationship with her mother, we should not find it astonishing that her fiction, when set in the private home among mothers and daughters, is anything but serene. But we do well to remember that angry mothers, like the first Mrs. Rochester, have their own history. When Némirovsky tells us a story about a little girl who is scalded to death after her mother, intent on an assignation with her lover, leaves her alone in a kitchen where a huge pot of water is boiling, we will think, as we are probably intended to, of all those myths and fairy tales where mothers disguised as evil stepmothers abuse their daughters cruelly. But we also need to remember that we are living in a historical world, where many upper-class children were left almost exclusively in the care of servants, where women were encouraged to value themselves for their appearance, dress, and appeal to men, rather than to develop their intelligence and see their possibilities as full actors in a social and political world. This world, taken for granted by most of its inhabitants in 1910, fell victim to a cataclysmic revolution eight years later. The connection we sense between, on the one hand, a mother's emotional violence and a child's agonizing death and, on the other, the seething anger of Russian revolutionaries faced with savage czarist repression is fully historical and political.

Yet unfortunately some of the stereotypes about domestic fiction persist in the claim, rather frequently made, that Irène Némirovsky was not a political or historical novelist. Nathan Bracher, in an otherwise insightful discussion of the ethical dimension of *Suite Française,* nonetheless concludes that Némirovsky "does not seem capable of understanding the war and the Occupation in terms of intellectual or political history as does [Jean] Guéhenno," author of the *Journal of the Dark Years, 1940–1944* (258). Guéhenno was a professor of literature who lived through the war in Paris, where his frank espousal of free thought, anchored in the tradition of Montaigne and Voltaire, whom he taught enthusiastically, annoyed the authorities. But while Némirovsky's fiction lacks Guéhenno's systematic discursiveness, it embodies a historical consciousness every bit as politically and intellectually sophisticated as his.

To read Némirovsky well, we need to think about how historical consciousness can be embodied in a novel that never reads like a history textbook or a newspaper editorial. Perhaps the first step is broadening our idea of how history is written. All of us are familiar with history as a narrative of Great Men and Famous Battles and Important Legislation; this is the version we studied in high school, and we would be lost without it. But even in Némirovsky's lifetime, her contemporaries in history departments were interested in reshaping and rewriting this traditional practice. France was home to the *Annales,* an influential journal whose historians rejected both *l'histoire événementielle,* the chronicle of military and political events, and a history of ideas focused on a few brilliant thinkers. Those drawn to what was later dubbed the "history of mentalities" wished to explore the "collective, automatic, and repetitive" elements that shape a "particular view of the world" that people of an era share. Jacques Le Goff called it "what Caesar shared with his soldiers . . . and Columbus with his sailors," the unconscious assumptions that we do not even recognize because our world takes them for granted (Chartier 56).

Natalie Zemon Davis's *The Return of Martin Guerre* (1983) provides a useful example of a history of mentalities. Relying on court records and notarial contracts to supplement two long-forgotten texts published in 1561, Davis tells the story of an imposter who appeared in a Languedoc village in 1556, claiming to be the Martin Guerre who disappeared several years earlier. Martin's wife Bertrande welcomed him back, bore him two children, and fiercely defended him when Martin's uncle had him tried for fraud. Only when the real Martin Guerre turned up and his sister had verified his identity did Bertrande admit that she had been deceived. The imposter was hanged, and Bertrande and the real Martin resumed their life together. Two popular accounts of the case were published in 1561, and Montaigne speculated about the judge's "boldness" in sentencing the imposter to death. The story fascinated Davis, not because either of the Martins was important in his own right, but because of what it tells us about implicit views of identity shared by sixteenth-century peasants and the better-educated classes responsible for adjudicating their debates. Moreover, Davis, who used novelistic devices of suspense to develop her courtroom drama, also emphasized ambivalence, uncertainty, and complexity as conditions that afflict contemporary historians. As Davis later pointed out, the question of where "reconstruction" ends and "invention" begins in a historical text is central to her book, an "analogy on the uncertain border between self-fashioning and lying built into my narrative" ("On the Lam" 572).

A similar impulse can be found developing in England and the United States, as historians struggled to recover what is sometimes called "history from below": the history of the working class or of enslaved Africans or of women. Such people did not lead battles, rule nations, or draft legislation; and so they had been largely ignored in school history texts. And when a historian decided to write about slaves, for example, it would do no good to go looking for their books, their letters, and what the leading newspapers had to say about them. A whole new body of information became telling: ship's logs, auction notices, records of corn and cotton harvested and sold, music sung, oral stories passed from one generation to another.

Jean Guéhenno: Wartime Journal of a Public Figure

When Jean Guéhenno wrote about the occupation, he was living in Paris, regularly meeting friends, including the novelist François Mauriac and the editor and publisher Jean Paulhan, who were major intellectual figures of his time. When a right-wing acquaintances sneered that the former (and Jewish) prime minister, Léon Blum, was "doubtless in London," he assured him that on the contrary he "spent the morning with Blum the day before yesterday" (7). The fascist editor of *La Nouvelle Revue Française,* Pierre Drieu la Rochelle, sent him copies of his new books and invited him to contribute an article on Voltaire. Guéhenno refused and was disappointed when Paul Valéry allowed one of his poems to be published there. When he listened to a speech read by the Vichy minister of labor, Marcel Déat, he remarked that "he has the same Auvergne accent that he had twenty years ago," when they both attended L'École Normale Supérieur (62). He was frequently in public to attend the latest Jean-Paul Sartre play or to visit the Museum of Man, where he met Jean Blanzat, who, as he mentioned only in his postwar preface, was then a key figure in the Resistance group associated with that institution. He was a dissident, in real danger, but still a man of his time living at the center of political and cultural activity.

When Irène Némirovsky wrote about the occupation, she was living in a small village, forbidden to travel to Paris, to practice any profession, or even to attend a concert or play. As in Germany and at first directly because of the actions of the Vichy government, Jews had been driven out of public life. So of course she did not share Guéhenno's connections to institutions and movements or his anguished reflections on his generation's responsibility for the defeat. Her only publications would appear under a pseudonym; then that avenue was also cut off. While she retained a warm correspondence with André Sabatier, the literary director at her publisher, Albin Michel, most of her famous friends had abandoned her.

If Guéhenno was someone the occupiers wished to co-opt, she was someone they planned to exterminate. As fluent in German as Guéhenno was, well educated and as much at home in the French literary tradition as he, she had to occupy an entirely marginal position. The French authorities would demote him, ensuring that he was teaching twelve-year-olds by 1943; but they would arrest her and turn her over to the occupiers. What would any of us do in her position? We would probably stay quiet and avoid attracting attention. But since the people around us, not just the Germans but the Vichy French as well, had the power of life and death over us, we would watch them closely, noting nuances in their speech and gestures, assessing their character, their reliability, their unstated intentions. No irony, such as the contradiction between a poster showing a beaming German officer handing out sandwiches to small children and one caricaturing Jews and their "detestable tyranny," would escape us (*Suite Française* 198).

So when Irène Némirovsky wrote a historical novel, we should expect it to resemble her earlier novels of manners. It would contain sociological, political, and historical information, but only as those topics were reflected in the everyday behavior of ordinary-seeming people. We would not watch the Germans crossing the border from Belgium in their tanks, but we would see a German officer, quartered on a French widow, pacing up and down her carpet, noting that her bookcase and piano were both locked, and finding the French words to ask for the keys. And we would feel her sense of being invaded, of losing the simple power to protect her books and her piano, her culture, as thoroughly as if the German were threatening her with a gun. This is the same history of France as a prison, its values and its pride apparently defeated, that Jean Guéhenno told. But it was told from a different position, through a different sensibility, by an elusive narrator who would not survive.

Chapter 1

Monstrous Mothers

Under "hatred of mother," the index to Philipponnat and Lienhardt's *The Life of Irene Némirovsky* lists fifteen entries. Even without the biography, we might suspect the author's sentiments from the frequency with which mothers in her novels turn into monsters. Némirovsky's earliest novel, *The Enemy,* published under a pseudonym in 1928, uses the word in its feminine form, *L'Ennemie,* as a synonym for mother; "ogress," the synonym for mother in a late story, "L'Ogresse" (1941), is no softer. *The Ball,* a novella, and the novels *Wine of Solitude* and *Jezebel,* all available in English translation, also reprise the theme, transforming a melodramatic tale of adolescent resentment and revenge into substantial works of art.

The historical Fanny Némirovsky served as a model for these fictional mothers, who share many features with the original. This mother, a great beauty, is never motherly. She alternately neglects and abuses her daughter, preferring the company of a series of young lovers; her husband is frequently absent and always occupied with making the fortune that his wife spends extravagantly. He is remarkably tolerant of the lovers and disinclined to interfere in his wife's treatment of their daughter, who may or may not have a loving French governess. Obsessed with remaining young and beautiful, the mother dresses her daughter like a child well into her adolescence. The daughter's sexual maturation precipitates a crisis; in two of Némirovsky's novels, *L'Ennemie* and *Le Vin de Solitude* (*The Wine of Solitude,* 1935), the lover becomes infatuated with the daughter, offering her the prospect of vengeance, of depriving the mother of his attentions and her illusion of youth. In *Jezebel* (1936), which begins with the title figure, a mother, on trial for murder, the backstory of mother and daughter is quite similar. In *The Ball,* the mother only fantasizes about finding a lover, while in "L'Ogresse" a lethal stage mother drains her talented daughter's life. The most significant difference between Fanny Némirovsky and these avatars is that none of them are Jewish.

We have no way of knowing if the infatuation between daughter and lover has a parallel in Irène Némirovsky's life or whether it simply plays out the implications of the family dynamics. She grew up in a household where her mother's sexuality was impossible to ignore, yet where Irène was expected to retain the innocence of childhood into late adolescence. We know that Fanny Némirovsky, who grew up in a poor Jewish family, strove to conceal her social origins while acting out the nouveau riche role her husband's business success made possible. The episodes where Némirovsky's fictional mothers rage at their daughters, belittle them, and occasionally slap them in public are drawn from life. Yet as often as Némirovsky recurs to this unhappy relationship, we notice how many changes she rings on it; she returns not simply to relive grievances but to reshape their context and meaning. We see Némirovsky developing distance from her unhappy childhood and multiplying the meanings her bad mothers suggest.

Since Némirovsky wrote fiction, rather than spilling out her story to a sympathetic bartender or therapist, we also need to recognize that lethal mothers, frequently disguised as stepmothers, have a long history in fairy tales, mythology, and literature. Then, too, once the Fanny Némirovsky story enters a twentieth-century domestic novel, it encounters a literary genre with its own conventions about mothers and families. Examining these will give us a better sense of what Némirovsky's fictional mothers do and mean.

Domestic Fiction: A Brief History

Domestic fiction is set in the home; it is often, though not always, written by women; and its central figure is usually a woman, a Pamela or an Isabel Archer, even when the author, like Henry James or Samuel Richardson, is male. Since the domestic novel arose in the late eighteenth century at roughly the time in which the division of men and women into separate spheres was solidified, we may be tempted to see it as simply reflecting social reality. And we may, if classic examples such as Odysseus traveling the known world while Penelope stays behind with her child, her maids, and her weaving lead us to think of separate spheres as timeless and eternal. Yet we need to remember that the distant past offers many counterexamples: the Cro-Magnon woman gathering while her husband hunted was not a homebody; the traditional farmwife on the prairie, with her garden and her dairy, was not necessarily more restricted to the farm than her husband plowing its fields. While gender roles have always been more fluid than the generalizations we make about them, the Industrial Revolution created the factory as a place where people went out to do many things, such as weaving cloth, which earlier generations had done in the home. At the same time, bureaucratization led to the growth of offices, hospitals, government agencies, and even department stores, where people went out to work instead of working out of the home. And thus the nineteenth century sharpens the distinction between the public world of men and the private world of women.

In an important book, *Desire and Domestic Fiction: A Political History of the Novel* (1987), Nancy Armstrong argues that women and the domestic novels they wrote actively contributed to shaping the perception of gender-defined spheres in the English-speaking world; moreover, they empowered women by doing so. Even though she acknowledges that society hurt women by limiting their political or professional roles, Armstrong stresses the cultural and ideological power nineteenth-century women gained in their homes. In *Jane Eyre* a poor and unconnected woman marries a rich landowner but only after discovering his secrets and resisting his amoral plea that she become his mistress, and then only after he undergoes an ordeal by fire, followed by an amputation and a spell of blindness.

Jane's power is political, according to Armstrong, for "domestic fiction actively sought to disentangle the language of sexual relations from the language of politics and, in so doing, to introduce a new form of political power." Rochester's genealogy, social position, and wealth, traditionally decisive in marriage matters, are trumped by Jane's psychological force and moral insight in a new world in which "only the more subtle nuances of behavior indicated what one was really worth" (4). The Brontës' "literary language . . . allows emotion to overpower convention and become a value in its own right, blotting out all features of political person, place, and event" (197). A woman in her home dominates "over all those objects and practices we associate with private life. To her went authority over the household, leisure time . . . kinship . . . under her jurisdiction the most basic qualities of human identity were supposed to develop." Thus, "to consider the rise of the domestic woman as a major event in political history is not . . . to present a contradiction in terms, but to identity the paradox that shapes modern culture" (3).

Lesley Walker builds on Armstrong's analysis of the ideological implications of domestic fiction in her *A Mother's Love: Crafting Feminine Virtue in Enlightenment France* (2008). Reading novelists generally less well-known abroad than Armstrong's, such as Élisabeth Vigée Lebrun, Stéphanie Félicité de Genlis, and Jeanne-Marie Roland, Walker argues for the significance of their "maternal discourse," which idealizes a wise and benevolent mother who may or may not have corresponded in any direct way with lived experience (23). In Jeanne-Marie Le Prince de Beaumont's enormously popular *Lettres de Madame du Montier . . . à sa Fille* (1756), we see a new mother, "understanding and gentle," whose "love provides the matrix out of which the ethical or virtuous daughter appears" (26). Such mothers flourish in French fiction throughout the second half of the eighteenth century. However, the "virtuous daughter," not only kept safe from "rakes and villains" but persuaded to avoid sexual passion altogether, is not a figure of liberation. Walker sees Madame Germaine de Staël's *Delphine* (1802) as marking the end of this "maternal discourse." Delphine's "suffering is needless and wrong," and her suicide, rather than being romanticized, is seen as scandalous and brutal (191).

So what do *L'Ennemie, The Ball, The Wine of Solitude,* and *Jezebel* have in common with these examples from the past? Certainly we notice familiar features, settings, and themes. In Némirovsky's domestic fiction we find characters in the comfortable settings enjoyed by their earlier counterparts, fashionably dressed and having apparently unlimited leisure for dining, taking tea, or dancing in glittering salons. Personal maturation and growth drive the plot, and though an occasional lurid event takes place, suspense and adventure are missing. Like many of the English domestic novelists, Némirovsky often depicts an outsider making her way into a higher social class. However, unlike Jane Eyre or the Fanny Price of Austen's *Mansfield Park,* Némirovsky's strivers fail to erase the signs of their difference, remaining permanently marked as vulgar or scandalous. Fanny Price deserves Mansfield Park, but when Bella Karol's husband in *The Wine of Solitude* buys the silver of a fleeing aristocrat, we note that its monogrammed initials remain those of the original owner and look out of place in the Karols' cluttered dining room. Though Némirovsky's domestic fictions do not detail business affairs, they show us an often absent, often exhausted husband whose fortunes rise and fall. The process by which money is made and the instability of wealth are more visible than they usually are in, say, Henry James.

But the major difference, which we notice at once, is that the wise and gentle mother Walker describes is replaced by a dangerous figure who fails to nurture her child. Where the heroine of a Brontë or Austen novel is often motherless and therefore lacks maternal guidance, a Némirovsky daughter typically finds in her mother the greatest obstacle to her moral development and emotional health. The daughter who resists, who forges an independent identity, will live and prosper; the daughter who submits will, quite literally, die young.

L'Ennemie and *The Ball* were both published under the pseudonym "Pierre Nerey," the latter a close anagram of "Irene." Though female writers of the nineteenth century used male pseudonyms, such as "George Sand" and "Currer Bell," because, as Charlotte Brontë said, "authoresses are likely to be looked on with prejudice," Némirovsky's motive seems to have been self-protection. She had reason to fear that her mother would recognize herself in the unflattering portraits of Francine Bragance and Rosine Kampf. Némirovsky called *The Ball,* published one year later, the "quintessence of *L'Ennemie*"; we might also think of it as a "distillation," much shorter, tamer, and better crafted than the earlier version—yet, in some significant sense, the same story.

The Enemy

If we imagine a young Irène Némirovsky pouring out her story to a therapist, we will conjure up a narrative more like *L'Ennemie* than any of her other novels. Divided into four parts, each containing five chapters, it reads like one of those undisciplined, sprawling novels of nineteenth-century realism that Henry James called "loose, baggy monsters," even when written by Tolstoy and Dostoevsky. Individual scenes are memorable, such as the one in which Francine is off for a winter stroll with her lover, her ill-dressed and hungry daughters straggling in the background, afraid to interrupt her. The cruelty of her negligence and the indifference of passersby could hardly be more economically conveyed. But the overall effect is of too many melodramatic scenes in succession, with too little attention to tone and motivation; as Olivier Philipponnat puts it, "sounding the depths of her heart, the young novelist only succeeds in exposing a monstrous pool of grief and gall" (*OC* 1: 251).

In this 1928 novel Némirovsky uses the familiar triangle: mother, mother's lover, and father, all seen through the unforgiving eye of a daughter. This time, however, we begin with two daughters, eleven-year-old Gabri and six-year-old Michette. Michette dies dreadfully in the fourth chapter, after she scalds herself by tipping over a giant laundry tub left boiling on the stove. Gabri has briefly left her sister alone and returns to her screams. Although the neighbors summon a doctor, Michette dies before her mother returns home at daybreak. The child's death conveys the point that Francine's behavior is not just self-indulgent but criminally negligent; moreover, the world's indifference to neglected children is reaffirmed when "everyone" pardons her because her grief is so hysterical.

This wholly invented episode, only too transparent in its intention to make the reader share Gabri's "exquisite hatred" of her mother, loses credibility if the reader asks questions (PL 18). Would a doctor in Paris really have failed to report the cause of the child's death? And who set that tub boiling on the kitchen stove? Francine does no housework, and it seems unlikely that a maid would start the laundry and then leave for the day. These problems are not insuperable, but the author's failure to address them suggests that villainizing Francine overcame her normal discipline about preserving probability.

One could raise similar questions, for example, about the family's sudden acquisition of wealth after the First World War, when Gabri's father, Léon (a name he shares with Némirovsky's father), is inexplicably offered what is described only as a "good job in Poland" (*OC* 1: 258). Two years later, he sends a telegram announcing that he will arrive home the next Monday, accompanied by Gabri's young cousin, Charles. When Gabri asks what her cousin is doing with her father in Poland, Francine responds vaguely that Léon had invited him there to make his fortune. She expects the pair to return as poor as when they left, but in fact they are rich, having bought factories the Germans had confiscated during the war at bargain rates and put them back into production.

Since Charles's business role is never clarified, we suspect that he was produced to play an essential domestic role, the mother's lover. Gabri immediately senses the attraction between them, and when Charles moves into the flat below her parents' new home, she knows exactly why. Charles treats her like an encumbrance, remarking that she should be sent to boarding school; Francine, however, has "acquired not only wealth but principles" and insists that her daughter be educated at home with a governess and tutors. Having spent much of her childhood unsupervised, in the streets of a working-class neighborhood, Gabri resents "the tyranny of a teacher who doesn't leave you alone any more than a jailer would, the discipline of a prison" (275).

In this version of the familial story, there is only a much-disliked English governess, Miss Allen; no loving figure based on Zézelle will soften Gabri's life. After she pleads unsuccessfully with her father to find a place where they could be happy together "without mama," she turns to books (291). She is increasingly preoccupied with her "savage and irrational hatred" of Francine and fantasizes about the power her knowledge of the affair gives her. One day she drafts an anonymous poison-pen letter to her father informing him of his wife's unfaithfulness. She writes to relieve her feelings, with no serious intention of sending the letter, but Francine catches her with the draft and snatches it up. She demands to know the source of the letter, so Gabri claims to have found it on the floor and attributes it to Miss Allen.

The discovery of the child's secret writing is a key incident that Némirovsky reprises in *The Wine of Solitude.* It suggests that Gabri, like the child Jane Eyre, always watching from the sidelines where no one notices her, is becoming powerful because she is a knowledgeable witness. Implicitly, she identifies with the morality of a middle-class society by which women like her mother, or Jane's harsh aunt and bullying cousin, are judged deficient. So even though she is a child, her correct observation aligns her with social forces that have real power outside the family; she need not remain helpless forever. Moreover, that Gabri expresses her power through writing suggests a liberating possibility that Némirovsky explores further in *The Wine of Solitude.*

Unfortunately, the invitation to consider these possibilities is weakened by another failure to preserve realism: would even so negligent a mother as Francine be unable to distinguish between the handwriting of her teenage daughter and her daughter's middle-aged English governess? But an excuse for dismissing the governess is needed so that Gabri will once more be unsupervised. She reacts by finding Babette, a teenage confidante with an equally negligent mother, and spending hours at a dancing hall in Pigalle, where she becomes involved with a Russian émigré, Génia Nikitof. Their relationship remains ill-defined for months but, as one might expect, ends badly. Nikitof commits what we would now call date rape, and Gabri is too inexperienced and afraid of attracting attention to call for help. It is a "long struggle, brutal and odious"; and when it is over, she resolves never to return to the dance hall and to break off relations with not only Génia but also Babette (310).

How would we expect an inexperienced teenager to respond to such an ugly experience? Certainly Gabri's decision to remain silent and suffer from unresolved anger is one many young women continue to make. Further, that a neglected child who grew up condemning her mother's promiscuity would blame her for the attack is entirely probable: "This horror, this filth, she would have never known it if her mother had been a real mother" (311). Gabri's response is realistic, even as it slides from pain into persistent revenge fantasies. Lacking adult support, Gabri fails to construct a positive plan to pull herself away from "that need for destruction that an evil passion unleashed in her" (312).

Since Francine's blindness to her daughter includes failure to realize that she is growing up, a plot development is needed to jar insight. Time for another poison-pen letter, this one from Génia Nikitof, who remains infatuated with Gabri and thinks he can blackmail her into a love affair. He follows through on his threat to send Francine the extravagant love letters Gabri had written to him when they first met, and Francine reacts angrily. But Gabri, for once, confronts her mother directly, citing her neglect, bad example, and failure to teach her daughter to distinguish right from wrong. She does not, however, tell her about the rape.

The chief problem in this scene is that the distance between the narrator's and the character's voices collapses, as may happen when a novelist draws on highly charged personal experience. The narrator is the first to label Francine hypocritical, observing that "there is something sadly comic in this sudden horror of lying shown by a woman who had been cheating on her husband for years" (324). When, four pages later, Gabri continues the same line of attack—"of course I lie, you never taught me to tell the truth"—narrator and character have become indistinguishable (328). At this point, then, the novelist's point of view is Gabri's—adolescent, non-ironic, unable to imagine alternatives. Some readers might identify with her and sympathize; most will probably feel themselves tiring of melodrama or even tempted to supply the missing irony and laugh at the purple prose.

Némirovsky briefly introduces the possibility that this hysterical slanging match between daughter and mother will be therapeutic. Francine apologizes and tells Gabri that some women were not meant to be mothers; Gabri, for the first time in her life, buries her head in her mother's shoulder and feels as if an "enormous sac of bile" has burst (333). Yet of course the damage is too great and the exchange too limited to provide real healing. Charles has only to remark to Francine that Gabri is growing up, and Gabri's vague notions of seducing him crystallize into a plan: "Voila! My revenge!" (313).

It is true that she has second thoughts about seducing Charles, particularly when the narrator's observation that "she was more like her mother than she thought" occurs to Gabri herself, wondering about their resemblance (315, 335). This is another potentially acute point that the novel does not develop: Gabri's attempt to use seductive skills learned from her mother to avenge her sister's death and their unhappy childhoods only reveals that she is made of softer stuff. So she behaves seductively with Charles, puts him off for a while, and finally yields. The melodramatic denouement comes when Gabri, waiting for Charles in his hotel room, is surprised by her unsuspecting mother; she has only to see Francine's ravaged face to imagine her voice crying out, "Parricide, parricide!" (350). When Gabri flings herself over the balcony, the stronger woman has the novel's last words, sobbing over her daughter's body, demanding that God tell her why he has struck this blow against her.

The Ball

The Ball, published only a year later, is a remarkably stronger story. Although she still felt the need to publish it under the "Pierre Nerey" pseudonym, Némirovsky edited out much of the melodramatic incident of *L'Ennemie:* the death of the little sister, the poison-pen letters, the governess's dismissal, the daughter's rape, her seduction of her mother's lover, and her subsequent suicide. Instead we have a story where the stakes at first seem much lower: Mme. Rosine Kampf, a socially ambitious mother, plans to stage an elaborately catered ball; her fourteen-year-old daughter, Antoinette, resents her mother's refusal to let her stay up for it and takes her revenge. The awkward shifts in perspective that characterize *L'Ennemie,* where the narrator sometimes seems distinct from Gabri and at other times indistinguishable, are replaced by a tightly controlled narrative voice and an ironic perspective that occasionally permits sympathy with the characters but never identifies with them. This time, rather than being tempted to laugh as lurid events follow too closely on each other or as characters fall into melodramatic cliché, we begin by being amused at a small-scale domestic conflict. Only gradually, as our understanding deepens, do we realize how deeply Rosine has damaged Antoinette and how accurately the daughter has gauged her vengeance. Némirovsky succeeds, as Jane Austen and Henry James often do, by offering us a story of apparently limited scope and gradually encouraging us to hear its resonances.

Like *L'Ennemie, The Ball* is set entirely in Paris; it depicts people who have experienced a great change of fortune in a short time and desire a higher social status than the one their new money automatically confers. A daughter feels unloved, and while her English governess is younger, Antoinette is no fonder of Miss Betty than Gabri was of Miss Allen. Like Gabri, Antoinette considers the regime of the schoolroom and the lessons "slavery, prison"; like Francine, Rosine is deliberately thwarting her daughter's desire to grow up because she fears aging (160). Both works imagine a psychic universe akin to the one we see in a fairy tale such as *Snow White,* where a conviction that only one woman can be beautiful at a time justifies cruelty to a younger rival. Some of the themes of *L'Ennemie* are preserved but muted: Rosine has a promiscuous past but only fantasizes about a young lover; Antoinette frequently thinks about suicide, even once visualizing herself jumping out a window and lying on the street "covered in blood," but such thoughts seem a product of adolescent self-dramatization, not a plan for action (161).

The Ball is focused and economical because it revolves around one episode: Rosine Kampf's plan for a ball and her daughter's sabotage of it. Rosine makes the mistake of forbidding Antoinette to stay up for even fifteen minutes of the ball but has no problem demanding that she address all the invitations, presumably because Miss Betty has taught her genteel penmanship. The scene where the Kampfs and their daughter do the invitations is comic, both revealing the social abyss they are attempting to bridge and the fluid state of fashionable society. Alfred Kampf is Jewish, as his wife is not, and their daughter is raised as Catholic. Of course his Jewishness, like Rosine's working-class origins—she was his secretary—are barriers to social acceptance, but ones that other people have overcome successfully.

So they work out their guest list, cheerfully including someone who was once imprisoned for fraud but now is invited everywhere; an extremely rich woman who was "mixed up . . . in the famous orgies in the Bois de Boulogne," whose husband does business with Alfred; and the Count and Countess Poirier, whom they once knew as Abraham and Rebecca Birnbaum (152).[1] They even include Antoinette's detested piano teacher, Isabelle Cossette, a cousin of theirs; when Antoinette protests, Alfred wonders why "that old madwoman" should be included. But Rosine has a good answer ready: "How do you expect my family to hear about it otherwise?" (156). When the Kampfs finish the invitations, there are 172 of them, and they smile in "weary triumph" at the prospect of an evening spent among so many people they barely know or heartily dislike.

The next day, Antoinette is dispatched to her piano lesson with an invitation for Mademoiselle Isabelle; Rosine sends along Miss Betty to mail the rest of the invitations. But Miss Betty uses the lesson time to meet her young lover, and when Antoinette encounters the two together, Miss Betty, to extend her rendezvous by a few minutes, sends Antoinette off to the postbox. Seeing Miss Betty kissing the young man further arouses Antoinette's resentment at being treated like a child, and she feels "the wild need to do something outrageous and evil"

(167). Impulsively, she rips up the invitations and throws them into the Seine.

So Antoinette and the reader know that the ball will be a disaster. The narrative takes us abruptly from the scene of the invitations' destruction to the evening of the ball, to Rosine rushing about in a frenzy of preparation. Here, Némirovsky allows us a closer glimpse of her psyche than we ever had of Francine's. The information comes mostly from her distracted interjections to herself, her daughter, and her servants; at one point, the Kampfs have a surprisingly honest conversation. Nothing we learn about Rosine is calculated to make her lovable: she remains the harsh-spoken caricature of a pushy arriviste she always was.

Nonetheless, we see her experiencing acute anxiety and fear of being hurt or humiliated, and these are emotions with which we can identify. She claims to have been sleepless for three nights, to feel that she is going mad. She is briefly aware that she is uncertain of how to act and may even notice that the maître d' looks at her with "ill-concealed contempt" (171). Her cry to her husband—"Oh, if you knew how frightened I am!"—seems entirely genuine, and when she adds that "I must seem ridiculous," we sense an unsuspected self-awareness (170, 171). This successful depiction of what is at stake for the Kampfs caused Jean Cocteau to call *The Ball* a "masterpiece," because "a ruined ball is terrible for a man of the world, even if he has the elegance of soul of [Proust's] Charlus" (356).

Just before Rosine comes down, Antoinette slips into the reception room like "an amateur assassin drawn back to the scene of a crime" and hides herself behind a settee, from which perspective the room looks "as if it were the stage of a theatre" (176). Of course, the concealed witness is the very definition of dramatic irony, and theatrical allusions keep the comparisons alive. For example, Isabelle, the poor piano teacher who turns out to be the only guest, "flapped with both hands as if she were one of the ridiculous courtesans in a Molière play" (177). The metaphor is telling: Rosine and Alfred are only playing at being fashionable Parisians, and the flowers, champagne, and caviar in their home are so many stage props. The theatrical metaphor, as Philipponnat notes, makes Antoinette, off-stage, the author or director of the scene that plays out. (*OC* 1: 355)

Moreover, as Antoinette assumes authorship, the inevitable aging and dying of the mother, which in the normal course of nature leaves the daughter as survivor, seems to result from her own decision to claim her independence: "Rich with her future, Antoinette can see her mother becoming lost in the shadows: adolescence is a coup d'état" (*OC* 1: 355). Further, adds Philipponnat, this transformation mirrors the "alchemy of art," which can make personal "bitterness into a dramatic wellspring" and make the "intimate" feel "universal" (*OC* 1: 355).

When the catastrophe is complete, when Isabelle has gone home and the caterers and musicians have been dismissed, the hosts quarrel bitterly. Alfred storms out after calling Rosine "an old woman with the manners of a fish-wife," whom he had picked up "out of the gutter" (183). Antoinette emerges from her hiding place only when mother and daughter are alone. We might expect Rosine to order her to bed, but their relationship has changed. Rosine makes no effort to hide her misery or her need for daughterly consolation. So the scene ends in an embrace, with Antoinette repeating, "poor mother," over and over. But as the narrator tells us, Rosine, her head buried in Antoinette's shoulder, cannot see that Antoinette is smiling. We understand then that she will not allow herself, as Gabri had, to become suicidally entangled in her mother's psychodrama.

The Ball was a transformative step for Némirovsky, producing, out of the same childhood and adolescent trauma that lent melodrama and purple prose to *L'Ennemie,* a highly sophisticated and very Parisian story. This story's success, however, comes at the cost of editing out several autobiographical events; one, the date rape, never returns. But in *The Wine of Solitude,* Némirovsky goes back to her childhood, to the daughter living in a triangle formed by her father, mother, and mother's lover. She also returns to her childhood's setting in prerevolutionary Russia and exile, Finland as well as Paris, and fills in ethnic details that were suppressed or elided in *L'Ennemie* and *The Ball.* As we recall, the family were all French and native born in the first novel, which leaves Léon Bragance's sudden acquisition of factories in Poland awkwardly unexplained. In *The Ball,* Alfred Kampf is Jewish but a native of France whose ethnicity draws little attention.

The Wine of Solitude

In *The Wine of Solitude,* the ethnic and political context is much more carefully evoked. Although Bella Karol, like Rosine, is a Christian who married into a Jewish family, the Jewish context is explored further than it was in *The Ball.* Russia and the experience of emigration are as crucial for young Hélène as they were for Némirovsky herself. In particular, the historical context permits the author to show Hélène's maturation, to make credible her avoidance of the psychological trap into which Gabri Bragance fell. Hélène's independence is also established through her relationship with Mademoiselle Rose, who replaces the unloved English miss of the two earlier texts and is clearly based on Zézelle, the governess Némirovsky loved as a mother. On the other hand, if *The Ball* required a certain softening of the family scandal, *The Wine of Solitude* makes no such concessions: the mother's young lover is brought back as the bane of her daughter's childhood, and as in *L'Ennemie,* the daughter contemplates seducing him.

No one would characterize *The Wine of Solitude* as a historical novel—it does not describe battles nor does it take us inside a terrorist cell or a government office. But where *The Ball* seemed set in an eternal upper-middle-class Paris, in which 1888 and 1936 look much the same, every section of *The Wine of Solitude* is anchored in a particular time and place. Political and historical details we do not usually associate with domestic fiction play an important role in shaping its meaning.

The first page of *The Wine of Solitude* evokes "the part of the world in which Hélène Karol was born" and specifies places: "the Ukrainian plains," the "Ural Mountains," the "Caspian Sea," and the "Dnieper River." Hélène's family has its own history, interwoven with the history of czarist Russia. This history is represented by the grandparents who join her and her parents for dinner in the first scene. George Safronov's first reflection, that his son-in-law is "lucky to have married" Bella, alludes to his own loss of an inherited fortune and subsequent need to marry his daughter off to an "insignificant little Jew" (9, 14). The social status of Jews in Russia will be an important issue in the book, as will the prestige of French culture to upper-class Russians. The French governess at table with the family, the French fashion magazines through which Bella Karol leafs as she eats, a conversation about the family's last vacation in Nice, even the Napoleonic soldiers with which Hélène plays—all underscore this point.

Similarly, Boris Karol's fortunes are tied to history. When eight-year-old Hélène expresses her hope that there will not be a war, Bella dismisses her anxiety, pointing out that papa's textile factory will have more business if there is. In 1914 and 1915, he and his friends become rich selling goods to the army; after the February and October revolutions, they hoard paintings, jewelry, and fine china and silver, all hastily sold by fleeing aristocrats. But even before the revolution, Hélène had caught glimpses of Ukrainian realities. She saw sick pilgrims in filthy rags marching through city streets on their way to the Dnieper monasteries and learns later that they may have brought the epidemic in which one of her playmates died. Revolutionary violence is on view from her bedroom window, where she watches an execution and sees "a group of anarchist terrorists in an old Ford decorated with a skeleton's head . . . fire a machine gun into the empty streets" (111). Out for an evening walk with her governess, she observes a group of men cutting up a dead horse in the street and breathes in "the sickly odour of filthy air from the Neva," knowing that it has grown worse since the February revolution, when the city stopped cleaning the canals (73). Her own relative privilege is unmistakable: "all over the city people carried dead children to the cemetery tied up in sacks, for there were simply too many to afford a coffin" (121).

Historical events establish Hélène as a character whose attention, unlike Gabri's, cannot be forever focused on the dysfunctions of the family hothouse.

Less isolated than Gabri or Antoinette, Hélène visits other Russian-Jewish families, where mothers are warm but where signs of marital boredom, even tolerated adultery, also appear. Further, Mademoiselle Rose provides her with love and attention, and proposes more benign interpretations of Bella's behavior: she may be spoiled, for example, rather than "evil" (24). Given this foundation, we would expect Hélène to prove herself stronger than Gabri.

This strength emerges in a scene that obviously reworks the episode in *L'Ennemie* where Francine pounces on Gabri's poison-pen letter, never meant for circulation. In *The Wine of Solitude,* Hélène is studying German from a text in which an idealized German family seems to mock her own. She crosses out the story, replacing the German mama and papa with "the husband, the wife, and the lover" and adding that "every household is the same . . . full of greed, lies, and mutual misunderstanding" (105). Hélène rubs out the word "lover," then writes the word again, then disguises it, feeling "enthralled" by the "evil air" it emits. Bella, perhaps sensing Hélène's intensity, seizes the book and pronounces her a "horrible liar" (106). Even though authorship is clear this time, Bella lashes out at the governess, dismissing her for having turned her daughter against her. Boris Karol permits this injustice and orders Hélène out of the room when she offers to tell him "the word he couldn't read" but finds "he didn't want to know anything" (109).

Initially, the dismissal seems crueler than the one in *L'Ennemie,* for Hélène loves Mademoiselle Rose. And her loss is permanent. The next evening, when the two go walking despite a thick fog, Mademoiselle Rose becomes disoriented, muttering incoherently about her own childhood and insisting on staggering forward long after she has exhausted herself. Eventually she disappears, and Hélène's shouts bring no one, for "calling for help in those days only made the rare passers-by rush faster toward their homes" (118). The next day, the Karols learn that the governess died in a hospital where passing soldiers had taken her: "she must have been ill for a long time" (120).

Were Hélène more like Gabri, she might blame herself for writing the words that led to Mademoiselle Rose's dismissal and be overwhelmed when she dies. True, Hélène briefly considers throwing herself into the Neva, imagining that she wants to die, but "she knew very well that she was lying" (119). Suicide might have been the right gesture, but "everything, right down to her feeling of despair, drove her to choose life." "'No,' she decides, 'I won't let them do it to me'" (119). Perhaps her resolution is stronger because the scribbled words Bella insisted on exposing were not aimed at her: Hélène was rewriting the family story for herself. Her version is true, even though she was punished for writing it, and she gains the confidence to assert, "I am stronger than all of them" (123). She refuses to shed the tears that make her heart "as hard and heavy as a stone"; she will never again say Mademoiselle Rose's name to anyone in her family (121). But she also recognizes that this death took place in the middle of a revolution, when "so many people were dying that no one . . . had time [for] consoling" her (120). "These days," the "life and health of a human being" have little worth (121).

Two days later, the Karols are in Finland, the setting for part 3, which closely follows the Némirovsky path into exile. The Communist revolution, having begun in St. Petersburg, quickly spread to Finland, which declared independence from Russia in December 1918. Civil war ensued, as in Russia, between White and Red factions; a draft constitution for "Red Finland" appeared on February 23, 1918; and Lenin signed a treaty with its government on March 1. "Red Finland," never a fully Communist state and never including the vast stretches of the country north of Tampere, was short lived; in May the Whites declared victory and established a democratic republic. Perhaps confusingly for modern readers, the Karols, like the Némirovskys, flee Russian Communism to take refuge in Red Finland.

Part 3 is largely set in a boarding house in the countryside, filled with Russian refugees who quickly overcome the mutual suspicions that divide Christians and Jews at home. Even with crowding and a monotonous rural diet, Hélène finds communal life utopian. Regular mealtimes reassure her; middle-class women teach her to sew and support her against Bella, "a caricature of a mother" (134). Much is made of the fresh country air (contrasting so strongly with the foul odors of St. Petersburg), the wholesome food, and the healthful exercise Hélène enjoys once she is free to spend hours walking in the forest or playing in the snow with younger children.

This idyll includes an extended flirtation with Fred Reuss, a handsome young married man with whom she spends hours, sometimes accompanied by his children, sometimes not; when they join a barn dance where village girls wear Loyalist red, his wife is left behind. Hélène's pleasure in her renewed physical health is accompanied by her first sexual stirrings. She and Fred are attracted to each other, but as he points out rather churlishly, she will be grateful later that he did not take advantage of her inexperience. When four local Red Guards are killed by Whites, the refugees disperse, fearful that their refuge is turning into a battlefield. Fred goes off with his own family, a development Hélène takes in stride.

Hélène's new sexual awareness, however, prompts the fantasy of wreaking revenge on Bella by seducing Max. Meanwhile, the lovers are beginning to quarrel; news that Max's mother has died in Constantinople heightens his guilt about refusing to join her in exile. Part 4 takes Max and the Karols to France in July 1919, just after the Treaty of Versailles is signed. Boris is once more rich but ruining his health with long hours of work, followed by nights in the casinos. Unlike Némirovsky, who enrolled at the Sorbonne, Hélène lacks friends and occupation. As a result, part 4 assumes something of the hothouse atmosphere of *L'Ennemie,* with Hélène and Max, like Gabri and Charles, having unlimited leisure for "guilty love" (196). Bella, convinced that Hélène remains a schoolchild, actually encourages their relationship.

This time, however, our heroine is stronger. Hélène recognizes that she is only playing at being in love, and that to seduce Max would not set her free but bind her more tightly to the familial psychodrama. After hearing Mademoiselle Rose's voice telling her that "real courage" is not playing "dangerous games," she formulates the challenge: "I've spent my whole life fighting against my hideous bloodline. . . . If I don't learn how to conquer myself, this bitter, cursed blood will win out" (194, 207). Hélène persuades Max that she means what she says, and he leaves for London. She remains at home until her father's death and walks out of the house the afternoon of his funeral. At the end she is free, looking up to see a blue sky framed by the Arc de Triomphe. She is homeless, jobless, and has only a small legacy to sustain her, but all the signs announce her ready for a new life.

Lethal Grandmothers: *Jezebel* and "The Ogress"

Two other lethal mothers, both bearing more than a passing resemblance to Fanny Némirovsky, appear after *The Wine of Solitude.* The more important work is a novel, *Jezebel* (1936), which begins with the murder trial of Gladys Eysenach. Gladys, the Jezebel of the title, is a familiar figure: the glamorous, scandalous beauty showing signs of aging. She is accused of killing a young man, Bernard Martin, whom everyone assumes was her lover. Gladys admits to this "terrible crime" but refuses to explain her motives. A series of character witnesses appear, and then the narrative leaves the courtroom for good, moving back to Gladys's youth and ending with the actual murder.

Gladys's own mother had been "a cold woman, harsh and virtually mad, an elderly painted doll," who moved her daughter across Europe and America. Gladys discovered her love of pleasure and her power over men early, finding happiness in her second marriage to Richard Eysenach, "a famous financier of dubious origins." Theirs is a vaguely sadomasochistic relationship in which he caters to her need for luxury while encouraging her to play at being childish and helpless: "this unspoken vice that was appeased through her was a pleasure for both of them" (57). His death leaves her lost, craving excessive male adoration, flattery, and attention; her daughter, Marie-Thérèse, lives in her shadow "and like everyone else who knew Gladys . . . strove only to please her, to serve her, and to love her" (58).

Then the destructive cycle sets in. Gladys insists on concealing her daughter's age and dresses her as a schoolgirl into her late adolescence. Marie-Thérèse grows up, falls in love with Olivier Beauchamp, the son of one of Gladys's first admirers, and the two wish to marry. But Snow White's wicked stepmother cannot bear competition: Gladys forbids the marriage. When Olivier tries to change her mind, she is so offended that he sees her only as his fiancé's mother that she fantasizes briefly about seducing him. No, she does not want her daughter to hate her as "she had hated her mother," but no, the marriage must be put off a year (99). The First World War breaks out, Olivier is drafted, and by October he is dead.

But the die is cast. Marie-Thérèse and Olivier had not waited for marriage; she is pregnant. Gladys recommends abortion but then insists that the pregnancy must be concealed. Her daughter must not go to a doctor or hospital; only her friend Carmen Gonzales, a nurse with a side-specialty in abortion, can be trusted to deliver the child discreetly. But Marie-Thérèse suspects, with justice, that if she lets Carmen attend her, the baby will be spirited away before she is strong enough to resist. As a result, she gives birth alone in her room, where one morning Jeanne, the maid, discovers a blood-stained bed in which Marie-Thérèse lies, a crying baby boy held "tightly against her lifeless breast" (125). When Jeanne reminds Gladys that she is the baby's grandmother, Gladys screams that she hates him. Jeanne offers to adopt him and takes him off with her to the provinces.

The little boy, named Bernard Martin, grows up hearing the story of his birth repeated endlessly. When he is old enough to attend university, he moves to Paris and visits his mother's grave, calls on Carmen Gonzalez, and comes looking for his grandmother. Bernard finds Gladys just as he expected and despises her. When she visits his flat, his lover comments that she might be his mother: "you both have a murderous look in your eyes" (178). Since he has inherited her character, he will not be satisfied with her money: she must publicly admit that she is his grandmother. When she predicts that Aldo Monti, her current lover, will leave if he learns how old she is, Bernard knows exactly what to do. Following her into her home, he vows that "I'm going to tell your lover that you're an old woman" (198). The telephone rings, Bernard reaches for it, and she shoots him dead.

In "The Ogress," one of Némirovsky's last published stories, a man recalls a few weeks of his adolescence that he spent at a seaside hotel, out of season, with his mortally ill father. As they sat in the hotel's reading room, an older woman lectured his father on the health benefits of classical art, recommending "distractions of an elevated order" to assist his cure. She is soon off on a story about her daughter, an actress who won prizes both for tragedy and comedy in 1920. When she names her daughter, the narrator's father expresses sorrow to hear of her death, for he remembers her as a "diamond" who stood out in an otherwise deplorable *Romeo and Juliet* that played in the provinces after the Great War. This short, polished story turns on its carefully framed unreliable narrator. The woman believes herself to be describing her daughter's talent and her own devotion to it, but what emerges instead is the story of a fragile beauty driven to death by her mother's insistence that she keep up a hectic schedule of performances despite suffering all the classic symptoms of tuberculosis. As she finishes her tale, her awkward and plain younger daughter, Édith, an actress whom the teenager immediately judges as too "vulgar" for the stage, comes up to be introduced, and mother and daughter go off with her director. The boy and his father overhear the director tell Édith that she will not be renewed for the next season. The mother interrupts her daughter's protests to propose a new talent for his music hall: a six-year-old who is even prettier than Shirley Temple and dances and sings to perfection. She is her granddaughter: "I trained her myself" (OC 2: 1175). This lethal mother who forced her children "to eat the fruit she had been forbidden, who forced them to swallow the skin, the pulp, and the stone until they choked," is transforming herself before our eyes into an equally lethal grandmother (1175).

Life Imitates Art

Fanny Némirovsky was always a survivor: she fled to the unoccupied zone after the French defeat, and then, having managed to obtain a Lithuanian passport, successfully posed as an Orthodox Christian. Her grandchildren had a more difficult war. Some two months after their mother's death at Auschwitz, her daughters, Denise and Élisabeth, then twelve and five, were summoned to the "*préfecture* at Autun" along with their father, Michel Epstein. A German officer showed them a picture of his little daughter, "who was as blonde as Denise . . . and told the girls he would give them forty-eight hours to get away" (PL 384). Michel was soon deported, but his daughters remained in Issy-L'Évêque under the care of Julie Dumot, a family friend. Denise was at school when Vichy police arrived to arrest her, but a sympathetic teacher hid her and returned her to Julie, who immediately took the children into hiding. She enrolled them in a convent school in Bordeaux, under false names, until February 1944, when "a cycle of hiding places, bombardment, and fear" began (PL 386). The liberation of Bordeaux on August 28, 1944, made it possible for the children to return to school. A poor diet, however, and long periods spent hiding in cellars, had left Denise seriously ill, perhaps with pneumonia.

Feeling desperate, Julie Dumot brought the children to their grandmother's door in Nice, pleading for help. It was not a good plan. Philipponnat and Lienhardt quote Fanny Némirovsky as saying, from behind a closed door, "I have no grandchildren" (386). Denise Epstein told the *Sunday Times* of London in 2007 that her grandmother had added, "If you are orphans, go to an orphanage" ("My Sweet Mother"). Readers of *Jezebel* will recognize this voice immediately.[2]

Establishing that the real-life Fanny Némirovsky was no better than her fictional avatars does not, however, tell us what the monstrous mother means for the domestic novel. That most of us loved our mothers and are still shocked if someone admits to having hated hers, reminds us how powerfully transgressive the ogress is. Medea, the wicked stepmother, and Gladys Eysenach remind us that the domestic setting is no haven from cruelty and violence. Moreover, these strong women are full of passion: Medea wants to punish Jason for spurning her; Snow White's stepmother and Francine Bragance lust for men's admiration and give the lie to any version of the "proper lady" or virgin mother we might prefer. If the doctrine of "separate spheres" was designed to protect women, the domestic novel suggests that putting a woman in charge at home was downright dangerous. Not only does a society that fails to prosecute child abuse tolerate others evils, but most of the evils we ascribe to the political world already live in the bosom of the family. The domestic worker, the cook or the nanny, is as oppressed as a factory worker; the silver spoils of a ruined aristocracy are displayed at the family table. The happy family of the German textbook belies the child's experience of growing up in a home where most of the evils bourgeois morality has banished to the margins, to the streets or gambling dens, flourish under a thin veneer. When we say that a writer treats domestic topics rather than great social and political issues, we are assuming a separation of spheres that in Irène Némirovsky's novels, as in reality, is illusory.

Chapter 2

The Russian Fiction

No one knew better than Irène Némirovsky how rapidly a revolution destroys houses, fortunes, and basic civil rights. Many Western writers, on the other hand, who followed the violent upheavals only in the newspapers, remained enthusiastic about the ideology and avowed intentions of the new Soviet government for decades afterward. To take one example: in 1934, on a visit, the illustrious novelist André Malraux praised Stalin publicly for building the White Sea Canal with prison labor. That 140,000 people, most guilty only of dissent from the official line, perished during its construction was an unpleasant detail that Malraux might have inferred from closer attention to Russian émigré accounts. But the documentation was then imprecise, and as Frederic Brown puts it, Stalin "held high the torch of anti-Fascism," blinding many to the harshness of the gulags and even the deaths by starvation of some four million Ukrainians in the famine years of 1932 and 1933 (210). As the Stalinist show trials began in August 1936, the famous French writer André Gide renounced the Communist Party, but the U.S. writer Lillian Hellman published "An Open Letter to American Liberals" with eighty-eight cosigners. This letter denounced not the trials but their critics, and not until the Hungarian Revolution of 1956 did the last holdouts abandon their admiration for the Soviet Union.

If we remember how much at odds the experiences of such Russian émigrés as Vladimir Nabokov and Irène Némirovsky were with the accepted views of so many intelligent Westerners, we can better appreciate why her depictions of revolution are always so thoroughly anchored in realistic description and so little concerned with the ideological claims of the combatants.

"The Birth of a Revolution, Seen Through the Eyes of a Little Girl," the long title of a story she published in the June 1938 issue of *Le Figaro littéraire,* depicts events she witnessed in St. Petersburg in February 1917.[1] What Némirovsky saw marked her political consciousness indelibly, and although she understood that further interpretation was needed, the child's perspective, what the eye innocent of political theory simply takes in, remained crucial for her. In *Les Mouches d'Automne* (1931), translated as *Snow in Autumn* (2007), we see the events of 1914–21 through the eyes of another innocent, the elderly nursemaid who raised two generations of an aristocratic family. Apparently nostalgic, Tatiana tells a story that prompts the reader to ask questions she herself cannot formulate. The narrator of *L'Affaire Courilof* (*The Courilof Affair,* 1933), "Léon M.," is a blood-stained veteran of revolution, a would-be assassin turned officer in the KGB's precursor, the Cheka, ending his days as an exile in France. Yet Némirovsky insists on framing even him as a child of revolution; born in Siberia, he lost his father, "the terrorist Maxime Davidovitch M.," in early childhood, and emigrated to Switzerland with his mother (242). She lived in poverty, losing two children to tuberculosis before dying herself, having entrusted ten-year-old Léon's further education to a "Revolutionary Committee" (245).

"The Birth of a Revolution"

Written after the two novels, "The Birth of a Revolution" distills what seems an apolitical reading of the Russian revolution. Based on an actual incident, with clear autobiographical resonances, the story presents a narrator who seems younger than the author was in 1917 and contains no hints of the instability and disorder of the Némirovsky household. The first line asks, "What is the exact instant when a revolution is born?" (*OC* 1,1827). The story goes on to define this "instant" as the time when the revolution becomes visible not only to the revolutionaries or the rulers but to the masses, even to a child. In the winter of 1917, says the narrator, she witnessed this time.

She sketches first the ways a child might hear about revolution: as a vague threat evoked in conversation, as an instance of "politics," which is the subject of newspapers, or "history," the subject of texts about past generations. One moment, "revolution" brings to mind the history of France or the novels of the elder Dumas; the next moment it is here, alive, part of the present for everyone, a signal of the dislocation and upheaval of everything. Its first signs are puzzling but can be accommodated into one's normal frame of reference. Such is the moment when the child sees a demonstration of working-class women, many accompanied by small children; she remarks on how pretty one sleeping baby is, and the young mother smiles. She asks the adults in her family what is going on, what the women want, but they do not answer; finally, she understands that they want bread. The child has never experienced poverty, but bread at least is familiar, and only the size of the demonstration, its masses extending farther than she can see, frightens her. Having come to clear a path for cars, the police take the child home.

Several days later, however, she hears shouting and blows coming from the street, and looks out her window to see peasants at the door of a bakery. The sounds of strife are replaced by laughter and applause as the crowd sees a novel sight: soldiers from the barracks next door jump over its walls into the street, crossing it and disappearing. Though the forces who kept her safe are deserting, their actions still seem like harmless fun; fundamentally her home remains so peaceful that she assumes everything in it has always existed and always will, "just as the earth always keeps turning" (1828).

Then, suddenly, she hears the first gunshots, more surprising than frightening. Within a few days red streamers fly from every building, trams are draped in red, and red flowers are sold in the street. This, she says, is the "triumphant revolution," which has not yet shed blood, or at least not very much blood; people are joyous, magnanimous, hopeful (1828). This is its proud, beautiful face, so soon to be altered, to be distorted "by the frightful passions of men" (1829). The revolutionaries are still searching out the last agents of the police who had defended the old regime, and suddenly she hears the cry of the people transformed into a mob. It is an "unforgettable clamor of hatred and madness," a cry that "demands blood, that no longer contains anything human" (1830).

The child sees that the mob has captured Ivan, the *dvornik* in her own building. Such men—part doorkeepers, part janitors—often spied for the police; this man's son-in-law is a police agent. As the child's mother warns her not to look, she remains rooted, staring as the revolutionary soldiers command the frightened man to say his last prayers and kiss his children good-bye. He props himself up against a wall; they blindfold him; a shot is fired. The child looks again: the *dvornik* is still alive, having suffered only a minor flesh wound, which the soldiers are already bandaging. Dazed like a patient coming around from anesthesia, he smiles at them weakly, lets them pat him on the back. They had only wanted to frighten him. "The Russians," remarks the child's French governess, "are mad" (1831).

The child can see the cruelty, the incoherence and gratuity of this action, and wonders how anyone could participate in it. As an adult, however, she remembers this mock execution "as the instant when I saw the revolution being born" (1831). This is the moment when the revolutionary is not yet stripped of his pity and humanity, when he is not yet possessed by the demon, when he can still stop short of murder. But the demon is already close; it already "troubles his soul" (1832). "What demon?" asks the narrator, and she says that everyone who sees it calls it by a different name. But those who have survived a war or a riot will never forget its face, which always has the same look: haggard and mad.

Némirovsky echoes here Edmund Burke's *Reflections on the Revolution in France* (1790). In Burke's classic conservative argument, the goals of a revolution may be thoroughly just. Violence, however, even when loosed in a defensible cause, quickly becomes self-perpetuating, destroying not only the enemy but the conditions of civilization itself. Revolutions, wrote Burke, show us "that criminal means, once tolerated, are soon preferred. They present a shorter cut to the object than through the highway of the moral virtues. Justifying perfidy and murder for public benefit, public benefit . . . soon become[s] the pretext, and perfidy and murder the end,—until rapacity, malice, revenge, and fear more dreadful than revenge, could satiate their insatiable appetites. Such must be the consequences of losing, in the splendor of these triumphs of the rights of men, all natural sense of wrong and right" (70). Burke further argued that a state founded on violent revolt naturally devolves into a military dictatorship, for "the nature of things requires that the army should never act but as an instrument. The moment that . . . it shall act according to its own resolutions, the government, be it what it may, will immediately degenerate into a military democracy: a species of political monster which has always ended by devouring those who have produced it" (179).

One could argue that long periods of representative democracy in modern France belie Burke's predictions, even if we take into account the Terror, the First and Second Empires, and Vichy. On the other hand, as a description of the Stalinist Terror that began with the assassination of Sergey Kirov in December 1934, Burke's words are uncannily acute. Stalin was the only member of the six-member Politburo of the 1917 revolution to survive the 1930s; much of the rest of the leadership of the party and the Red Army, the notable intellectuals and artists who supported the Revolution, and millions of other Soviet citizens were shot or died in the Gulag. The number of those killed in 1937–38 alone, according to Michael Ellman's carefully argued "Soviet Repression Statistics," was "about a million" (1162).[2]

In addition to pessimism about revolution, Némirovsky's story also evokes a famous incident in the life of Dostoevsky, whose *Demons* offers an apocalyptic vision of anti-czarist terrorism. In his youth Dostoevsky held liberal views, and at twenty-eight he was arrested for his membership in a secret society called the Petrashevsky Circle, whose members discussed progressive ideas, including the theories of the French socialist Charles Fourier. Dostoevsky was sentenced to death; at the last moment the sentence was commuted to a mock execution followed by four years in Siberia. Though the child narrator does not make the connection, for an audience versed in literary history, the dvornik's ordeal evokes this famous incident in all its symbolic savagery. It is a moment of political theater, of the symbolic violence that she explores at greater length in the *Courilof Affair.* With Dostoevsky's shadow, Némirovsky also introduces the complex relationship between writers and revolution, between violence and its representation.

Snow in Autumn

Before we begin *Les Mouches d'Automne,* we should note that its title is the only one Sandra Smith does not translate literally; in French *Snow in Autumn* is actually *The Flies of Autumn,* a much less romantic image. The key phrase occurs in a sentence evoking the lives of affluent Russians reduced to shabby exile in Paris: "Back and forth they went, between their four walls, silently, like flies in autumn after the heat and light of summer had gone, barely able to fly, weary and angry, buzzing around the windows, trailing their broken wings behind them" (213). Although this powerful image of a dying aristocracy is worth keeping in mind, Smith's title is also apt, since we see snow in the novel's first scenes, when the sons are going off to war, and learn that Tatiana Ivanovna's unfulfilled longing for snow in Paris is the last of her disappointments.

One of the models for a novel set in a revolutionary era is the nostalgic saga of a lost, golden age. Margaret Mitchell's *Gone with the Wind,* the film version as much as the novel, is the epitome of the "plantation novel," a genre originally designed to counter the negative image of the American South projected by Harriet Beecher Stowe's *Uncle Tom's Cabin.* Told from the perspective of slave owners plunged into poverty by the end of the Civil War, *Gone with the Wind* presents the antebellum South as a gracious, romantic era when beautiful young white women wearing floating dresses fell in love with handsome young men and moved into their elegant houses to preside over medieval kingdoms of fairy-tale harmony and prosperity. Book and film include faithful portraits of the horrors of war—the burning of Atlanta, Sherman's march to the sea, amputations performed without anesthesia, survivors facing hunger. But none of the violence associated with slavery and none of the hardships of daily life in the slave quarters are suggested. An essential feature of the genre is the faithful servant, someone like Scarlett's Mammy, who identifies completely with the values of the ruling class and remains devoted to her white owners in even the most difficult times. Mammy, we remember, lectures Scarlett about how ladies must eat before a party so they are not tempted to stuff themselves like farmhands in front of gentlemen. She does not bring up malnourishment among enslaved children, a subject about which few of her real-world counterparts would have been ignorant.

Tatiana Ivanovna is, in many respects, a version of this faithful retainer. A nursemaid for two generations of Karines, she remembers their infant selves better than anyone else. Having nearly forgotten her own dead husband and child, she focuses her emotional life on the noble family and its estate, Karinova. She understands nothing about history or politics as these subjects appear in books, but when she watches Youri preparing to leave for the Great War in 1916, she remembers Alexandre Kirilovitch, possibly his grandfather, dying at thirty-nine in the 1877 war between Russia and Turkey. The grown family members sometimes forget to visit her in the nursery or even mock her gently, but she is a permanent part of the family, someone they look to for comfort. Nicolas Alexandrovitch, father of the two young soldiers leaving for war in the first chapter, comes up to Tatiana Ivanovna's room after they depart, for "where could he cry freely, if not with her?" (198).

Yet Tatiana Ivanovna, for all her devotion, sees imperfections in the Karines: she remembers that before Hélène Vassilievna's first husband died and she married Nicholas Alexandrovitch and became the mother of his four children, she was the Countess Eletzkaïa. Even in middle age Hélène Vassilievna notices "how [Tatiana Ivanovna] recoiled from her . . . as if she was still that young adulteress running to meet her lover" (192). Tatiana Ivanovna's favorite child, Youri, "had the heavy, youthful features of a serf," unlike his brother Cyrille and sister Loulou, who "had the beauty, the sparkling eyes, the contented and cruel features of the Karines before them" (191). At the beginning of chapter 3 she is alone at Karinova, for the Karines "had fled . . . in January 1918," and the one other servant left behind has died (200). Although she still has no political opinions, her naïve consciousness records "the flames in the air" and the "sound of people screaming" as the nearby town of Soukharevo burns. And although she would not criticize the Karines directly, she remembers the old cook before his death, urging her to drink to forget that "we're all alone, abandoned like dogs" (200). He had even begun to sympathize with the revolutionaries, for the nobility "have bled us enough . . . the dirty bastards" (201).

As Soukharevo burns, Tatiana sees a man with a "pale, exhausted face" standing on the path to the house (201). It is Youri, barely recovered from typhus and six months in prison, with a Communist "death warrant" on his head. Naturally Tatiana Ivanovna takes him back to his old room, where "slightly delirious" he sleeps, interrupting himself at intervals by reaching out to touch familiar objects like the old calendar, still bearing the czar's portrait and the date, May 18, 1918, and muttering, "I don't understand, I don't understand" (203). Once he asks Tatiana to identify a background noise. She suggests "thunder," but he immediately corrects her, "that's cannon fire" (203).

Both realize that the war is getting closer and that Youri is in grave danger; Tatiana Ivanovna wants him to leave immediately and take shelter with her brother. But he argues that the whole region is unsafe, so he might as well stay: "At least here, the serfs know me, I've never done them any harm" (205). So the stage is set for the single scene that represents the revolution in this novel: Youri, in the nursery, peacefully dining on potatoes and drinking one of the remaining bottles from his father's wine cellar, his table set with "fine linen" and "antique silver," hears a knocking at the door (205). Tatiana tells him to hide immediately, but Youri recognizes the voice calling his name. "It's me,

Ignat," calls up the family's former coachman, with whom he had played when they were both children.

Youri understands Tatiana's warning but refuses to heed it: "'If *he* wants to hurt me,' Youri suddenly thought, 'then everything be damned, and me with it'" (206). He welcomes Ignat as a friend, pours him a drink, and then asks him if he has enough to eat, whether he still plays the accordion. Ignat smiles broadly but insists that Youri accompany him to the village. Catching a look in his eye, Tatiana Ivanovna starts screaming, calling him a "bloody bastard" and asking, "Who do you think you are to be giving orders to your master?" (207). Youri rises to go with him, only remarking calmly that his old friend could have waited a day. As he pauses at the doorstep, Ignat points his revolver at Youri: "The second bullet went right through his neck, killing him instantly" (208).

This is a classic encounter, of course: childhood friends meeting as adults, on opposite sides in a war. Tatiana Ivanovna, faithful servant, instinctively sides with the old regime and its values. And to the extent that the killing illustrates the triumph of ideology over an ethic of personal relationships, we may say that Irène Némirovsky agrees with her and sympathizes with Youri's unwillingness to go on living in a world where ideology trumps friendship. Four months later, when Tatiana Ivanovna arrives at the door of the dark room in Odessa where the Karines have taken refuge, having survived a terrible trip with the family's remaining diamonds sewn in her skirts, she encounters an equally ideological response from Cyrille.

She must explain that Youri is dead, and when Loulou asks why he was killed, she replies that the peasants were afraid he had come back to reclaim the estate. Because he had always been a good baron, "they wanted to spare him the pain of a trial and execution" and thought "it was better to kill him that way" (210). Instead of expressing gratitude to her for having walked hundreds of miles to rescue his family from penury, Cyrille shakes "his fist at the old woman with a kind of hatred. 'Bloody serfs,' he shouts; 'we should have been harder on you when we were your masters!'" (210). Here, even more clearly, the old nursemaid's faithfulness to an ethic of personal relationships has the author's sympathy.

Tatiana Ivanovna is reunited with the Karines in chapter 4; the narrative sketches out the two difficult winters they spend together and brings them to France in May 1920 "on the last French boat leaving Odessa" (211). The remaining five chapters of the novel take place in Paris, where the family, along with many other Russian émigrés, rents a shabby apartment in Passy. Just enough money remains to send the youngest, André, to a boarding school. Cyrille leaves, taking up with a rich actress he met in prison. Only Loulou remains at home. This is the chapter where Némirovsky compares the diminished Russian aristocracy to "flies in autumn," sketching out the Karines' frustrations with the limitations and squalor of their new life in the heat of a Parisian summer they find intolerable. The immigration experience is of interest in itself, but we can also note that these chapters complicate the book's political perspective.

Loulou, who will eventually find work as a model, spends the first few months in Paris missing the "dangerous, exciting" life she led in Odessa, and her face acquires a new look, "strange, weary, and cruel" (214). She starts going out drinking in the evenings with other young people, who return home "and start drinking again, caressing each other in the darkened rooms" (214). One morning Tatiana Ivanovna finds her in the sitting room, sleeping next to a Russian émigré whom she recognizes from his childhood days as the lace-clad prince, George Andronikof. The nursemaid is shocked by the squalid scene, the half-dressed couple in each other's arms, amid empty bottles, scattered phonograph records, and over-spilling ashtrays. "You are offending God," she says, recognizing Loulou's hasty assurance that she is still "innocent" for the lie it is. The émigré prince, staggering to his feet only to collapse in a chair, muttering, "I'm utterly drunk," completes the picture (217).

Loulou believes that she is doing nothing wrong and associates her sexual freedom with the dangers of her recent past. She remembers a night in Odessa spent in bed with a lover, now probably dead, watching together "walls of flame engulfing the port" (217). When Tatiana Ivanovna reproaches her with stories of Loulou's aunts, allegedly chaste at the same age, coming in to tell her about their dances and picnics, she becomes nostalgic about the beautiful nights in the forest and the family's fine horses. Loulou, glancing around the "dingy" room, remarks, "The décor has obviously changed" (217). And though Tatiana Ivanovna is quick to say, "That's not all that's changed," we have only to remember her "adulteress" mother to realize that Loulou is telling the truth. Her parents were really no more conventional than she; Tatiana Ivanovna's nostalgic perspective does blur sexual propriety with aesthetic elegance.

A moment later Loulou is sobbing in Tatiana Ivanovna's arms; she is, after all, her nurse. "I want to go home . . . home," she wails, and asks, "Why have we been punished like this? We didn't do anything wrong!" To which Tatiana Ivanovna responds, "It is God's holy will" (218). At this point both women are real people caught up in powerful political history neither can begin to explain. We can sympathize with them humanely, but we are unlikely to believe that the Russian aristocracy is wholly innocent or that God's will is the best explanation for their sufferings.

Chapter 6 similarly centers on how émigrés remember and interpret the past. The family gathers to have a Mass said for Youri; his siblings loved him but have found ways to cope with his death. Cyrille says that "Youri was the best of us," and he and Loulou, looking at a picture of him as a child, project onto it the sense that their brother always knew he would die young and is now at peace. Hélène Vassilievna also thinks of him at peace, happier than her living children, but the narrator points out "that of all her children, Youri was the one she had understood the least, loved the least" (220). The Mass triggers other memories for her and her husband. They each remember how attractive the other once was, and Nikolai Alexandrovitch reflects on how much he had loved his wife.

He grows impatient as Hélène Vassilievna and Tatiana Ivanovna reminisce about details of lost furniture and moiré silk, reflecting, "If only he didn't have all these memories in his heart, life would be bearable" (221). He briskly urges his wife to come out to dinner with him, and she agrees, murmuring conventional sentiments: it was God's will, and at least they still have each other. Indisputably, the second point is true, and as the couple head out the door, we understand they are committing to living in the present. The Karines are becoming real survivors: "They were beginning to like this city and its people" (219).

Tatiana Ivanovna, however, is seventy-four and beginning to fail. She can no longer lift heavy laundry; she will seem to hear nothing and then burst into reminiscence if someone mentions a Russian place. She is the only one who remains faithful to the past: at Youri's Mass, she is the only one who prays for "his salvation and eternal rest" rather than for herself (219). Alone in the apartment after the family has left for dinner, she remembers the day of his birth, "his first sharp, plaintive cry . . . the others didn't cry like that" (222). She is the one who dreams about him, sitting in the old nursery, playing with jacks, and she "feels extraordinary joy" although she knows that he is dead (230).

Loulou becomes irritable with the old nursemaid, and everyone admits that they could find a better apartment if they didn't have to worry about Tatiana Ivanovna's inability to climb a long flight of stairs. But abandoning her never occurs to them. Tatiana Ivanovna has never spent a winter in Paris and cannot understand Nikolai Alexandrovitch's attempt to explain that the "snows of autumn" for which she longs will not come. On New Year's morning, while the family members are still asleep, she mistakes a white fog for snow and leaves the house alone. She sees the Seine and assumes that it is frozen over; she thinks "that all she had to do was cross the river and on the other side would be Karinova" (233). She slips into the water and tries to cry out because it is cold, but she is dead before she can say a word.

This is another death from drowning, like the death of Mademoiselle Rose in *The Wine of Solitude,* which we can read as replaying the death of Irène Némirovsky's beloved Zézelle in St. Petersburg. The scene is steeped in the pathos of Tatiana Ivanovna's loyalty to the past, which, realer to her than the present, eventually takes the form of a fatal delusion. We are certainly invited to respect Tatiana Ivanovna's bravery and her capacity for love: her impressions of people and events, whether of Yuri's first cry or the sight of Soukharevo in flames, define the facts of the story. Hers is the innocent eye; what she takes in is indisputably real. She is not, however, the embodiment of the novel's political perspective. We never forget that she has the limitations of her experience and her illiteracy, that other people know more about the Great War or the climate of northern Europe than she does.

Snow in Autumn ratifies neither a Marxist nor a czarist perspective on the Russian Revolution. Some people would say it is not really about politics at all, but as we have seen, all of the significant events of story are triggered by war and revolution. Although the novel fails to analyze the causes of the Bolshevik's success or the failures of czarist policy, it presents human beings whose lives are anchored in a political history that overwhelms them. No character in the book believes that he or she can effect political change; the best one can do is to survive, adapt, or emigrate. This is neither a progressive nor optimistic view, but it represents the way millions of people actually experienced the Russian Revolution. Its positive ethical vision focuses on private behavior and interpersonal ethics, matters often regarded as secondary during times of political crisis and danger. Perhaps for Némirovsky ethics emerge most forcefully in private cases, in personal relationships. Only *Suite Française* will define a threat to civilization so great that it forces one to choose sides, to identify with the movement, the group, or the nation at the expense of a personal relationship.

Plots of Terror

The Courilof Affair, set in Russia in the first decade of the twentieth century, is the most overtly political of Némirovsky's novels and the one for which she did the most historical research. In an insert included with the first edition, she recalls reading "a huge amount of biographies, memoirs and letters from that period, as much in Russian as in French. I drew a great many authentic details from them, going so far as to use phrases that were actually spoken or written . . . which I put into the mouth of my hero" (PL 200). Unfortunately, she recorded the title of only one, Trotsky's *My Life* (1930). The genre in which she composed it, the terrorist tale, has its own history as well.

In the decades between 1881, when Czar Alexander II was assassinated by a bomb thrower from the radical People's Will movement, and 1914, when the assassination of the Austrian Archduke Franz Ferdinand and his wife by a member of Young Bosnia triggered World War I, Western Europe, Russia, and the United States were rocked by revolutionary violence. Some of the rebels were nationalists, like the Young Bosnians and the Irish Republican Brotherhood; others were anarchists like Leon Czolgosz, who killed U.S. president William McKinley in 1901. Although orthodox Communism deplored terrorism, many organizations advocating the establishment of a socialist state along Marxist lines practiced it. Bombings as well as assassinations seized newspaper headlines; the Houses of Parliament and the French Chamber of Deputies, along with military barracks, newspaper offices, train stations, and packed cafes, exploded. Not only did these incidents fill the newspapers, but they also inspired a popular genre of fiction. And as pulp fiction stories about sinister men with foreign accents plotting terror in backrooms multiplied, more literary novelists also adopted the genre.

One theory is that the alliance between terrorists and journalists threatened writers of serious fiction. The steam-powered rotary press and dynamite, both inventions of the mid-nineteenth century, provided features essential to modern terrorism. Isolated cells of plotters could plant bombs in public places, eluding the capture that traditional assassins had courted, and the next day headlines about bombing, soon accompanied by illustrations, could sell newspapers. The *Illustrated London News,* or the pulp novel with a plot snatched from the headlines, sold by the hundreds of thousands while the literary novel languished. Dostoevsky's *Demons* (1872), Henry James's *The Princess Casamassima* (1886), and Joseph Conrad's *Under Western Eyes* (1911) all presented terrorism, a symbolic form of violence drawing its strength from cheap publicity, as a threat to rational political discourse and culture. *Demons* portrayed the terrorist bent on installing a reign of terror as the son of a foolish liberal academic, and *The Princess Casamassima* portrayed a would-be a terrorist who commits suicide rather than commit an act that might destroy the class that always patronized art, music, and literature.

English-speaking reviews of The Courilof Affair often evoke Joseph Conrad's Under Western Eyes, a tale of Russian revolutionaries. Nobel Prize–winning novelist J. M. Coetzee even goes so far as calling Némirovsky's novel "redolent of Conrad's *Under Western Eyes*."[3] Although no one offers definitive proof that Némirovsky read *Under Western Eyes, The Courilof Affair*'s similarity in setting, plot, and tone is remarkable. Both books take place among revolutionaries underground in St. Petersburg or exiled in Switzerland; both plots are based on actual assassinations of czarist officials early in the twentieth century; and both combine melancholy reflections on the futility of revolution with an interest in the revolutionary as a writer.[4] Conrad's Teacher of Languages observes, "The scrupulous and the just, the noble, humane, and devoted natures; the unselfish and the intelligent may begin a movement—but it passes away from them. They are not the leaders of a revolution. They are its victims" (113). Némirovsky's terrorists also include idealists and intellectuals; some of them, too, are victims of the movements they supported.

The Courilof Affair

In the "Prologue" a man sitting alone on the terrace of a café in Nice is accosted by a stranger who claims to recognize him as the revolutionary "Marcel

Legrand." "Weren't you in charge of the Courilof affair, in 1903?" he asks, identifying himself as Ivan Baranof, formerly one of Courilof's bodyguards. Seemingly weary and almost indifferent, Léon M., as he is identified to us, will not give his name. He looks up only when Baranof claims to have been with Courilof for ten years and asks what happened to Courilof's family after the revolution. A wily survivor, Léon M. parries most of Baranof's questions, admitting only to having been a "subordinate" member of a terrorist group based in Switzerland. When pressed to say if he had later been "at the top" of the Cheka, the revolutionary secret police, he concedes only that "I did a bit of everything" (238). Baranof then asks him, "How many others did you personally bag . . . in total?" He responds with an anecdote, telling a story about an American journalist interviewing him in Russia, asking, "how many men I'd killed since I'd come to power" (240). Of course he refuses to answer the question both times but repeats in Russian, "how many people did die? 'In answer to our prayers'? With our help?" Baranof shrugs and claims to have been "acting under orders." Léon M. wearily mutters, "Fair enough," and disappears into a waiting cab (240).

The rest of the story, as Némirovsky tells us, transcribes the contents of a manuscript, "The Courilof Affair," found after Léon M.'s death. It begins frankly, even shockingly: "In 1903 the Revolutionary Committee gave me the responsibility of *liquidating* Courilof" (242, italics in original). But after this straightforward statement, the story begins to take on the style of Léon M.'s conversation with Baranof: cryptic, full of unexplained gaps. The writer plans an autobiography, and the Courilof story is "linked to the rest of my life in only a minor sort of way" but "forms the beginnings of my life as a revolutionary" (242). Giving credence to Baranof's suspicions about the Cheka, Léon M. notes that fourteen years passed between the Courilof Affair and "the time I came to power" (242). Almost as an aside, and one he will never fully explain, he adds enigmatically, "I changed sides afterwards" (242).

Told decades after the events it describes by an exile in a foreign country, the story suggests political pessimism from the onset. The damp night in Nice, Léon M.'s shabbiness and isolation, and the story of his death at some vague time after Baranof's interrogation put us in a world antithetical to the glorious future Soviet propaganda anticipated. Nor does anything in the memoir he leaves behind relieve the gloom. Born in Siberia in 1881, Léon M. was a child of revolution.[5] His father, "Maxime Davidovitch M.," died in prison when his son was six: "prison and exile do not lend themselves to a close-knit family" (242). His mother, worn-out and elderly at thirty, was a writer of sorts, forging passports and other documents, teaching languages, struggling against poverty to keep alive two little boys who died of tuberculosis before she succumbed to it herself. Since Léon M. himself suffered from the disease, from which he is never fully cured, his mother's political friends sent him to live in Switzerland with Dr. Schwann, a revolutionary who also directed a sanitarium.[6]

Léon M., then, was indoctrinated in radical politics in childhood, with a career in terrorism available to him as a place in the family business would be to a bourgeois. He grew up believing that "a social revolution is inevitable, necessary, and fair, as fair as anything to do with human affairs could ever be." To these were added what he called "my love of power" and "my desire for a certain kind of human affection that I lacked"; the revolution "was the only place that I found it" (249). If he has changed his mind, Léon M. does not say so, but he is disillusioned enough to admit that "I no longer appreciate the romantic side of the Revolution as much as I should" and no longer cares about changes in the party (247).

Léon M., equipped with documents falsely identifying him as a physician named "Marcel Legrand," arrives in St. Petersburg in 1903 to assassinate "the Minister of Education, Valerian Alexandrovitch Courilof, who was universally despised" (254). Courilof is a fiction, but in 1901 N. P. Bogolepov, the real-life czarist minister of education, was killed by "Peter Karpovich, a disgruntled ex-student" (Kassow 126). Although Courilof is not modeled closely on Bogolepov, to understand the novel we need to understand the smoldering discontent of Russian students during the last decades of the czar's rule.

Russian universities, unlike their Western European counterparts, were of modern origin; the state that had founded them also monitored them closely. For most of the czarist period, university students were required to wear distinctive uniforms, even when off campus, making them easy to spot during strikes and demonstrations. During the first university strike in St. Petersburg in February 1899, police attacked students with whips, and on July 29 the government issued the notorious "Temporary Rules, which empowered special boards to conscript students involved in disorders, for varying periods of military service" (Kassow 115). Though even army officials protested the idea, 183 student protesters were actually drafted in December 1900, and the following year 775 more were expelled and given jail sentences. But the resultant publicity was too negative, and by fall most of the conscripted or jailed students were back in school.

Lenin and other Communists, who believed the proletariat should lead the revolution, initially had little respect for student protests. In the decade before the revolution, students and faculty debated whether they wanted to limit their protests to matters of educational policy, such as ending the bans on admitting Jews and women, or to consider themselves full participants in the workers' political struggle. The students' political relevance was greatest during this early period, which culminated in the 1905 Revolution. Although Russia was closer to having a representative, constitutional monarchy afterward, its reforms were too limited to satisfy Communists. As for the universities, they were shut down for two years following the 1905 revolution; when they were reopened, after some reforms such as removing barriers to women and Jews, they were no longer centers of political agitation. Léon M. dates his departure for Western Europe from the 1905 revolution; in 1917 he returned to Russia as a Bolshevik.

This brief survey explains why terrorists might have targeted a czarist minister of education in 1903. Indeed, when Léon M. arrives in St. Petersburg, he finds Courilof widely characterized as "savage, ambitious" (265). At first sight he loathes the man and almost relishes the thought of assassinating him, "seeing this superbly decorated mass, that harsh face explode in 'flesh and bones flying in all directions'" (266). He blames Courilof when he hears that sixty students have been arrested for protesting a history professor's refusal to answer questions about the Paris Commune; later some are killed. Léon goes to the university and sees Courilof with a man at his side writing down names as eight bodies are carried out: "I had just enough time to see the minister lean back in the corner and pull his hat down over his eyes. I have never lost the impression of intense horror I felt at that sight" (269).

Owing to a fortuitous introduction from the Swiss Embassy, Léon M. is soon installed as an attending physician in Courilof's home, where his first encounter with his patient reveals that he is mortally ill. Seeing Courilof thrashing in pain, he injects morphine, feeling moved when the weight of the blanket he lays over him provokes a "bestial moan" (272). He summons Courilof's regular doctor, Dr. Langenberg, who confides that Courilof has a tumor of the liver, probably cancerous. Normally he would operate to prolong the patient's life, but the risk of being blamed if this czarist official dies is too great. "You don't know this country!" responds Langenberg when the narrator demurs; other doctors have also refused to operate (278). In short, the despot he imagined is nearly helpless, his high political position preventing him from receiving the care that doctors would offer an ordinary bourgeois.

For Léon M., the knowledge that Courilof is dying is an argument against assassinating him, but the revolutionary leadership disagrees. From a terrorist's perspective, the goal is not ending Courilof's life but creating a spectacle for foreign newspapers to publicize. Léon's assignment from the first is to kill Courilof publicly and in front of foreigners, so that czarist censorship cannot prevent the story from making the headlines in London, Paris, and Berlin. When he argues that Courilof is "just a poor fool; if you get rid of him, the next one won't be any better," an "infuriated" party leader rebukes him: "you know very well we're not killing a man, we're killing a regime" (340). The revolutionaries want to kill the minister of education to show the vulnerability of czarist officials: should Courilof lose his post, he would no longer be a target for terrorism.

So the terrorist plot, with its political motive, is almost immediately set up against another plot involving machinations within the czar's inner circle, where an ethnic German named Dahl wants Courilof's office. Only the narrator understands the ironic stakes: if Courilof remains minister of education, he will be assassinated; if Dahl replaces him, Dahl will be the new target. Yet Courilof refuses to resign. For one thing, he needs "the illusion of influencing people's fate" (344). A czarist ministry ensures his historical, even transcendental significance: he declares that "Russia will forget my enemies, but she will not forget me" and that "I am the holy guardian of the traditions of Empire" (321, 357). Moreover, his political ambition meshes too closely with a social ambition—to force respectable St. Petersburg to recognize his second wife, Margot.

Courilof's love for Margot puts him on a collision course with the religious ethos the imperial family wishes to project. Courilof's first wife, the mother of his son and daughter, is described as resembling the Empress Alexandra, a religious obsessive: "By the end of her life [the first Mme. Courilof] was completely mad" (291). For fourteen years, Courilof "lived openly" with Margot, a notorious beauty with a past that includes a long alliance with Prince Nelrode, still occasionally a guest in the Courilof home (266). The fading beauty par excellence, Margot resembles Fanny Némirovsky in many externals, with the difference that she seems genuinely capable of love, remaining at Courilof's side for hours when he is in pain. Courilof sees his second, recent marriage as divinely sanctioned: "In her, God has given me a friend" (302).

That Margot is a social liability at court is a reality Courilof cannot accept. So the wheels turn in a third plot, where it seems possible that Courilof will destroy his career by insisting that everyone, including the czar and his wife, be willing to receive Margot. He forces the issue by inviting the royal couple to a birthday ball for his daughter Irina, refusing the face-saving accommodation Prince Nelrode proposes, that of sending his wife out of Russia beforehand. No, he tells his archenemy, Dahl, his "wife will not be leaving St. Petersburg and will not do so until she has paid her respects to her sovereigns" (325). If the emperor refuses to come, he will resign his office. He does, however, yield to Dahl's suggestion that Courilof set aside a special room in his house, the Malachite Room, for receiving the royal visitors. He even visits the royal family at the Winter Palace, pressing his invitation, which they accept "vaguely . . . as if they might cancel at any time" (330).

Léon M. soon becomes an intimate of the Courilof family, all fluent speakers of French. By concealing his knowledge of Russian, he multiplies his opportunities to eavesdrop. It seems to surprise him that some supporters of the monarchy dislike the emperor himself intensely. Courilof's "hatred [which] he could barely disguise" is evident to all. No matter how much he covets a visit from the emperor, he cannot stop himself from taking satisfaction when it looks as if a stage set up in his Malachite Room might collapse: "If only they would all go to hell! Disappear into a hole in the ground!" (331). Prince Nelrode also complains of how the sovereigns' "coldness and hostility" have replaced their former "trust and goodwill." "I cannot," he adds, "sacrifice the little time I have left to these ungrateful rulers" (297).

And if Courilof and Dahl and the Prince Nelrode do not provide edifying lessons in political morality, they are more reflective than the narrator might have expected. When Dr. Langenberg proposes "a secret society with the purpose of exterminating all these damned socialist, revolutionaries, communists, free thinkers, and all the Jews, of course," Courilof makes no response but alone with Prince Nelrode wonders aloud how they can "prevent ourselves from leaning towards the liberalism we're reproached for at court" when they hear "such stupidity . . . heart-breaking" (299).

Léon M. is also starting to hear echoes of the revolutionary rhetoric he has known since infancy in the monarchist talk. Prince Nelrode had been responsible for the brutal suppression of a Polish uprising, sending the cavalry out after a battle to trample the bodies of dead Poles beyond recognition. But he defends that action in moral terms: the "horses . . . couldn't do them any more harm . . . and inspiring terror did them good; it stopped the insurrection and so saved human lives" (300). The prince says he "behaved rationally": "I will never regret having been humane" (299). Of course, the terrorists also rationalize violence, killing symbolic targets such as Courilof for the sake of influencing public opinion. But the narrator remarks that although he first heard those words with "ironic disbelief," he later "understood there had not been an ounce of hypocrisy in what these men said. They simply had a short memory, as we all do" (299). At the time, however, they only led him to "musing and wondering whose . . . speculations about the future . . . were fair," a contemplation that left him "sad and tired, but filled with feelings of blissful savagery" (305).

Léon M.'s life in Courilof's household not only shows him a side of powerful people he had never imagined but also changes his view of political power. He comes to understand not only that powerful people seldom feel powerful but that their actual power is hedged in ways invisible to the public. Prince Nelrode is offended when protestors blame the ruling class for wars: "No one ever wants war or any other sort of crime, but that doesn't stop it. Because the people in power are weak human beings, not blood-thirsty monsters, as everyone imagines. . . . *Lord,* wouldn't that be preferable!" (296). Léon M. remarks that Courilof spoke "the truth" when he adds something similar: "Ministers, princes, what puppets they all are! True power lies in the hands of madmen or children, who don't even know they have it. The rest of humanity is chasing after shadows!" (346).

Courilof does not analyze the kind of power that children or madmen unconsciously possess, though we may remember Némirovsky's description of a mob possessed by a "demon." However, Courilof's relationship with a Jewish woman who pleads for compensation illustrates the gulf between the unlimited power ordinary people attribute to officials and their actual ability to control outcomes. Sarah Aarontchik had denounced her son's tutor, who turned out to be an undercover agent for the Ministry of Education and who retaliated by demanding a hundred rubles. When she could not pay, he planted papers and books in her son's room so that he would be expelled. Sarah Aarontchik brings documents to Courilof that support her claim, including a confession from Courilof's agent. Courilof agrees to investigate and recommend that her son be allowed to resume his studies. But no, she cries, that will not do: her son committed suicide, so she wants Courilof to compensate her for the loss of income she expected from him, which she needs to educate her other children.

Although Sarah Aarontchik's plight is terrible, her denunciation of the tutor puts her in an unattractive light, and Courilof hates to be blamed for matters outside his control. So he flies into a rage, laughing hysterically afterwards and wondering aloud, "Do such creatures deserve any pity?" (314). But in the end he softens and sends the money, a good deed that comes back to haunt him. Dahl will claim that Sarah Aarontchik had once performed an abortion on Margot and Courilof is only giving into blackmail. As for Prince Nelrode, her past lover, he is blown up by an anarchist bomb, which deprives the Courilofs of the protection he offered them. Now it is even easier for Dahl to spread vicious rumors about Margot, which the Czar encourages, suspecting Courilof of favoring his brother, Prince Michael.[7] Meanwhile, right-wing Russian papers at home are denouncing Courilof for his liberality to the grieving mother, while revolutionary papers abroad report that the son "had been murdered by Courilof's agents" (316).

Although Léon M.'s reservations about killing Courilof began as soon as he saw how ill he was, he feels them even more intensely after he lives in the household, even though Courilof's ministry continues to treat protestors harshly. His contact among the revolutionaries, Fanny, increasingly presses him to action, meeting him nightly to talk about "the harassment in the universities, the disturbances crushed with unbelievable violence, the students who'd been arrested and deported" (327). Léon M. believes her accounts but finds Fanny, her "voice quivering with passion and hatred," increasingly distasteful (309). "The idea of killing this man filled me with repulsion and horror," he declares. "He was a blind creature already living in the shadow of death" (321). But he is also beginning to like "the married couple, the Killer Whale and his old tart; they moved me, I don't know why" (318). When Fanny questions him closely about what Prince Nelrode said to Courilof, he realizes that though both men "were feared and hated . . . [they] seemed as imperfect and unhappy as anyone, including me" (309). When he realizes that Courilof is more absorbed in the secondary plot, Dahl's efforts to replace him as minister of education, than in the primary question of how university protestors should be addressed, he sympathizes: "My poor Courilof! I had never been as close to him, never understood him so well, despised him so much, felt as sorry for him as I did on those days" (343). Léon M. has stopped thinking as an ideologue; what binds him to Courilof is the ethical obligation imposed by their personal relationship.

Perhaps it is a flaw in the story that its triple plots dissolve so quickly at the end. The emperor and his wife do come to Irina Courilof's ball, but the next week the emperor urges Courilof to seek a divorce and replaces him with Dahl when he refuses. The political situation deteriorates rapidly; Léon M. scarcely can enjoy his relief from the pressure to assassinate Courilof before another student killing occurs. Courilof is warned in advance by a delegation of frightened teachers who, refusing to accept his loss of power, beg him to prevent something terrible from happening. The next day the army fires on a group of protestors trying to petition the emperor and kills fifteen people, including the son of a teacher from the delegation.

As Courilof predicted, the massacre puts Dahl in an impossible position: the czar can accept violence when it happens at a distance but does not want to see "dead bodies underneath his windows" (348). Courilof is back in the ministry, and Léon M., understanding "the intensely bitter joke destiny had played on us," is "devastated" (356). But within days he must flee Russia because Courilof has become suspicious and is having him followed: "At that very moment, I could have happily held a gun to his head and pulled the trigger" (358). Back across the border in late September, Léon M., accompanied by Fanny, carries the bomb into the cathedral where the long-awaited visit with the kaiser is being celebrated. At the last moment he cries, "I can't kill him" (361). Fanny grabs the bomb and throws it at Courilof. They are arrested; Léon M. takes the blames for the bomb and is sentenced to be hanged. Fanny gets life in prison.

"But," says Léon M., "you should never count on death any more than you count on life" (362). His death sentence is commuted on the birth of the emperor's son; he is sent to Siberia and then released sometime after the beginning of the Revolution of 1905, only to return in 1917 as a Bolshevik. He will be "head of the Special Branch," most likely the Cheka, and will be "chief administrator" of the Red Army when it battles the Whites, led by Nikolai Yudenich, in the same seaside area where he had once visited Courilof's villa (333, 271). Although we have no detailed, coherent account of Léon M.'s activities as a Bolshevik, we know that he did "terrible work": he speaks of having machine guns installed in Fanny's former home "once we'd taken Kiev" to mow people down as they came out of church and recalls a conversation in prison with a "grand duke dying of hunger, his face smashed by one of the guards" (251, 259, 285). "When the policies of the leaders changed," he tells us, "I was sent into exile" (251).

Just as he had noticed that revolutionaries and monarchists both rationalized violence, he had long been aware of their tendency to fall into the same clichés. When the "famous terrorist," fated to be "executed by the Soviets in 1918," insists that Courilof must be assassinated, he adds, "Those people deserve no more pity than mad dogs" (339, 341). He remarks that Langenberg had used the same language, and we recall how Courilof briefly believed that Sarah Aarontchik deserved no pity. In his last conversation with Courilof, Léon M. asks him if the innocent deaths he has caused keep him awake and receives a surprisingly honest answer: "Every action, every battle brings death. If we are on this earth, it is to act and destroy. . . . When one is acting for a higher cause it isn't easy to live a good life" (357). His rationalization for sending "men to their deaths . . . who . . . were like my brothers, my very soul" is similar: "as long as we are on this earth, we have to play the game" (334–35). No decisive political action, he seems to believe, can remain innocent.

Léon M. has not resolved the dilemma he articulates: abstract slogans such as "eliminate the unjust for the good of the majority" become problematic as soon as we ask, "And who is just?" He seems to agree with Prince Nelrode that "human nature is incomprehensible—the good have been cruel, the intelligent foolish" (303). At times he is nostalgic for Russia and the suffering he endured on behalf of the revolution; he would die "happy and at peace . . . in one of those prison cells I knew so well" (252). But elsewhere he despairs of any political message: "A revolution is such a slaughterhouse! Is it really worth it? Nothing's worth the trouble, it's true, not even life" (332). But is the fact that "it is unbearable for a hunter to kill an animal he has looked after and fed" tantamount to a prohibition on all killing? (334). Léon M. seems to die with the question unanswered. Doubtless Irène Némirovsky, looking to the Soviet Union in 1932, believed that the hopes of the idealists of 1917 had been betrayed. The question would become harder for her in 1940, when the Nazis and their French collaborators were in power.

Chapter 3

David Golder, the Controversy, and One "Revision"

As the introduction noted, Némirovsky's portrayals of the upper-middle-class Jewish milieu in which she lived can distress twenty-first-century readers. Critics correctly point to her portrayals of characters with stereotypical traits, such as avarice and vulgarity, which were so commonly associated with Jews in fiction written before World War II that only her Jewish critics remarked on them at the time. Some have further deplored her failure to write about Jewish spirituality and culture or to balance portraits of overbearing and flawed characters with warm-hearted, generous, and likeable Jewish people. In any case, today's readers, who have grown up fully aware of the Holocaust, its memory shaped by decades of research, documentation, and artistic representation, will find any text problematic if it echoes slurs from the centuries in which Western culture stigmatized Jews as an alien race.

The Controversy

This consciousness of the Holocaust helped create a favorable climate for *Suite Française* in the early years of the twenty-first century, when most readers were keenly interested in the experiences of people who, like its author, were deported and murdered. But this same climate made for a difficult reception of Némirovsky's fiction from the 1930s, as it came back into print and then was translated. The most problematic text is the one that established Némirovsky's reputation, *David Golder.* This story of a successful businessman who loses his fortune and then wins it back through a struggle that kills him, struck some reviewers, most notably the *New Republic*'s Ruth Franklin, as "an appalling book by any standard." In "Scandale Française," she argued that its "Jewish caricatures are shocking" and found the publisher's framing of Némirovsky as a Holocaust writer not just "spin" but "a fraud." The real-life Némirovsky, in Franklin's debatable interpretation of Jonathan Weiss's biography, gained her considerable success "by trafficking in the most sordid anti-Semitic stereotypes."

Franklin, a recipient of the Guggenheim Fellowship and author of *The Thousand Darknesses: Lies and Truth in Holocaust Fiction* (Oxford, 2011), is a highly qualified reader whose arguments deserve serious consideration. She first pressed her case in a review of Sandra Smith's one-volume translation of *David Golder, The Ball, Snow in Autumn,* and *The Courilof Affair,* citing offensive passages from *David Golder.* As additional evidence of Némirovsky's "self-hatred," Franklin accurately noted that she had many friends in right-wing literary circles and published in journals such as *Candide* and *Gringoire,* which had anti-Semitic editorial policies and content. After Philippe Pétain became the Vichy marshal of France, Némirovsky wrote to him asking to be distinguished, as "an honorable foreigner," from other, presumably poor, Yiddish-speaking refugees from the East. She noted that after Némirovsky's arrest, her husband, Michael Epstein, wrote a letter to the German ambassador, Otto Abetz, stating that although Némirovsky was indeed Jewish, her writing was "anti-Semitic."[1] And finally, acknowledging Weiss's argument that Némirovsky's portraits of Jews "moderate" in 1939, Franklin expressed dismay at the absence of Jewish characters from *Suite Française,* speculating that "perhaps Némirovsky was incapable of creating sympathetic Jewish characters."[2]

Although Ruth Franklin's attack was the first and most thoroughgoing, it was not isolated. In 2009 Naomi Price reviewed Sandra Smith's translation of *The Dogs and the Wolves* (1940) in London's prestigious *Times Literary Supplement.* Characterizing it as steeped in "crude anti-Semitism," Price went on to observe that "had a Nazi publishing house commissioned a novel stipulating the perpetuation of racial stereotypes, they would not have been disappointed with this as a result." Similarly, when the distinguished novelist Francine Prose reviewed Philipponnat and Lienhardt's *Life of Irène Némirovsky,* along with Bridget Patterson's translation of some of Némirovsky's short fiction, *Dimanche and Other Stories,* in the *New York Times Book Review* in May 2010, she repeated the charge that Némirovsky "was the author of several anti-Semitic novels as well as a regular contributor to xenophobic and racist French journals." She quoted a passage from one of the *Dimanche* stories in which a Jewish refugee is described as looking "almost like a monkey" to prove her point that Némirovsky's "inability to distinguish caricature from character is the hallmark of a writer unable to see the problem with doggedly insisting on the 'honesty' of repeatedly painting slight variations on the all-too-familiar portrait of a long-nosed, scheming, unhygienic, miserly Jew."

Némirovsky, of course, has not lacked defenders, whom we will consider after we read *David Golder* closely. We note, however, that her most vocal detractors reject the most obvious defense, that Némirovsky could not have anticipated the rise of Hitler when she wrote *David Golder* in 1929. "If Némirovsky's crude anti-Semitic stereotypes were banal in their time," argued Franklin, "then they are even worse to behold, since they were then just the common currency of a racist culture." Némirovsky's critics seem to expect her to anticipate the twenty-first-century perspective of people familiar with Holocaust studies, although her death assured that she would not live to hear the term "Holocaust" applied to events she experienced at first hand. While no one is quite willing to say that she deserved her fate, it seems to elicit little sympathy or be accompanied by unprovable assumptions. Thus Price characterized as a "savage irony" that she died "having been unable to prove any traces of Aryanism," a phrase suggesting that Némirovsky actively sought to conceal her origins. As Némirovsky told Nina Gourfinkel in 1930, "I'm Jewish myself and say so to anyone prepared to listen" (PL 164). Price failed to note that Némirovsky was arrested even before the infamous round-up of Jews in Paris on July 16–17, 1942, normally seen as the first stage in the escalation of Vichy's deportation program. This round-up, which led to the temporary incarceration of over thirteen thousand Jewish people in the Vélo d'Hiv, or Winter Cycling Stadium, in horrifying conditions will be familiar to those who have seen the 2010 film *Sarah's Key*. Némirovsky's early arrest can be traced to her decision to live openly in occupied France, wearing the prescribed yellow star.

The charge that Némirovsky was, if not anti-Semitic, at least "self-hating" has been reprised in the popular press and on the Internet so often as to constitute one of those rare cases in which a critical debate is well known to people who have never actually read the author in question.[3] As a result, few readers today can pick up *David Golder* unaware of its reputation for anti-Semitism. Moreover, reading the first chapter will be enough to confirm Franklin, Prose, and Price's contention that she draws on anti-Semitic stereotypes. This novel is grounded in old associations between Jews and moneymaking, and recognizes that they are often thought to be outsiders whose business practices involve the secrecy and manipulation, sharpness and slyness, for which Shylock made his name. The novel's first word, "No," underscores the title character's refusal to lend money to his business partner of twenty-six years. They are both Russian Jews, men who have made a fortune buying and selling oil wells, among other commodities. Marcus, whom David Golder has detected in a plot to double-cross him, goes off to commit suicide in a brothel, and the next day Golder calls on his widow, finding her bargaining with the funeral director for a cheaper coffin. Golder offers the widow some money but only after removing documents bearing his own name from the dead man's desk. Plot and characterization are in fact grounded in familiar stereotypes; the only real question is whether the text simply reproduces and ratifies them, or whether it critically modifies and therefore undermines them.

Arguing that *David Golder* undermines anti-Semitic stereotypes requires us to think clearly about the difference between propaganda and the literary novel. Where propaganda simplifies in order to enlist its audience's allegiance to a political movement, literary novels tend to ambiguity, irony, and complexity. Their authors do not intend to move readers to take simple actions, and their texts do not provide a justification for making generalizations about whole ethnic groups. Literature tends to find difficult cases, to draw us into the grey areas where the assumptions we bring to the text may be put in question. Audiences are often asked to identify with unsympathetic characters or at least to find something human and recognizable in them.

How much weight we give to historical context is another issue. We can only read Némirovsky, in Angela Kershaw's excellent formulation, "after Auschwitz," after an extermination campaign that was unthinkable even when it was taking place. We have to keep in mind, even if we cannot precisely calculate, the transformation in historical, political, philosophical, and theological consciousness that the Holocaust produced. We will also need to look closely at the difference between Némirovsky's treatment of Jewish themes in her early work, published well before Hitler came to power, and later work that clearly grapples with the crisis that brought so many Jewish refugees to France after 1933. Yet another issue we need to understand historically is the term "self-hating Jew," which Némirovsky's critics frequently deploy. Rather than simply serving as a passive bad example of the phenomenon, Némirovsky recognized it and actively used it to delineate character.

This analysis will not lead to a full-fledged refutation of Franklin's arguments, although it will certainly question many of them. Indeed, it will argue that *David Golder* haunted Némirovsky, who told a reviewer that she would write such a novel differently in 1938 (PL 164). Several of her subsequent works, from *Le Pion sur l'échiquier* (*The Pawn on the Chessboard*, 1934) to *La Proie* (*The Prey*, 1938) to *Le Maître des âmes* (*The Master of Souls*, 1939) to *The Dogs and the Wolves* (1940) can be read as rewriting key issues from *David Golder*. Certainly the theme of the ambitious outsider continued to preoccupy her, and she made efforts to present it both as a part of Jewish experience and as a story that could be divorced completely from her own culture.

David Golder: The Text

While *David Golder* initially introduces anti-Semitic stereotypes, the novel's narrative strategy soon begins undercutting them. All racisms involve dehumanizing another group of people, presenting them as objects that burden the majority and, like pests, need to be controlled, possibly eradicated. Once a novelist enters into a character's subjectivity, presenting the world from his or her point of view, she is committed to representing the character's humanity. From the moment the narrative leaves readers alone with David Golder, they experience his self-doubts, his uncertainties, and his pain. In his Paris apartment after the scene with Marcus, Golder feels alien rather than at home, surrounded by objects such as "winged Victories in bronze with black marble bases" that he "particularly detested" (8). He has bought them for others, having no other role than "to pay" and wonder where he "will get the money" (8). Even as he tries to justify his refusal of Marcus by saying, "Let *him* start over. . . . *I've* had to do it often enough," their last conversation replays itself in his mind (8, italics in original). He is again uneasy.

Already an aging man, sixty-eight, his face "deathly pale and waxy," and beset by fatigue, insomnia, and a racking asthmatic cough, Golder suffers his first terrifying attack of angina as he travels to Biarritz to join his family after Marcus's funeral. The pain traps him on his sleeping car berth, where he feels "as if earth were being pushed into his mouth, as it was . . . the dead man's . . . Marcus" (21). When the pain fades, his thoughts return to his partner: "'I see it now . . . It's Marcus. But why? Why?' At that moment he felt he could see within himself with extraordinary lucidity" (25). But then he dismisses the idea of "remorse" and moves back to self-justification: "'I have nothing to regret'" (25). Yet the dead man remains the only person with whom he identifies, for he thinks of the businessmen gathered at Marcus's funeral as "dogs, bastards" and is almost as hostile to "the others . . . his wife . . . his daughter . . . Yes, even her, he was no fool. He was nothing more than a money machine" (23).

The reader's first acquaintance with Golder's wife, Gloria, and his daughter, Joyce, in Biarritz bears out this bitter characterization. When he contemplates the purple awning Gloria purchased for the terrace of their Biarritz, he can only think of Marcus's wife describing her husband's last moments, his "mouth full of foam and blood" (28–29). Both wife and daughter ask for money within minutes of joining him. At the point in a reunion where she might be expected to ask her father about himself, Joyce asks him if she is "growing beautiful"; Gloria asks if he notices how much weight she has lost (33).

The society Gloria and Joyce have gathered around themselves seems to confirm Golder's view that they are "all the crooks, the pimps, the old whores on earth" (30). Like Thackeray's *Vanity Fair* or Fitzgerald's *The Beautiful and Damned,* the novel portrays a society where baptized Christians are as materialistic and vulgar as anyone else. There is Gloria's long-term lover, Hoyos; the destitute White Russian prince Alexis, Joyce's suitor, who may really prefer men but is currently the lover of an elderly rich Englishwoman, Lady Rovenna; and the rich old businessman, Fischl, who prides himself on having been jailed for fraud in Austria, Russia, and France. Later there will be Joyce's friend, Daphne Mannering, "with her mother and the German man who kept them" and a Maharajah with "his wife, his mistress," and two daughters, along with a dancer from Argentina and a Japanese general (37). Of all these people, only the Golders and Fischl are Jewish; their society is so international that we may not notice immediately that none of them are French.

On the evening of his return, Golder takes his wife's advice and heads toward home with his daughter at the wheel of Daphne Mannering's car. Joyce instead takes him to a casino, knowing that once he sees its lights he will not want to leave. Before he goes off to play, as she had intended, she cries, "Oh, Dad, I do love you so!" (48). Through a long night she alternately fears he will lose and fantasizes about using his winnings to pay for a trip to Spain with the penniless Russian. The next morning Golder emerges, having lost and then regained a million francs, with an additional fifty thousand, which he hands to Joyce. After filling her hand with banknotes, he collapses "with a deep, dull moan that seemed to rise up as if from the living roots of a falling tree that has been struck right through its heart" (50).

At this point, we may deplore the novel's presentation of Jews as plotting financiers, but we see a degree of self-doubt and complexity in David Golder that none of the other people in his environment, whether Jewish or Christian, demonstrate. We hear the evidence confirming Marcus's betrayal; we understand the pain and panic his angina creates because we experience them through his consciousness; and we largely share his view of Hoyos, Prince Alexis, and Daphne Mannering because nothing in their dialogue or behavior suggests hearts of gold or hidden depths. Golder's heart attack, however, provides an occasion for demonstrating the pathologies of his marriage, and the language of its dialogue and commentary provides critics with fodder for their accusation of anti-Semitism or self-hate.

When the doctor tells Gloria the truth, that Golder has had a heart attack, suffers additionally from angina, and "will have to stop working," she translates his diagnosis into hard economic fact (53). Golder cannot quit working because he has put every penny of his profits back into his businesses: "Millions on paper, of course, but cash in hand, not a penny" (54). The family regularly spends so much that a million francs "would only last six months" (54). Moreover, a future of nursing "a useless, bedridden man who was dying" is unacceptable. Worse yet, what if a tranquil existence were to allow him, as the doctor believes possible, to live on for fifteen years? "No, no. . . . She detested him. He was mean, old, and ugly" (54). She briefly acknowledges that she has put some money aside, "but that's my money, mine and mine alone!" (55). No, she will not support him, and she will not pass on the doctor's advice that he retire immediately.

So the medical history is subsumed in an economic melodrama. The doctor may tell Gloria the truth, but he also tells her, in the usual dogma of his times, to conceal it from her husband. As a society doctor, however, he finds an excuse to change the diagnosis as soon as he realizes how little truth she wants. "I am now inclined to believe we are dealing with an attack brought about purely by nerves," he equivocates, and this is the line she takes with her husband (57). Golder suspects the truth, interrogating his nurse closely when she discourages travel and even drafting a telegram to a specialist in Paris, but confronting his death is no more attractive to him than it is to Gloria. So he remains ignorant, and the family dysfunctions continue to play out against economic chaos. A business associate arrives to tell him that the most dreadful rumors about Marcus's suicide and Golder's illness are destroying his credit: the Bank of England plans to sell off his collateral if he does not pay his overdraft of four million within the week. Golder's major hope of restoring his credibility depends on meeting with Tübingen, the German with whom Marcus had secretly negotiated, who subsequently agreed to buy out Golder and take him into his own company, and wants him to go to the Soviet Union to negotiate an oil concession.

Though in no condition to travel, Golder recklessly commits to a series of meetings in Paris, London, and New York. Meanwhile, the family keeps undermining his convalescence; Joyce demands more money and storms off when he refuses it. When Hoyos lectures him about handling Joyce more forcefully, Golder pounds on the table and then physically shoves his wife's lover. Golder's travel plans alarm Gloria enough to heed her lover's advice about arranging to put the title to the Biarritz house in her name. But Golder demonstrates backbone on this occasion as well, refusing to hand over any more of his assets and taunting her with his knowledge of how much wealth she has secretly amassed. He points out that he has subsidized her many lovers and even, in the case of Hoyos, provided enough money for them to pass on to other women. Everything that remains will be reserved for his daughter. "Your daughter!" exclaims Gloria and reveals that Joyce's father is really Hoyos (88). His lurid memories of a visit from Gloria when he was building a railway in the American West confirm the story; all too obviously, she visited him only to provide a cover story for her pregnancy. For once, he must believe Gloria: he has no biological daughter.

This ugly scene, which will become uglier when we look at the inflammatory language that accompanies it, is of course too much for the sick man to withstand. He reviews the hard struggle to make money, the moral compromises, and even acknowledges, "Yes, I killed Simon Marcus" (92). A few hours later, the business associate finds Golder half-dead in his bed. It is too late for him to travel to London; he is not even conscious enough to sign his name to his letters. "Three days later, David Golder's crash on the Stock Market was over, dragging down many other fortunes along with his own, like a senseless tide" (93).

Self-Hatred

The Jewish "self-hatred" of which Némirovsky's critics have accused her is the subject of Sander Gilman's masterful *Jewish Self-Hatred: Anti-Semitism and the Hidden Language of the Jews* (1986). Gilman did not invent the term, which appeared in Germany shortly after World War I, but he has explored its history, its meaning, and its American manifestations more thoroughly than anyone before him.[4] He explains that he decided to write this book after noticing the degree to which his female graduate students, newly admitted to the Ivy League, had absorbed the very prejudice against women that previously excluded them. Gilman postulates that members of any excluded or disadvantaged group are painfully aware of the disparaging terms in which the majority sees them and have good reason to wish to assimilate themselves to the majority by demonstrating their own divergence from stereotype. Némirovsky's letter to Pétain would be a classic example of this impulse.

"The liberal fantasy," as Gilman puts it, is that outsiders can share power with insiders if they act exactly like them. But the real insider is already inside. As Hélène grasps in *The Wine of Solitude,* what one wants is not to become French but to already be French.[5] What the outsider really hears from the insider is: "The more you are like me, the more I know the true value of my power, which you wish to share, and the more I am aware that you are but a shoddy counterfeit, an outsider." This is a classic double bind, which the outsider represses, "saying, in effect, The contradiction must be within me, since that which I wish to be cannot be flawed [*sic*]. Perhaps I truly am different, a parody of that which I wish to be"(Gilman 2–3).

Jewish people might experience the impulse to assimilate, to share the insider's advantages, as self-hatred, a dislike of the difference they find in themselves and their Jewish family and friends. But for Gilman, this "Jewish self-hatred" is a syndrome shared with all people who have experienced exclusion. It is an understandable fact of life, not a moral flaw, or, as Susan Suleiman has put it, "an analytic concept, not a bludgeon" ("Jewish Question," 12). Indeed, when writers implicitly contrast a "self-hating Jew," a Kafka or Philip Roth or Némirovsky, with "self-loving" Jews like themselves, they replicate the "splitting" that the concept was designed to analyze. "Such splitting," according to Suleiman, "excludes precisely the possibility of ambiguity and ambivalence, concepts I find more useful in discussing psychological attitudes towards . . . any minority group identity" (13).

If we accept Gilman's general characterization of self-hatred as a social phenomenon, we also acknowledge that a writer may actively observe and portray it. When Golder's nose is described as "enormous and hooked, like the nose of an old Jewish moneylender," one certainly can imagine the phrase appearing in

Der Stürmer. But when Martina Stemberger notes that such phrases are usually set in the consciousness of a Jewish character or occur in dialogue between two Jewish characters, one can begin to see them as cases where the author observes "Jewish self-hatred" in action (Stemberger 114). It is Gloria who is looking at her husband's nose, seeing it transformed by illness: "It had never been that shape before" (58). And since Gloria is the constant object of her husband's and, it would seem, the narrator's scorn, her observation carries a note of irony rather than a summons to join in the ethnic slander.

This Jewish self-hatred is most visible in the terrible scene in which Golder and Gloria relive all their financial and marital grievances, which ends with the revelation of Joyce's parentage and the physical collapse that results in bankruptcy. Gloria starts it all when she demands the title to the house, stringing together insults to her husband's manhood—"wimp," "coward"—with reminders of his Jewishness: "You're still the little Jew who sold rags and scrap metal in New York, from a sack on your back" (85). He responds in kind, reminding her that she was not called "Gloria" when he met her in her "moneylender father's" shop: "'Havke! Havke!' He hurled the Yiddish name at her like an insult, shaking his fist" (85). The ugliness of the slurs matches the ugliness of the actions: "His old teeth were savagely biting into her flesh beneath her pearls" (85). And they serve a function, underscoring the poverty from which these two antagonists rose and the desperation of their need to disown it. It also reflects Clement Greenberg's insight that "hatred is as intimate as love," which accompanied his explanation that he would rather be called a "self-hating" Jew than a self-alienated one (Reitter 44).

After Golder's bankruptcy, he leaves Gloria behind with her savings and her lover; she and Hoyos take Joyce and Alec, the Russian prince, with them on a cruise. Golder returns to Paris, watching with "sardonic pleasure" as removal men strip the apartment of objects he always disliked. After one visit from Gloria, in which he struggles to control his temper and warns her that her speculations in the stock market will lead to ruin, he is alone. He has just enough money to eke out a simple existence; his only visitor is "an old German Jew," Soifer. This man's "meanness bordered on madness," since initial losses in the German inflation brought home to him "the way revolutions and war" could erase wealth. Now rich, he has invested his fortune in jewels, which he keeps in a safe in London, but lives like a pauper. Too frugal to buy dentures, he eats "only cereal and puréed vegetables" (104).

Soifer is presented ambivalently; even his physical appearance sends mixed signals, a "head crowned with beautiful . . . silvery white hair" and a "look of pathetic nobility" offset by a "gaping, sputtering mouth . . . that inspired a feeling of revulsion and fear" (104). In a much cited line, the text anticipates his "death, all alone, like a dog . . . buried in the cheapest cemetery in Paris by his family who hated him, and whom he had hated, but to whom he nevertheless left a fortune of thirty million francs, thus fulfilling till the end the incomprehensible destiny of every good Jew on this earth" (104). Here we are neither reading dialogue nor a transcription of a character's thoughts; the aloof figure who pronounces on "the destiny of every good Jew" must be a narrator and could easily be confused with an omniscient one. Negative generalizations always convey bias, and this one recalls the anti-Semitic association of Jews with single-minded acquisition of wealth. Some readers also find an allusion to Fanny Némirovsky's financial demands on her husband here or even a trace of the author's daughterly guilt. Note, too, that Soifer's asceticism seems more like a parody of Christian virtue than anything in Jewish theology, which is not in the habit of cringing away from the body or its normal needs.

This ambivalent attitude toward Jewishness seeps into David Golder's consciousness as well. Initially he is given to mental assessments that draw on stereotype: "Golder looked with a kind of hatred at Fischl, as if at a cruel caricature. Fat little Jew . . . comical, vile, and slightly sinister" (31). The phrase "as if at a cruel caricature" seems an example of Gilman's definition of "Jewish self-hatred"; Golder sees this man as the kind of Jew who confirms anti-Semites in their prejudices. But as he becomes older and sicker, his thoughts recur to Judaism. In a moment of despair, when he thinks he is dying, he whispers, "*Adenoi* . . . suddenly remembering the forgotten name of the Lord" (63). He finds companionability in Soifer, "who possessed a kind of dark sense of humor that was very similar to Golder's" (104). When Soifer insists on a restaurant in the rue des Rosiers, Golder refuses to order food but nonetheless feels nostalgic: "He stretched out his hands towards the glowing stove that had just been lit" and "a kind of sensual warmth . . . seeped deep into his bones" (109).

Through his association with Soifer, Golder is brought closer to a Jewish community vulnerable to history and politics, war and deportations. Soifer asks him if the "dirty Jewish neighborhood" near rue des Rosiers reminds him of anything, and though Golder snaps back, "Nothing good," we understand that he has made a connection with his youth (108). Within a page he is "transported back in time to the old country, was seeing once again those familiar faces" (108). Soifer reminds him of traditional Jewish poverty, remarking that it "preserves the Jews like the brine preserves the herrings" (109). And Soifer makes the only contemporary allusion to the legal disabilities of Jews in France when he complains, "If I don't renew my identity card right away, I'll be deported" (106).

Isolated as he is, Golder soon receives two visits in quick succession. One is from Tübingen, who tries to talk him into reviving their connection and going to the Soviet Union to negotiate a deal over oil wells in the Caucasus. Golder initially says no because of his heart condition, but he relents after Joyce pays him a visit. Even though her irresponsibility enrages him and he understands that she is not his biological daughter, he feels a stir of compassion when she tells him she is engaged to Fischl, "the cruel caricature" (115). Initially the prospect amuses Golder, as he imagines Joyce cheating on Fischl with "your little gigolo": "This was how you were meant to end up, you little slut, it was written all over your face" (116). But Joyce grows increasingly hysterical, reminding him that Fischl is a "dirty old man" and threatening, like Marcus, to commit suicide: "you'll have my death on your conscience too" (117). But then he softens: perhaps she is his daughter after all; perhaps it does not matter. Besides, the thought of people saying that Golder's daughter had to marry Fischl wounds his pride. He promises Joyce he will make more money, only for her, by traveling to the Soviet Union for Tübingen.

We know that the trip will kill Golder. First there is the long journey by train, then eighteen weeks of negotiating with Soviets in smoke-filled rooms, enduring sleepless nights, every nerve poised to detect efforts by his Communist adversaries to smuggle in language that will allow them to break this contract as they have broken others. Finally, he slams his fist on the table and insists that the talks are over, demanding that all of its seventy-four articles be read aloud to him, even as he, looking "pale and wan as a corpse," tears open his shirt to massage his chest (124). The papers signed, he endures a twenty-one-hour car trip to the port city, presumably Odessa, which he had left forty-eight years earlier. He spends the night in a rundown hotel with bullet holes in the walls and collapses in a storm that starts up as soon as his ship moves away from the port.

Staggering below deck, he is joined by a young man whose accent he recognizes immediately:

> "You're a Yid?"
>
> The man laughed nervously but seemed cheered. "Yes," he murmured. "You too?"
>
> "Me too," said Golder. (135)

Now listed in English dictionaries as an offensive word, *yid* has a similar status in most other European languages, although in its original Yiddish it simply means "a Jew." The two men do not seem to view it as an insult but as the basis for a bond that needs to be articulated in desperate circumstances. Golder watches him speaking "with a kind of sad, poignant pleasure" for "that feverish desire, that nervous energy . . . he too had once possessed them: the hungry exuberance so particular to young people of his race" (136).

As Martina Stemberger has demonstrated, the association of Jews with feverish, burning energy, with restlessness and ambition, has a long history in anti-Semitic discourse and therefore seems troubling when it appears in Némirovsky, along with the word "race." In a context where anti-Semites focus on ruthlessness and unrestrained greed, we can understand that feverish ambition might not always be admired. Yet we may also wonder if anything in the context of this scene makes the drive to succeed that poverty and discouragement can inculcate in intelligent and talented people problematic. And if money is the object of such a drive? Golder tells the young man that if he wants to get rich, he should take a good look at his own devastated face: "Do you think it's worth it?" (137).

That they are both Jewish is the bond that quite literally enables communication in the last hour of Golder's life, when "the forgotten language of his childhood unexpectedly spilled from his lips, and he started speaking Yiddish" (140). With superhuman effort, Golder dictates instructions to Tübingen and his lawyer with their Paris addresses. He asks to sign the note, which the boy thinks he will not be able to manage, though he does, "with a kind of madness and terrified determination" (141). Then Golder makes the youth swear "before Almighty God" that he will deliver the message and invites him to take all the money in his wallet in exchange. Shaking, the young man slips the addresses under his belt and puts the money in his pocket, leaving behind the man he believes to be already dead.

The novel's remaining paragraph, however, returns to Golder's mind. He imagines himself touching Joyce's hair and then feels her pulling away. Then he sees Marcus. Then all he can see is "a street from his childhood, a candle set behind an icy window" and hears a voice calling, "David, David." This, we are told, "was the last sound he was to hear on this earth" (142). If the first chapters of the novel present David Golder through the lens of anti-Semitic stereotype, the final chapter presents qualities that such a lens could not register. The Golder we see dying is flawed but fully human: a man who acknowledges responsibility for his friend's death and makes extraordinary efforts to leave his wealth to a young woman who has shown him little love. And when he dies, if not sentimental about his Jewish past, he at least associates it with light, warmth, and recognition as well as poverty.

David Golder in France: The 1930s

If we see David Golder being transformed from a ruthless, "self-hating" financier into a morally conscious human being whose flaws seem understandable, we will disagree with critics who find the book a thoroughgoing example of anti-Semitism. As for Franklin's charge that Némirovsky grew rich catering to prejudice, it is useful to remember the wide range of political and cultural anti-Semitism available to readers in the 1930s. The old anti-Semitic novelists of the Dreyfus Affair, Maurice Barrès and Charles Maurras, were still influential figures; by 1937 Louis-Ferdinand Céline's *Bagatelles pour un massacre* was on the shelves; and Robert Brasillach, Drieu la Rochelle, and Louis Rebatet were publishing regularly in the anti-Semitic press, which included the notorious *Je suis partout*.[6] At a time when so many books, magazines, and newspapers urged anti-Semitic actions ranging from deportation and imprisonment to extermination, a literary novel devoid of calls to action would seem quite tame. As Angela Kershaw has concluded, *David Golder* is "an ambivalent work of fiction which uses negative stereotypes of Jewishness but which does not propose anti-Semitic arguments and is (unlike the work of Drieu or Céline) politically disengaged" (116). Stemberger would add that Némirovsky also deserves credit for avoiding another convention of the anti-Semitic novel, the division of the world into "good" and "bad" Jews (17).

But should we be satisfied with the view that Némirovsky remained politically disengaged, or is her disengagement problematic? This is a harder question. In 1930 Nina Gourfinkel interviewed Némirovsky for *L'Univers israélite*, asking whether she was concerned that depictions of financiers like Golder, Marcus, and Soifer provided a weapon for anti-Semites.[7] In that year Némirovsky's answer was clearly no, as she insisted that her portraits of them were not based on stereotypes but on accurate observation. She knew these people: "that's how I saw them" (PL 165). Gourfinkel, who drew Némirovsky out on her "partial, dreary and narrow" experience of Jewish life, ended by concluding that while Némirovsky was "certainly not anti-Semitic," she was barely Jewish at all (166, 168).

But was Gourfinkel's concern about providing ammunition for anti-Semites justified? On this issue, we can turn to Angela Kershaw, who has closely studied early reviews of *David Golder*. These indicate that many critics praised the novel for its "Balzacian" realism and paid little attention to its specifically Jewish themes. Others, influenced by the popularity of the "Jewish novel" in the 1920s, praised it while assuming that readers could avoid overgeneralization. Thus Benjamin Crémieux, himself Jewish, lauded the novel "as an expression of the Jewish soul, but not of the Jewish soul in its totality, which would be impossible, but of the Jewish soul seized at the point at which it is no longer supported by religion and family tradition, and before Western civilization has refined and moderated it" (Kershaw 129). But one anti-Semitic critic did praise it for portraying "one of the Israelite financiers who govern the market," and another regretted that although "for over a hundred years" novelists had been portraying men like Golder in "horrifying terms," they had not so far "caused any damage to their power or prestige" (126). In this case a reviewer who wanted to see Jews damaged regretted that novels had failed to do so, perhaps because they lacked the clarity of straightforward political propaganda. Only in the Jewish press did reviewers complain of anti-Semitism in *David Golder*.

But a defense based on truthfulness or aesthetic quality will not satisfy all critics. To use a more contemporary example, the film version of *The Color Purple* struck Ishmael Reed as a "Nazi conspiracy," while Tony Brown labeled it "the most racist depiction of Black men since *The Birth of a Nation* and the most anti-Black family film of the modem film era" (Bobo 43). Reed and Brown were perfectly aware that incest is universal and has been a theme of Western literature at least since Sophocles. They were not arguing that incest never occurs in African American families but that a mass American audience, which is all too ready to see black men as sexual predators or to assume that African Americans are "primitive," does not need a Steven Spielberg film to ratify those prejudices. Artists, in this view, have a responsibility to understand their audiences and the messages their work will send, and neither the truth nor aesthetic merit nor the purity of the artist's intention should be used to defend a work that reinforces bigotry.

And this, perhaps, is the best argument that can be made against *David Golder.* To anyone who sees politics as trumping aesthetics, who believes that the Holocaust—or, for that matter, the murder of nine South Carolina Christians by a white gunman whom they had welcomed to pray with them—results at least in part from long-tolerated images of Jews or African Americans in art, the issue is clear. Members of a group should not lend support to bigots. Some people, who argue for greater aesthetic independence, may find themselves resisting it in normal times and then drifting the other way during an emergency. Thus Irène Némirovsky, speaking to another interviewer from *L'Univers israélite,* Janine Auscher, in 1935, said, "It is absolutely certain that had there been Hitler, I would have greatly softened *David Golder.*" But even then she had doubts, saying that she would have been wrong to do so, that "it would have been a weakness unworthy of a real writer." Besides, the book also depicted "genuinely racial virtues: courage, tenacity, pride" (PL 164).

The Master of Souls

Like David Golder, Némirovsky also seems to have been uneasy. After publishing *The Ball* in 1930, she avoided Jewish subject matter until 1939, when Hitler was a clear and present threat to France. Then she explicitly returns to Jewish characters faced with dangers in an increasingly right-wing France. These novels, as we know, would not be received any more warmly by Némirovsky's detractors, but they reflect her knowledge of the dire circumstances facing European Jews in the late 1930s and will require their own chapter. It is interesting, however, to consider Némirovsky's untranslated novel of 1939, *Le Maître des âmes,* or *The Master of Souls,* as it reframes some of the issues of *David Golder.*

Like David Golder, Dario Asfar was born in poverty and migrated to France as an ambitious, hard-working young man. Némirovsky deliberately avoided making him Jewish, though the prejudices of the time may have made "a little Levantine from the Near East" too close to Jewishness for comfort.[8] She did not want to risk "suspicions of anti-Semitism" but wanted to tell the story of a "charlatan in the most conventional, the most bourgeois of worlds" (PL 266). A doctor, Dario Asfar seeks out French patients; once he is successful, his associates are never members of the international set we saw at Biarritz in *David Golder.* Nor does Némirovsky create a medical milieu comparable to the business world of David Golder: he usually appears with a patient or in a fashionable social gathering. Where Golder's past is glimpsed only briefly, in flashbacks, Némirovsky establishes Dario Asfar's motivation by explaining how the miseries of his struggles as an impoverished medical student and emigrant lead him to become a charlatan. Since *David Golder* begins with a fully formed protagonist, readers may suspect that his Jewishness, whether cultural or genetic, explains his character. By making Dario Asfar "Levantine" and isolating him from any "Levantine" society, Némirovsky eliminates any genetic explanation; instead this charlatan is formed by his experiences in France. Since his suffering is vividly real and reinforced in a whole series of events, the reader understands how narrow the range of his choices is. The suggestion here is that anyone who suffered from poverty and exclusion, for whom hard work and sacrifice were never enough to ensure a basic standard of living, might well become a con man to survive.

Another way that Némirovsky distances Dario Asfar from David Golder is by giving him a sympathetic wife, daughter of a Jewish clockmaker. As Kershaw helpfully summarizes Stemberger's argument, "anti-Semitism and matrophobia" are indelibly linked in Némirovsky, where negative stereotypes do not convey "hatred for Jews in general, but . . . most often, hatred for the bad mother" (110). We have noted that the "monstrous mothers" in *L'Ennemie, The Wine of Solitude, The Ball,* and *Jezebel* are all gentiles. Gloria Golder, however, is an exception to that practice, and this hard, grasping character who pushes her husband toward death and her daughter into marrying the hateful Fischl, conforms to anti-Semitic stereotypes. She, unlike Golder, is almost entirely seen from the outside and has no opportunity to attract the reader's sympathy by assessing her responsibilities. By introducing Dario's wife, Clara, in a maternity ward and always depicting her as loving, generous, and motherly, Némirovsky avoids any repetition of that toxic mixture of matrophobia with Jewish stereotype that troubles Stemberger.

Moreover, Némirovsky is highly successful in conveying how wretched poverty and frustration damage an initially idealistic man. When we first meet Dario, he is visiting Clara in the hospital, where she has given birth to a healthy son some years after losing another to illness and poor nutrition. We feel Dario's acute hunger as he watches Clara with her hospital dinner tray, noting how eagerly he devours a piece of bread she gives him, even as he protests that he has already eaten. We share his anger when the Russian woman in his apartment building refuses him a loan, because even after fifteen years in France, even with a French medical degree, he has nothing to offer as collateral. We understand that Dario's shabby apartment and clothing make it hard for him to attract middle-class French patients who can pay their bills. When the Russian woman promises to change her mind if he will provide an illegal abortion for her daughter-in-law, we know exactly why he agrees to do so. And when, shortly thereafter, the daughter-in-law abandons her family and the Russian woman insists on being repaid immediately, even though Dario has already used much of the loan to pay his creditors and buy food and clothing, we understand his desperation. He has lost one infant to hunger, and losing another is unthinkable. That is why he turns to his last resort, a rich maître d'hôtel, Ange Martinelli, whose son he saved. The ten-thousand-franc loan Martinelli provides pulls him into disreputability, for the man is in a position to direct to him patients whose ailments, addictions, and injuries must remain in the shadows. Lounging in hotel lobbies and bars, Dario waits for referrals from the maître d'hôtel and thereby becomes complicit in his underworld.

Through Martinelli, Dario meets Philippe Wardes, a rich auto magnate with major psychiatric symptoms, a drinking problem, and a habit of beating his wife or, when she is out of town, bringing home a series of prostitutes. Wardes insists that he will never follow his regular doctor's advice about giving up drinking, smoking, gambling, and prostitutes in favor of a quiet life in the countryside. He thus will remain in Asfar's life, often as his patient, until both Wardes and Clara are dead and Dario marries Wardes's second wife, Elinor. Wardes becomes Dario's prototypical patient, first of a string of troubled rich French people who want "long lives but without having to sacrifice an atom of pleasure" (*OC* 2: 246). And rather than tell them to give up drinking or get more sleep, Dario gives them what they prefer to an accurate diagnosis: he keeps them comfortable, as "a great doctor would frighten them" (246).

For the rest of Dario's career, he is a rich, fashionable doctor promoting a therapy that, as he tells his patients, does not stop with identifying the cause of the patient's symptom but proceeds to "sublimation of the self" (293). "Sublimation of the self" is self-acceptance, particularly of anything that creates shame. The patient learns to see herself as having "an exceptional nervous organization" and to recognize that the source of one's shame is also "the germ of all one's most precious faculties." A "feeling of guilt" is the cause of psychic suffering and must be eradicated (294). Although Dario insists that his method is not psychoanalysis, it will be familiar to anyone who reads current bestselling self-help books. We might say it is a heresy of Freudian psychoanalysis that stresses the dangers of feeling guilty without encouraging reflection on how one's behaviors affect other people. Under his care, patients have the ear of a sympathetic confidant—a confessor, even—and mild prescription drugs that reduce insomnia or soothe the nerves.

Now Dario has "understood in his heart . . . that he agreed to sell his soul if that was the price of earning his existence" (274). This is, as Philipponnat says, the classic Faustian bargain (*OC* 2: 203). Yet *Master of Souls* is an entirely secular book that recalls Thackeray's characterization of the denizens of *Vanity Fair:* "as a set of people living in the world without God" (Saintsbury xiv). Despite Némirovsky's 1938 conversion to Catholicism and the numerous allusions to the Gospels in some of her other writing of the same period, this book has even fewer references to religion than *David Golder* did. So to whom does Dario Asfar sell his soul? There is some hint in a passage where he styles himself a "charlatan," someone who "cultivates the vices and illness of the rich as a plowman sows a field" (286). Ambitious to become a healer, he instead becomes complicit with the vices of a society that does not want to be cured. Again, although no Marxist, Némirovsky stresses the social and economic underpinnings of her character's behavior, showing us that, instead of introducing a contagion, he enables long-established vices of rich French people. We cannot judge this immigrant without judging the French class to whom he sells his soul.

There are times in this book where Dario's charlatanism seems harmless. He overcharges rich society women, but they can afford his fees, and by listening to them he makes them feel better. But Némirovsky casts a cold eye on him; if Dario has chosen the only path to survival, it is still criminal. He shares 50 percent of Wardes's fees with his mistress and plays on his fears until the man "feels shut up, by Dario's willpower, in a magic circle he lacked the power to escape" (360). When this mistress, Elinor, has become Wardes's second wife, she insists that her husband is "mad" and must step aside so that she can run his auto-manufacturing company. The easy, prosperous 1920s have passed, she argues, and in 1936 an irresponsible manager could send any firm into bankruptcy. Dario gives into her pressure, accepting a million francs from Elinor to convert "La Caravelle," his house in Nice, into a *maison de santé,* or care home, where Wardes can be shut up. Even worse, having nurtured Wardes's dependency, Dario suddenly stops answering his pleas for help until the sick man, who had placed all his hopes in him "as if he were God," kills himself (367).

Dario's own son, Daniel, regards his father's virtual imprisonment of Wardes as a crime and urges his mother to report it to the police. But Daniel's prosperous childhood ensures that he is completely foreign to his father. Large, well-muscled, and blond, he does not appear to share a bloodline with either parent. Although he adores his mother, from early childhood he has felt an aversion to his father, detesting "his long Oriental fingers" and his "too soigné" appearance, and always imagining that Dario, who never wears scent, smells like a woman.[9] When he argues about his father's treatment of Wardes, Daniel uses moral abstractions: "It's not a question of the individual, Maman, but of crime, for it is a crime, you know that it is a crime" (338). But his mother, remembering the years of torment that made Dario what he is, stresses that deep emotional connections should count for more: "even if he had killed or stolen, even if the whole world abandoned him, our duty would be to protect, love, and help him" (337).

As we noted, Némirovsky's stress on Dario's poverty and emotional anguish already introduces a mildly Marxist argument about how economic factors shape values. Dario himself articulates this view when he speaks to Clara about Sylvie Wardes, whom he met when she was still married to his patient. This woman embodies "what I came to find in Europe," not only wealth and comfort, but "culture . . . morality . . . virtues, everything that is higher than I, different from me, different from the mud where I was born" (257). She is a creature "without coquetry, without egoism, without avarice, for whom money and the things of this world had no significance" (267). But when Clara reacts jealously, he explains that she has no reason to feel herself inferior to Sylvie, who "comes from a race that has been preserved from hunger for centuries" and therefore "can permit itself the luxury of honor and disinterestedness" (268). When, at a crucial point in his career, Dario accepted ten thousand francs from Sylvie to pay off his debt to Martinelli, he felt shame and stopped seeing her. He was never her lover; he did not want anything to tarnish his idealization of her.

Thus we can read *Master of Souls* as, in part, a rewriting of *David Golder* meant to erase the stain of anti-Semitic stereotypes. Both novels trace the careers of immigrants to France whose single-minded ambition leads to significant financial success, though not to financial security or full social acceptance. By portraying Dario Asfar's evolution from idealistic but starving doctor to charlatan, Némirovsky makes his motivation understandable. The vices he enables are deeply French, belonging to the society and not to the alien. Is this wealthy world really ready to let him die, as his first son did, if he insists on practicing his profession with high ethical standards? Is this France concerned about its aliens, its immigrants, and its refugees, or is it prepared to cooperate with a more villainous invader, who will arrive with a more vigorous program for excluding them?

Master of Souls, under the title *Les Échelles du Levant*, was serialized in the anti-Semitic journal *Gringoire* during the summer of 1939, on the eve of World War II. Whether anyone noticed the contradiction between the novel's sympathetic reading of the immigrants' plight and the journal's call to "expel the aliens" the previous fall is unclear (*OC* 2: 205). Published on the cusp of war, the novel was little noticed at the time, and because it remains untranslated, it has not been reviewed in the English-language press. It is even possible, given the number of stereotypically Jewish traits ascribed to Dario Asfar, from his feverish ambition to his long fingers to his olive skin, that readers might not have noticed that he was labeled "Levantine," not Jewish. That the only Jewish character in the novel is the ever-sympathetic Clara might easily have gone unnoticed as well.

In other words, given a sufficiently anti-Semitic audience, this book too might have reinforced fears of brilliantly unscrupulous outsiders who grew rich at the expense of the natives. Perhaps some contemporary readers might find it offensive for that reason. Némirovsky, like other modernists, thought that an ambitious literary text, riven with ambiguity and nuance, should reflect the difficulty of knowing and judging people that we experience in our own lives. As such, it is clearly distinguished from propaganda that calls for action against whole groups of people. It is always possible, however, for such a text to be read as propaganda and used to buttress a dangerous prejudice.

How far a writer must go to avoid such misreading remains a question on which reasonable people will disagree. But for the reader who is willing to read closely, the transformation of David Golder from a pale shadow of Shylock into full humanity can be seen as a model of the process by which stereotype and rejection are transformed into understanding and sympathy. We might admire Némirovsky for confronting the stereotypes so directly, for taking readers from the villain they thought they knew to a complex human being they might hesitate to judge. We can see a suggestion, even in *David Golder,* that the protagonist's harshness is rooted in painful experience. Reading *Master of Souls,* we can agree with Philipponnat that Némirovsky "gives concrete form to the xenophobic climate which was rampant then in France, which few novels have presented to us so strikingly" (*OC* 2: 206).

Dario Asfar clearly retains his belief in the ideal France embodied by Sylvie Wardes, but he believes that the actual France is indifferent to his welfare and quite willing to let people like him starve in obscurity. That this view was plausible is clear when we remember that on December 11, 1938, Édouard Daladier's government published a decree authorizing the creation of internment camps for undesirable aliens. In September 1939 "foreigners of male sex from territories belonging to the enemy" were told to report to such camps; later, other categories, including women and children, were added. The miseries of their prisoners, which included hunger, filth, and sickness, are recorded in the testimony of refugee writers and intellectuals from Arthur Koestler and Lion Feuchtwanger to Hannah Arendt. A society that could permit such misery, even before the Nazi invasion, is already recognizable in *The Master of Souls.*

So we may legitimately argue that a Jewish writer should not depict characters who reinforce anti-Semitic stereotypes and reject Némirovsky's argument that she knew those people. Yes, she knew people like David and Gloria Golder, including her own parents, and if she had lived in our time she would have known about Bernie Madoff. When an audience is likely to draw illegitimate generalizations, however, we may want her to edit that part of the truth. But we should also recognize that in *Master of Souls,* she portrayed what she believed to be the truth about a significant layer of French society. They were not only beautiful and damned, like characters in F. Scott Fitzgerald, but they already had the social attitudes that would enable many of them to stand by complacently as the Vichy government collaborated with the Nazis in deporting 72,000 people, most to their death, who had lived among them for years. The novel comes from the heart of Irène Némirovsky's experience as a Jewish Russian never granted citizenship, who lived in France for twenty-three years before her death in Poland. This historical experience, whose reality cannot be doubted, demands acknowledgment, no matter how we label her.

Chapter 4

France and the Jews in the 1930s

In a study of Jewish writers active between the Dreyfus Affair and the outbreak of World War II, Isabelle Ebert has observed that during the 1930s most seemed to believe "that Jews should make themselves as inconspicuous as possible" (Malinovich 237). Nadia Malinovich cites the increasing wave of anti-Semitic propaganda coming from Germany during the period and the stream of Jewish refugees following the Nazis' rise to power as triggering this reticence. But France, as we have noted, had its own indigenous anti-Semitism, and some major players in the Dreyfus Affair, most notably Charles Maurras and his Action Française, took on new life in the 1930s.

One notable occasion for the resurgence of native French anti-Semitism was the 1934 Stavisky scandal. At its center was Alexandre Stavisky, a classic con man and, unfortunately for his compatriots, a Jewish Russian émigré. His most famous scam took advantage of the 1920 Treaty of Trianon, which officially ended World War I for Hungary and was followed ten years later by "international accords in The Hague and Paris [to] set up an agrarian fund to compensate" Hungarian landowners whose properties had been incorporated into other nations. The dispossessed soon "lost faith in their claims," but Stavisky offered to buy them at 90 percent, which turned out to mean far less than that in cash and by 1933 meant payment in bonds from the *crédit municipal* of Bayonne (Jankowski 146–49).

The *crédit municipal,* a distinctively French institution, is half bank, half pawnshop; it was founded to make a legal source of liquid cash available to citizens, with profits intended to be used for public welfare. Stavisky's initial inspiration was persuading the mayor of Bayonne to set up a branch of this institution in April 1931, the month, fortuitously, in which the Spanish king was deposed. Located virtually on the Spanish border, Bayonne was an ideal location for spreading rumors that the local *crédit municipal* was filled with jewels pawned by fleeing Spanish aristocrats. Soon the shop had raised forty million francs "on jewels no one had seen from desperate nobility no one had met" (Jankowski 108). Soon La Confiance (Confidence), an insurance company, had "bestowed on the Republic, the status guarantor, as unimpeachable a fiduciary as the borrower behind the annuities and treasure bonds they held," which of course included the worthless guarantees to the Hungarians (Jankowski 109). In the words of Janet Flanner: "The scheme which finally killed Alexandre Stavisky, his political guests' reputations, and the uninvited public's peace of mind, was his emission of hundreds of millions of francs' worth of false bonds on the city of Bayonne's municipal pawnshop, which were bought up by life-insurance companies, counseled by the Minister of Colonies, who was counseled by the Minister of Commerce, who was counseled by the Mayor of Bayonne, who was counseled by the little manager of the hockshop, who was counseled by Stavisky" (Flanner 109).

On January 8, 1934, as headlines reported, Stavisky barricaded himself in his bedroom and committed suicide as the police were arresting him. This story may have even been true but led many to speculate, as Flanner did, that "the police shot him to keep him quiet" (111). The unfolding story revealed fraud and collusion involving newspapers, police, government agencies, and elected officials, including deputies in the French parliament. In normal times one might expect bribed members of parliament or negligent regulators to be disgraced and legal loopholes closed. But this scandal, associated with a Jewish immigrant who had done exactly what anti-Semites always said foreign Jews did, aided by democratic institutions and elected officials, gave the French extreme right an opportunity to call the Republic, democracy itself, into question.

The writer Léon Daudet "hectored 'the government of Scum' day after day, while his fellow novelist Charles Maurras minced no words condemning 'the Jewish State, the Masonic State, the Immigrant State, the Protestant State.'" The Stavisky scandal, he argued, was but a "preliminary skirmish in the war between the 'legal State' constituted by usurpers and the 'real State' of true Frenchmen taking up arms against a 'judiciary of bandits, a police force of assassins, a government of traitors'" (Brown 199). The government of Camille Chautemps fell on charges of corruption on January 27, 1934; Édouard Daladier replaced him as prime minister but resigned on February 7, to be replaced by the conservative Gaston Doumergue.

Daladier resigned because of the riots of February 6, which took place in the Place de la Concorde, outside a French National Assembly attempting to conduct business. Some in the crowd were conventionally armed, while others threw rocks, set fires, and vandalized government buildings. Organized by a coalition of old rightists from the Dreyfus era, such as Action Française, the League of Patriots, and the Camelots du Roi, along with newer groups including the World War I veterans' Croix-de-Feu, the riots led to an armed battle that left fourteen demonstrators and one policeman dead; fourteen hundred more were wounded (Brown 203). The new Doumergue government, labeled a government of national union, preserved the Republic for a time, but the rightist struggle to replace the "legal" government with an (unelected, authoritarian) "real" government continued until June 1940, when the Vichy government, aided by military defeat, fulfilled this long-term indigenous goal.

To people on the French Left, the February 6 riots constituted an attempted fascist coup, an interpretation some later historians dispute. In response, the Left grew better organized and unions more militant; one culturally important organization, the Comité de Vigilance des Intellectuels Antifascistes, was founded in March 1934. Communists and socialists found new ways of working together and in 1935 joined forces to create the Popular Front, a party that won a resounding victory in June 1936. Its prime minister, Léon Blum, was Jewish and its policies popular with labor: a guaranteed right to organize unions, to strike, to work only forty hours per week, and have twelve-day mandatory paid leaves.

An American is tempted to think of analogies with our own recent past. The election to high office of a member of a group traditionally excluded from power marks democratic progress but can provoke backlash. The French Fascist Party (PPF) was founded on June 28, 1936, and quickly grew to 130,000 members. La Cagoule, founded the same year and funded by Eugène Schueller, founder and owner of L'Oréal, was a paramilitary organization for people who found the Camelots too mild; it was committed to "making France ungovernable with strategic acts of terror" (Brown 268). As Eugen Weber explained, "a dirty stream of undifferentiated hate distorted human and social realities. . . . Myths of pervading evil turned superficial disagreements into haunting fears and political differences into vendettas, and the French body politic became incapable of any kind of unity because all foundation for mutual trust had been shattered during these ruthless and bitter fights. . . . The plots of the Cagoule helped to convince both sides that all such plots were real" (Brown 268). Blum's first term ended in June 22, 1937, and four more governments succeeded each other before the German invasion in May 1940. When democracy, under fire for of most of the decade, was defeated, many French citizens, at least initially, welcomed Vichy.

Defining the "French" Novels

The increasing polarization of French politics in the 1930s and resurgent anti-Semitism "made talking about Jews a political act" (PL 260). Appearing early in the decade, the best-selling *David Golder* benefitted from the interest in ethnic literature characteristic of the 1920s. But it had also been criticized for anti-Semitism, and when political anti-Semitism was back in the headlines, championed by some of France's best-known novelists, the stakes were higher than they had seemed to Némirovsky in 1930. "Obviously," she wrote on April 11, 1938, "'the Jew' would be best, but non-literary considerations are a part of my fear'" (PL 260). Throughout the 1930s, she had consciously avoided even Jewish names, trying to avoid the trap into which she fell in *The Master of Souls.* It had not been enough to avoid calling Dario Asfar "*heimatlos*"—that is, homeless—because "that is another word for the Jews" (OC 2: 204); readers nonetheless read him as Jewish. In "Espoirs" (1938) she resigns herself to "calling her heroes Popoff or Arkady, since unfortunately they can't be Lévy or Rabinovitch" (PL 262). Similarly, she renamed a character in *Le Pion sur l'échiquier (The Pawn on the Chessboard)* "Beryl," because she judged it "less dangerous" than his previous "Jewish name Tedesco" (OC 1: 836).

One of the dangers was criticism from Jewish readers or antifascists more generally, but the other obvious risk was giving ammunition to the right. Because Némirovsky thought of the novel in a modernist way, as an art object rather than a political act, she was ambivalent about self-censorship, even for ethical reasons, as shown in her interview with Janine Auscher. In a journal entry from May 1938, she exclaimed, "I should vow to myself to do a Stav [Stavisky] and not to give a damn about the effect it would have on the condition of the Jews" (PL 260). But though we will find a fictionalized version of him in *The Prey*'s Abel Sarlat, she will not depict him directly, in full Russian Jewish colors, and the condition of the Jews was no matter of indifference to her. "Imbecile hypocrites!" she protested after reading a favorable review of *The Prey.* "Just as I expected, they aren't scandalized, because Daguerne is French. But I understand their point of view: accept from any Dupont or Durant what would be intolerable if it came from outsiders *(métèques)*" (OC 1: 1648).[1]

So Némirovsky's fiction of the 1930s and early 1940s includes four novels, *The Pawn on the Chessboard, The Prey, All Our Worldly Goods,* and *The Fires of Autumn,* in addition to *Suite Française,* which center on characters with French names. These novels focus on working- or middle-class Christians; or, at the very least, where a character might be foreign-born or *métèque,* they avoid exploring his origins, featuring instead historical events, the World Wars and the Depression, that affected French citizens as much as immigrants. Nonetheless, an attentive reader will note a recurrence of earlier Némirovsky themes: ambition and social exclusion, the conduct of business and its intersections with government. And more than once, a Jewish character will make a brief appearance, or the stereotypes conventionally attributed to Jews, from restlessness and hypersensitivity to the feverish glance, will be attributed to the native French. We will want to ponder what this return of the repressed means before turning later to the explicitly Jewish fiction Némirovsky published between 1937 and 1940.

The Great War

Irène Némirovsky arrived in France as the Treaty of Versailles was signed, in the summer of 1919. Unlike her fiction of the Russian Revolution or the German occupation of 1940–42, her accounts of World War I are entirely based on hearsay and reading. The Great War played a brief part in her earliest novel, *The Misunderstanding* (1926), which centers on a love affair between a prosperous married woman and a veteran whose family's fortune was lost during the war. Its depictions of battle are brief and entirely conventional, but the novel introduces a theme she develops later: the profound changes in young men who had gone to war enthusiastically and returned "with a strange, faraway look" and a "bitter hostility to towards others . . . because they hadn't suffered, hadn't seen" (14).

What they had seen and suffered is by now familiar from books and film. It can be intuited, doubtless only partially, in a painting like John Singer Sargent's "Gassed" (1919) with its line of stumbling men, apparently blinded, each with his hand on the shoulder of the man before him, or a novel such as Erich Maria Remarque's *All Quiet on the Western Front* (1929). Eight million four hundred ten thousand Frenchmen were mobilized; nearly 1.4 million of them were killed and another 4.2 million wounded, a casualty rate of nearly 75 percent ("World War I"). So few home leaves were granted to wartime soldiers that experts project that 1.4 million fewer births took place; as one consequence, the number of draft-age men was exceptionally low in the late 1930s, just as the danger of another war began to loom.

But it is also necessary to remember that the Western Front on which much, but not all, of the war was fought was four-fifths French (Martin 18). Four years of shelling and trench warfare left many regions unrecognizable. As Benjamin Martin has noted, the ten northern departments of France fully justified their designation as "devastated regions," and while only 10 percent of the population lived there, "60% of coal mining, 66% of textile production, and 55% of metallurgical production" took place there (18). French insistence that the Allies enforce the rigorous terms of the Treaty of Versailles is rightly remembered as a disaster for impoverished Germany, but at the time many French saw British and American reluctance to press for reparations as a betrayal by Allies whose own landscapes remained unscarred.

France suffered economically in other ways: Russian commercial bonds, as well as those issued by the Russian government, became worthless after the revolution, and French investors held 25.397 billion francs' worth of them in August 1914. In mid-January 1924, a "precipitous drop in the franc vis à vis the dollar and pound" rocked the economy further (23–24). Even before the Depression, many veterans found themselves unable to find decent work, and doubtless many of the over 1.1 million left with permanent disabilities were unable to perform it (17). César Fauxbras, a war novelist and activist now largely forgotten, was prescient in warning that "the victims of war were also casualties of unemployment" (Perry 172). As the title of his novel *Viande à brûler* ("Meat to Burn") suggested, "Mass unemployment prefigured future carnage" (173).

The Pawn on the Chessboard

"The man of 1933," as Némirovsky wrote in her journal that year, was the intended subject of her new novel, published as *The Pawn on the Chessboard* after her publisher rejected the title *A Man of Our Time* as unlikely to attract readers (*OC* 1: 835). Like Yves Harteloup, protagonist of *The Misunderstanding,* Christophe Bohun is one of the "new poor," a war veteran come home to greatly diminished prospects after the failure of the family business. Compelled to take up what he regards as soulless labor in a postwar world where blaring radios and phonographs distress him even more than his wife's desire to abandon their cavernous family home for a small modern flat with central heating, Christophe is a study in the inability to reimagine a disappointed life. As in *The Misunderstanding,* Némirovsky's gestures to the aftereffects of combat remain conventional, but she demonstrates an acute sense of the psychological consequences of a life that offers all the material necessities but leaves cravings for comfort, travel, and aesthetic satisfaction unfulfilled.

Christophe's life is anchored in contemporary economic news, of which he overhears snatches on the radio or from other people's conversation. The cinema offers him newsreel images—a "decline in the dollar, unemployment, budget deficits, a hunger march on London"—as well as the sounds of "drum rolls, German soldiers, a peace conference, Italian soldiers, airplanes, tanks, cannons" (*OC* 1: 842, 876). His whole temperament resists such messages, as he prefers to dwell on the past. At the novel's beginning, he and his wife and child are still living with his father, and he never seriously considers working for anyone other than his father's old partner, Beryl. Beryl and Christophe's father, James Bohun, belong to the older generation of businessmen, what Némirovsky calls in one notebook the "Golder era": a day of expansion, adventure, and international deals in steel and oil. Christophe belongs to a diminished era of contraction, caution, and small economies (*OC* 1: 835).

Whatever Némirovsky had sought to achieve by renaming her character Beryl she loses by telling us that he changed his name from "Biruleff" and having Christophe scorn him as "a little Jew, born on the marshes of Romania, my father's business spy" (839). James's origins are unspecified, but he is also a foreigner, without connections, *heimatlos* (the very word Némirovsky later privately identified as code for "Jew"), and never naturalized (866). Oddly, though our attention is drawn to Beryl's changed name, the text never explains why

James Bohun's first name is English.[2] After his death, when Christophe goes through his father's papers, he finds nothing about his father's childhood or his grandparents; nor can he recall any stories or memories, "barely the name of an obscure Greek village" (922). James Bohun and Beryl were in business, sharing an enthusiasm for long hours and taking legal and financial risks until the 1925 "Bohun crash" left James ruined and Beryl in charge. The collapse followed denunciations of James as a traitor and a merchant of human flesh when his 1924 efforts to start a war between England and France were made public. Although Christophe hopes that his father has secretly put away money for him, the legacy James leaves when he dies is only some old documents that prove Beryl's complicity in the old scandal.

With his father's death Christophe learns that his career with Beryl is based on blackmail; James has all along threatened to reveal the details unless his son is kept on Beryl's payroll. His father seems to have believed that Christophe would contact journalists and politicians, winning back the family fortune by exposing Beryl, but Christophe is the last person to engage in such a campaign. "Moi?" he scoffs. "Collar men like Beryl, buy newspapers, and turn over ministries! But I don't like to do things like that!" (925). Like his own son, Philippe, Christophe prefers passive resentment to action: "Is it my fault that everything that is worth the trouble of living costs money?" (925). He will do nothing more than show Beryl the incriminating letters and extract a promise that his job in the firm is safe.

Christophe's passivity and the author's unwillingness to explore the issues of immigration and assimilation that are so obviously built into the plot create major flaws for the novel. "My father," he muses, "was of Beryl's race, but I don't have the strength" (927). Like other writers before the Second World War, Némirovsky is at home with the word "race," which sometimes designates ethnicity but at other times merely identifies personal tastes, "the race of those who love," say, solitude. But here the slippery word creates problems, for Christophe seems to mean that he is of a different generation than his father, inherits none of his tendencies, and therefore faces no internal conflicts. He wishes that he had been born into his wife's family of small provincial "*rentiers*," that is, of people who could live on their investments before the war (925). But rentiers have died out, and then, too, he is largely contemptuous of his wife's family.

If she short-circuits the promising theme of acculturation, Némirovsky underscores the vibrant qualities of "Golder's generation." Christophe himself realizes that his father loved his business struggles and their risks. Even more important than having money is loving life: "their strength, those men, was that in defending their money they were defending their lives." He and Beryl were always fully engaged; they knew how to hate, how to take revenge (927). Christophe starts the novel being grateful to have gotten through another day, for having one less day left to live (837). "It's a filthy life" is one of his catch phrases, as he slips into one languorous distraction after another: alcohol, the cinema, long drives on back roads, casual pick-ups in bars (844). When his father's death deprives the family of two thousand monthly francs with which they had supplemented his three-thousand-franc salary, the family gives up its few remaining luxuries: the old apartment with its grand furniture, their car, the prospect of holidays. At the end of the novel, in a moment of melodrama, he cuts himself shaving but lacks the will to carry out suicide. He dies alone of blood poisoning, having attempted to summon a doctor from a public telephone, and then given up when the doctors all seem to be on vacation. An impatient reader might wonder why he does not just take the Metro to the nearest hospital.

The Pawn on the Chessboard is as close as Némirovsky ever came to writing one of those naturalist novels in which the environment slowly crushes human hopes. Its conscious model was Sinclair Lewis's *Babbitt*, to which she attributed "a sordid beauty" (*OC* 1: 835). Philipponnat believes that Léon Némirovsky's death was a model for James Bohun's and that, always the professional writer, she sometimes shared Christophe's frustration with the "little daily prison" of working for money. But in the end, the novelist with her accomplishments and her pleasures, her children and her novels, has little in common with this incessantly self-pitying character. To better illustrate the misery inflicted by the Depression, she would need to turn to characters whose struggles are accompanied by the self-determination, energy, and imagination she saw in the men of "Golder's generation." We have seen one such figure in the doctor, Dario Asfar, and another appears in the political operative, Jean-Luc Daguerne, protagonist of *The Prey* (1938).

The Prey

In an insert designed to be sold with *The Prey*, which had been serialized in *Gringoire* before Albin Michel published it in 1938, Némirovsky outlined her subject: "a young man of twenty years of age, who sets out to discover life, in a troubled world, our own" (PL 263). Referring to the ambitious hero of Stendhal's *The Red and the Black*, she called him a "Julien Sorel of the crisis," or Depression, and asked, "Does he have scruples? He will find out as he goes on" (*OC* 1: 1646). Only poverty, not ethnicity, makes Jean-Luc Daguerne an outsider. Perhaps twenty years younger than Christophe Bohun, he is the son of a World War I veteran who came back from a prison camp in Germany an invalid. Laurent Daguerne had been a successful architect before the war, but by the time the novel starts, he and Jean-Luc, the son of his first marriage, are living with his second wife and two more children in a dreary but solid suburban home originally designed as a summer villa. For the past two years,

Laurent has been unable to pay his son's tuition at the university, forcing Jean-Luc into a miserable life, exhausting himself between his schoolwork and his odd jobs—washing cars, translating crime novels, giving lessons at starvation rates (1662).

Sent off to boarding school at the age of eight after Laurent's remarriage, Jean-Luc is unsentimental about his childhood, shadowed first by his mother's death and then by a harsh stepmother with a family resemblance to Némirovsky's other maternal monsters. Yet the family expects him to support them when he graduates, though even a year later he still leads a wretched existence selling vacuum cleaners, radio parts, and bars of soap bought cheaply from bankrupt perfumers: "Nothing, not his brilliant diplomas, nor his courage, nor his work brought him the least security. . . . In Europe, in this autumn of 1933, intelligence was sold at bargain-basement prices" (1664).

This is poverty as Dario Asfar experienced it, and like Dario, Jean-Luc falls in love as a young man and initially aspires to be worthy of Edith, whom he idealizes and wishes to make "his wife, not his mistress" (1660). Yet he has nothing like Dario's calling to medicine, for bitter poverty has awakened in his generation only a half-avowed, resentful ambition: "with what joy they would have buried the old world!" (1665). Money had driven men throughout the 1920s, but the Depression has proved to them that money itself is unsure. All that remains for their "cruel and cold passion to succeed" is to fix on politics, the "sole human activity that can move them" because, as often as governments fall in the Third Republic, they cannot imagine a world without some kind of powerful political activity. It is raw power, not an idealized commitment to democracy or Communism or even fascism, that motivates them: the ability to influence elections, government spending, official appointments, and the exploitation of resources. Where James Bohun and David Golder sought to influence politicians to favor their business interests, the newer generation will eliminate the middleman. Yet as Jean-Luc knows, modern politics requires a network of contacts, the support of influential patrons, and introductions to the right houses far more than it requires ideological commitments.

The crisis that propels Jean-Luc out of poverty is Edith's betrayal. She is the daughter of a rich banker, Abel Sarlat, and neglects Jean-Luc, allowing her family to persuade her to become engaged to the repellant but very rich Bertrand Bolchère or, as Jean-Luc's friend Dourdan calls him in dated slang, "the very big *galette*," or pancake (1669). Jean-Luc is initially distraught but after a sleepless night resolves that he will not take after his father: "no one would ever feel sorry for him" (1672). Learning of Edith's engagement party from the newspaper, he crashes it, managing to introduce himself to her bewildered family and then pressing her into what the text describes as a "brutal caress" when they are briefly alone. Edith's resistance melts, and she promises Jean-Luc that she does not love Bertrand and their marriage will make no difference to her liaison with him.

The difference to Jean-Luc, however, is that he finally realizes that respecting Edith's chastity was a miscalculation; his main appeal for her is sexual. So with Bertrand conveniently off in the United States, Jean-Luc and Edith pursue a passionate affair that soon results in pregnancy. Edith breaks her engagement, and Jean-Luc plays the pregnancy card to gain Abel Sarlat's consent to the marriage. The wily old financier, however, does his best to keep Jean-Luc in his place, giving the young couple only a modest monthly income and warning his friends against offering the young man a job. On an evening in autumn, a disoriented Abel Sarlat appears at the young couple's door and, learning that his daughter is in labor, remains only until his grandson is born, vanishing after a brief glance at mother and child. The next morning, Jean-Luc learns that his father-in-law is dead, having gone home to swallow two packets of barbiturates.

Abel Sarlat's wealth and reputation have vanished in a massive scandal, which Philipponnat suggests may owe something to Stavisky (*OC* 1: 1647).[3] In addition to dishonesty, Sarlat, as his friend Cottu tells Jean-Luc, had two flaws: snobbery and an addiction to women. Keen to preserve his social standing while also rumored to be the sole support of a Parisian brothel catering to special tastes, he spent vast sums (1715). When he ran out of money, he gained ready cash for himself by selling some of his bank's commercial paper before its due date, guaranteeing these transactions with stocks in his own mining company. Like Stavisky with his municipal pawnshop, Sarlat knew that the mining company was not worth enough to repay his debts. But he also had numerous political friends and wrongly calculated that one of them, the ambitious Calixte-Langon, also a bank administrator, would take care of the problem. Langon, however, likely to be compromised in the "inevitable crash," refuses his help; as Cottu says, he is an "honest man" who had no clue as to what was going on in the bank (1714).

Once the debts are settled, Sarlat's estate leaves the young couple with only a thousand worthless bank shares. Edith and the baby are forced to live wretchedly on Jean-Luc's salary as a radio and perfume salesman. Cottu, however, has a suggestion: what if he were to buy those bank shares for forty thousand francs? Jean-Luc, having promised to think over the offer, spends hours trying to figure out what "lies hidden under Cottu's words. What does he know that I don't?" (1720). As he eventually realizes, paying for the worthless bonds would put Cottu in a position to file a lawsuit implicating Langon, his patron. This betrayal will ignite a fresh phase of the scandal, presumably for the benefit of some other politician whose future looks brighter to Cottu. If he accepted this arrangement, Jean-Luc explains to his friend Dourdan, the lump sum of forty thousand francs would be gone in a year. But if he in turn betrays Cottu by informing Langon of the plan, Jean-Luc might finally have an entrée into the inner circle of national politics. It is "a dangerous game," as Dourdan warns, but Jean-Luc plays it well (1722).

Langon's first impression is that Jean-Luc wants him to make a better offer for the shares, something he cannot afford to do. Jean-Luc, however, disclaims any attempt at blackmail; all he wants is to serve a man he admires. Politicians, he suspects, "seek power as a form of love," and "no trap is too crude if it is made sticky with flattery" (1729, 1726). To underscore the strength of Jean-Luc's determination and the deterioration of his marriage, Némirovsky arranges for him to come home from this meeting with Langon to find Edith groaning in pain. A doctor is summoned and determines that her ovaries are gravely inflamed; she needs an immediate operation. Edith, the child of privilege, insists on a private clinic, but Jean-Luc maintains that he has no way of paying for it. Instead she goes to the hospital, where, dressed in the coarse linen of a charity patient, she recuperates for weeks in a public ward.[4]

The chapter in which Jean-Luc agrees to serve as Langon's secretary for eight hundred francs a month ends with another Faustian shudder, as Langon asks him if he is "mine." "Entirely yours," responds his new employee (1735). Though the position will lead Jean-Luc to wealth, its initial salary offers no relief from near poverty. His real work will be "galvanizing Langon's nervous nature, which rallied as easily as it fell, which was capable of great courage, but only fitfully, and which only admiration—anyone's admiration—could sustain" (1736). He must help Langon understand that the Sarlat scandal has already made his position in his own party untenable; therefore, he must renounce it dramatically, in a blaze of glory. Doing so will require him to make peace with Armand Lesourd (the deaf), his oldest political enemy, to damage his own party, currently in power, and rupture its government (1737).

Given the ideological battles of the 1930s, one might expect to learn whether Langon started out as a conservative and later became a socialist, or vice versa. Alternatively, he could have moved from the center to either the fascist or Communist extreme. But although politics then was visibly a life-and-death matter, in this novel Némirovsky strips it of content. Langon at one point vaguely alludes to having saved France from a looming war, but whether he is referring to preventing Léon Blum from entering the Spanish Civil War on the Communist side, as many rightists feared, or to appeasing Hitler, who violated the Treaty of Versailles by moving his troops into the Rhineland a month after the February riots, bringing down two French governments in close succession, or to some other event remains unclear.[5] Similarly, early in the novel Cottu ridicules Armand Lesourd, whose father was a millionaire, for reviving a claim to having herded sheep as a child with the election cycle every four years. As we know, roots in the soil were more important to right-wing politicians than to socialists, but we can gather nothing more specific. In analyzing political temperaments and processes without specifying content, Némirovsky runs the risk of appearing indifferent to events that would prove catastrophic for her, but she also anticipates an analysis of a "mediated" politics that we today associate with postmodern theorists like Jean Baudrillard or Slavoj Žižek.

Némirovsky begins with the observation that we all long to be loved and recognized. Men like Langon who seek "power as a form of love" begin with an entirely human need; in the same way, Jean-Luc's early outburst, "I wish to be, to exist, to say 'I,'" is entirely understandable (1693). Yet our nature being what it is, the craving for love and self-expression is accompanied by an equally natural violence: "A creature is born with teeth, claws, muscles. He needs to seize. He needs to bite and chew" (1680). Moreover, radio, newsreels, and mass-circulation journalism encourage human beings to become so alienated from their own nature that they mistake celebrity and public approbation for love. A man like Langon will act without conscience in part because he is never alone but always "surrounded by an invisible audience," whose approval he always solicits, whose roars drown out quieter ethical authorities. When Langon tries to talk about "the authentic man hidden behind the mannequin the crowd sees," Jean-Luc can only hear how completely he has conflated them: "his voice now was intoxicated by tenderness and pity for himself" (17, 33).

When politicians gather, it is obvious that they constitute an elite coterie whose primary concern is to retain their membership in it, no matter how often they have to change their principles or betray their supporters. When Jean-Luc, who worked like a slave for years to educate himself and establish a career for himself, finds himself mingling with the Sarlat family, he notes the casualness with which they conduct their business and bestow their favors. How terrible to be young, to know how much ardor, desire, will, and lucid intelligence are inside you, and yet to be unable to act. But anyone in Sarlat's circle could change it all with a single word or gesture: "They all trafficked under the sign of friendship, of confidence, of services given and received, and so easily" (1705). What we now call "access" is the chief goal of politically ambitious outsiders: more than money, one needs to get close to people in power, to see how the game is played, to get over the initial barriers (1680). Lesourd and Langon visibly loathe each other, yet they attend the same dinners, speak to each other familiarly. Lesourd always claims to be a jolly fellow who forgives insults easily, and Langon cannot help believing that even his worst enemy has a certain tenderness for him at the bottom of his heart (1703).

Jean-Luc's first success as a political operative is to direct the "spectacle" that allows Langon to turn his back on his own party and embrace his supposed worst enemy, Lesourd (1743). The chapter describing this triumph begins with the observation that the National Assembly's red draperies no longer evoke the blood of revolutions but rather the pomp and scarlet of theaters (1743). Jean-Luc has written Langon's speech, but he is only the "obscure author" of the performance that depends on the skill of the "marvelous actor" who knows how to play "with his voice, his face, his sincerity" (1744). Jean-Luc researched all of the evidence pointing to Langon's innocence, but in speaking, Langon, "with a sure instinct," replaces the numbers and citations with "lyrical flight" (1745). The audience is excited into that "almost physical emotion that attaches less to the significance of words, to their content, than to the vibration of the human voice" (1745). Even Jean-Luc ceases to see the private Langon he has coached, having eyes only for "the public figure, offered up as a spectacle" (1745). Like a skillful actor's, Langon's voice rises over the clamor of the audience, "reaching the high registers with facility and grace, as if in play" (1745). By this point the reader will have forgotten that Langon really is innocent but will have no trouble recognizing the "triumph," the "ovation," the "furious applause" of the audience.

We are by now all familiar with the argument that mass media encourage audiences to confuse reality and spectacle. One can read Jean Baudrillard's *The Gulf War Did Not Take Place* (1995) for a highly nuanced argument that U.S. television coverage of bombing attacks on Bagdad, reported with video-game-like images of targets selected and destroyed from a great distance, reflects something deeply troubling about our inability to distinguish what he calls "simulacra," life-like images, from real world actions. Of course real people die in wars, but the argument is that comfortable people in the West are swayed to support it by "cool" images familiar from gaming and cinema and unwilling to hear arguments based on hard facts. Baudrillard did not live to see the Bitcoin economy, but it is a phenomenon, like Disney World, tailor-made for his theory. A popularized version of the same argument regularly appears in op-ed articles about the 2016 U.S. presidential election, whether the writer is deploring the infomercial aesthetic of a video aimed at convincing us that one candidate is just a regular suburbanite or analyzing another candidate's history on reality TV.

Némirovsky's decision to portray political behavior without reference to content suggests an almost nihilistic despair about political action. She imagines a political world in which decisions about matters of life and death, such as the French government's 1939 decision to intern all foreign males between the ages of twenty-one and fifty-five in special camps, are made as lightly, and by the same procedures, as decisions about building new post offices. It is not the same thing as complacency or indifference; it is a picture of an apparently democratic republic that has become something else—an oligarchy vulnerable to fascism, perhaps. But Némirovsky's vision of the primacy of the personal and emotional life suggests something like a natural limit to Jean-Luc's ability to succeed as a political operative.

In a passage that one early reviewer, Edmond Jaloux, criticized for too obviously foreshadowing the end, Laurent Daguerne warns his son against growing up too fast, for "ambition and calculation are the passions of maturity" (OC 1: 1647). A young person, the father says, must occasionally yield to wildness and folly; when these are stifled, "youth avenges itself" (1691). Of course Jean-Luc resents this advice, believing that poverty left him with no alternative to grim determination. But chosen or not, a life based on alienation—marriage to a woman chosen for her father's wealth, a career spent behind the scenes enabling a man he does not respect to garner votes and power—will prove unbearable. In the novel's main subplot, Jean-Luc becomes attached to Marie, the fiancée of his old friend Dourdan, who is serving a prison sentence for forgery. Because she is poor, he can safely allow her to see his suppressed misery and feels a profound peace when he is with her that leads to love. Though she always says she will return to Dourdan later, they become lovers.

Almost as soon as Jean-Luc allows himself to love Marie, he makes a significant miscalculation. Returning from a ball that he and Edith had attended with Langon, Jean-Luc notes a slight and instantly dissimulated movement of the politician's hand that reveals that his wife and his employer are having an affair. Almost simultaneously he realizes that he no longer wishes to be Langon's operative but to run for office in his own name. Edith and Jean-Luc return home to a bitter quarrel, disclosing a lifetime's resentments, which ends in a decision to divorce. Jean-Luc reports the upshot to Langon, who swears he would never have betrayed his faithful employee and then starts quoting Oscar Wilde about the tragedy of age being that one remains young. Jean-Luc sees him moving from the impulse to play the scene to creating "a certain image of himself, in his own eyes, which became reality" (1779). When Jean-Luc adds that his wife will retain custody of their son, he is astonished to see on Langon's face "a reflection of real emotion" as the politician acknowledges his satisfaction at finally having a family, a home (1779).

Now that he has agreed to divorce Edith so that Langon can marry her, Jean-Luc must find another source of income. He takes Langon's advice to propose himself as a candidate for deputy in the next election. Having apparently believed Jean-Luc's declaration that Langon has revealed his "deep nature" and shown him the difference between the public man and the human being, the politician assures him of success: "You have lived at my side. . . . I have taught you to know men" (1780). But what Jean-Luc has not fully considered is that although his divorce causes no emotional suffering, it leaves him "socially diminished." "This wife and child," he realizes too late, "made him the Daguerne that he had become, solidly anchored in life, assured, and rich" (1783).

For a brief period, Jean-Luc continues to see Marie, only partially aware of how much his love for her, rooted in reminders of his unhappy youth, has deepened. But then she makes excuses for avoiding him, and when she finally meets him at a coffee shop in the Quai d'Orsay, she appears with a small suitcase. Her fiancé, Dourdan, has been released from jail with the proviso that he remain outside the capital. Jean-Luc becomes distraught, protests that he loves her, that he can give her a far better life than Dourdan will. But Marie not only loves her fiancé but also doubts Jean-Luc's sincerity, telling him that he cares only for ambition and success. We understand how harsh this assessment is as we follow Jean-Luc through the aftermath, marked by all the signs of a major depression, including inability to focus on his upcoming election campaign. After four months, he travels to the village in the Loire where Marie lives wretchedly with Dourdan, who is ill and unable to work. Mocking Jean-Luc's propensity for bargaining and scheming, she turns down his proposal to use his political connections to bring Dourdan back to Paris.

Three other encounters between Marie and Jean-Luc illustrate his anguish, as he moves from vowing to take her away from Dourdan to trying to manipulate the couple into allowing him to use his political connections to help them move back to Paris. But nothing avails: soon a letter from Marie informs Jean-Luc that they are moving to South America, where Dourdan has found a job. A desperate trip takes Jean-Luc back to the couple's flat, where he argues vociferously with Dourdan: No, Marie may not leave France. Jean-Luc needs her. Does Dourdan not realize that she was his mistress? There is a scene, the two shove each other, and Jean-Luc finds himself alone on the street, with Dourdan still shouting for help, because Daguerne, "the hope of Lesourd's party" and the "son-in-law of Abel Sarlat," has just tried to murder him (1811).

It is the election season, and the country is filled with journalists on the lookout for scandal. The story of Jean-Luc's fight with Dourdan appears first in a small local paper and then is reproduced in Paris. Everyone had known, of course, that Jean-Luc was married to Edith, but the printed link to the Sarlat scandal, illustrated by a wedding photo, reawakens forgotten rumors. Journalists hostile to Lesourd take them up, amplifying and publicizing them. Langon, with his acting skills, could have easily assumed a handsome pose, made some promises, and escaped unharmed from such a trivial threat, but Lesourd is "unwilling to dissimulate" that it will be different for Daguerne. These groundless rumors without real substance are the worst ones to defend yourself against; all you can do is be silent and wait them out (1813). Jean-Luc understands the message: he withdraws his name from consideration in the face of certain defeat. Cottu will be elected in his stead.

What has undermined Jean-Luc is not so much love as, indeed, the revenge of his unhappy, stifled youth and its old habits. He has learned how to work with politicians but not really to be part of their bloc: as in youth, without Edith and Langon, he is fundamentally isolated. As he tells his ambitious half-brother, José, who has always envied his success, he was good at reading how other men would react, because doing so requires only intelligence. What is more difficult is knowing how you yourself will react, for that requires experience (1803). He is "the prey of himself, of everything that he never had . . . of everything he fended off, of everything that appeared shameful and low to him" (1804). Having lost his mother in childhood, he quite possibly spent his life trying to substitute success for love and now has neither. Or, we might say, he has understood that the world trades on images, publicity, and rumor, but his deepest nature demands to be acknowledged for what it irremediably is. His brother urges him to come out for a drink, but he says he must change first. In a scene that replicates the headlines of the Stavisky scandal, he goes into his bedroom and shuts the door. As José waits, a gunshot rings out.

We have seen the Freudian "return of the repressed" evoked in its most literal clinical sense in *The Prey.* A man whose career requires constant roleplaying, self-suppression, and calculation of effects is consciously suppressing his own real feelings, which, in a spatial metaphor, are driven underground, but basic instincts and needs do not die because they are ignored. As Freud argues in *Moses and Monotheism,* "the instinct . . . either retain[s] its forces, or collects them again, or it is reawakened by some new precipitating cause . . . since the path to normal satisfaction remains closed to it by what we may call the scar of repression, somewhere, at a weak spot, it opens another path for itself . . . which comes to light as a symptom, without the acquiescence of the ego, but also without its understanding" ("Return"). For Jean-Luc, losing Marie as his career is collapsing is this precipitating incident; his ego, which ordinarily would allow him to sort out options and plan rationally, is overwhelmed, flooded by pent-up, primitive need. Whether Freud's description of the "return of the repressed" is sound science is another issue, but clearly the metaphor is persuasive. And as Jaloux complained, we saw Némirovsky setting it up with Laurent Daguerne's warning of the "great danger" that a stifled youth will "avenge" itself (1691).

This same metaphor can help us see the effects of Némirovsky's deliberate suppression of Jewish themes, even Jewish names, in *The Pawn on the Chessboard* and *The Prey.* As we have seen, this suppression is incomplete; not only Beryl but also James Bohun share so many features of the driven immigrant businessman whose archetype is David Golder that the connections cry out for exploration. Christophe Bohun's nostalgia for a sheltered childhood and his inability to take any practical steps to change his life seem much less interesting than, say, Hélène Karol's struggle to free herself from the traces of her mother's promiscuity she recognizes in herself. Jean-Luc Daguerne, who is quite convincingly an ethnic Frenchman, is able to play the part of the ambitious outsider much more convincingly. Némirovsky may never have persuaded herself to write directly about Stavisky, but this repressed subject seems to return in the form of Abel Sarlat, whose ghost in turn seems to return to destroy his son-in-law's career.

As for the novel's politics, which suggest something like nihilistic despair about the connection between the actual needs of human beings and the government's capacity for responding to them rationally or helpfully, do they not finally seem to carry more than a trace of the novelist's history? The novel's insistence on the theatricality and spectacle of politics, the media's role in publicizing the calculated images and unfounded rumors that shape election results, the persistence of a political class that furthers its own interests at the expense of the public good, and the undisguised dependence of all of these on money seems redolent of a bleakness often associated with the postmodern. Not one politician in the book even talks about crucial public issues—immigration, unemployment, rearmament, the Spanish Civil War, the rise of fascism—let alone chooses a position based on moral or humanitarian grounds.

Of course, the era had humane and progressive politicians who spoke out about poverty, unemployment, the rights of workers to fair wages and decent conditions, and the plight of disabled veterans and refugees from Hitler. Not everyone was a stooge of the moneyed classes or a creation of the media. In France the most famous, Léon Blum, was a published literary critic before the Dreyfus Affair persuaded him to enter politics. He was prime minister for a little over a year (1936–37) and again for a month in 1938, and though some historians still excoriate him for indecisiveness, he had many moments of public heroism. He was featured on the March 9, 1936, cover of *Time* magazine lying in a hospital bed, his head wrapped in bandages after a beating administered by right-wing thugs. In 1938 Némirovsky contemplated a book on "Le Juif" (the Jew) that would explore three men who took risks. One of these was to be Leon Trotsky, another Stavisky. The third was Léon Blum. Although entirely different personalities, Némirovsky believed they were all motivated by "the fire in their blood," which Philipponnat and Lienhardt gloss as "race": "an unstable, audacious fluid, spurred on by adversity and propelled by otherness" (PL 260).

So Léon Blum was part of the real political record, along with much else, that Némirovsky repressed in her novel about French politics in the 1930s, even as she followed most of the conventions of realism. Had she merely wished to avoid Jewish issues, she might have imagined him without ethnic roots, an older brother, perhaps, of Christophe Bohun. But instead she created a nightmarish political world not only without heroes but also without humanitarians. One can deplore such a nihilistic vision of politics, arguing that the voices of ordinary people or principled people or outsiders can and must be heard everywhere. But if we allow ourselves to imagine what it must have felt like to be a Jewish woman in France, watching the headlines grow blacker while your applications for naturalized citizenship were rejected over and over, we can see how deeply its despair is rooted in and truthful to historical experience. Perhaps to write about France in the 1930s without Léon Blum is to underscore the failure, at least for the short term, of his humanitarian, progressive, and socialist vision. In 1942, when the writer was deported and the former prime minister was imprisoned at Buchenwald, the nightmare was a political reality.

Chapter 5

The "Bond of Tears" and Jewishness in the Late Fiction

To review briefly: Irène Némirovsky's early fiction centered on upwardly mobile Jewish families. One or two generations away from the *shtetl,* these families were determined to shed their Yiddish culture and the restrictions imposed on them by centuries of czarist rule. Some are first seen in Ukraine or Russia, but they soon emigrate to Paris, with perhaps an intermediate stop in Finland along the way. This fiction reflects the author's experience, but Angela Kershaw also argues that it responded to an interest in ethnic fiction French readers also evinced in the 1920s. Its assumed audience was French and Christian, rather than immigrant and Jewish, and its characterizations reflect this audience's stereotypes, as well as its interest in reading about Russian Jews as romantic, exotic strangers. And as noted, although most of her original audience seemed oblivious to social anti-Semitism, some early Jewish readers criticized Némirovsky for echoing old stereotypes about financial rapacity or for describing Jews with long-stereotyped Jewish features, such as large noses or sallow skin.

By the 1930s anti-Semitism was the law of the land in Germany, and significant political parties and influential cultural figures were promoting something similar in France, urging the nation to define itself through family origins and traditions "rooted in the soil." Ethnic literature was no longer popular, and the stereotypes that fill a novel like Paul Morand's *France-la-doulce,* which takes as its subject the filming of the French national epic, *The Song of Roland,* by a Jewish immigrant director, have a new ideological message. Along with assuming that a trashy movie based on a national treasure would be even more of a sacrilege if the producers were outsiders, Morand adopts the timeworn tradition of using misspelled words to mock foreigners' accents. He also directly ridicules the plight of Jewish immigrants, depicting them as spongers and parasites. Thus his novel depicts Jewish refugees along the same ideological lines that we find in Action Française propaganda and which Vichy would use to justify the deportations of 1942–44.

As noted, Némirovsky's movement away from Jewish characters and themes after 1932 reflects this changing political context. Anti-Semitism had become such a powerful political force by then that a novel with Jewish themes would inevitably be read in political terms, and she did not see herself as a political novelist. She did not think *David Golder* anti-Semitic, but she knew that some Jewish readers did, and her comment to *L'Univers israélite* in 1935 that she would have "softened the novel greatly" following Hitler's rise shows her unwillingness to give ammunition, even unintentionally, to fascists. And then, in 1936, she broke her rule, and wrote "Brotherhood," a story about an assimilated Jew encountering an impoverished refugee in a train station. *The Dogs and the Wolves,* published shortly before the German invasion of 1940, returns unequivocally to Jewish themes, tracing the rich and poor branches of a family first seen in czarist Ukraine to their life as immigrants in France in the late 1930s. What led Némirovsky back to subject matter she had avoided for five years?

Certainly anti-Semitism had not lost its political urgency, so we may speculate that Némirovsky's commitment to an apolitical literature was pressured by deteriorating events. The reluctance of the United States to admit Jewish refugees and the strong strain of isolationism in U.S. politics, which only Pearl Harbor would end definitively, discouraged any expectation of American military aid or even refuge. Great Britain and France failed to intervene when Hitler marched into Austria in March 1938; a few months later they signed the Munich Pact, permitting the German takeover of Czechoslovakia. Even the Soviet Union, long billed as the major ideological opponent of fascism, signed the German-Soviet Non-Aggression Pact on August 23, 1939, which pledged that neither nation would take military action against the other in the next decade. Meanwhile, as the already large numbers of refugees from Russia, Spain, Poland, and Germany were swollen with fresh waves of Jewish and other refugees from Austria and Czechoslovakia, anti-immigrant rhetoric and policies grew harsher in the major Western democracies. Irène Némirovsky might have preferred that the novel remain above or outside politics, but she knew that political events were overtaking writers' lives and transforming the institutions, including a free press and independent publishing houses, on which literature depended.

"The Spectator"

That an apolitical theory of literature might turn one into a spectator foolishly unaware of any personal vulnerability to political events is the theme of a story called, appropriately, "Le spectateur" ["The Spectator"], which Némirovsky published in December 1939.[1] We will start with this simple, even schematic story because it offers insight into Némirovsky's awareness of the personal and moral hazards of a neutral perspective, which allows one to observe history as if it were art without feeling the need to intervene. The spectator shudders for Duncan but does not rush the stage with a knife to save him from Macbeth. Based on his social attitudes, as well as his fondness for collecting porcelain, the central character, Hugo Grayer, seems to Olivier Philipponnat to be based on a Parisian critic of the 1930s, Pierre Loewel, whom Philipponnat also sees as the target of "Brotherhood" (OC 2: 388).[2] Without disputing Philipponnat's expertise, let us add that both characters also share many attitudes with Némirovsky herself; this implicit self-criticism piques our interest.[3]

"The Spectator" starts in August 1939, as Hugo Grayer is savoring the afterglow of a fine lunch described in a gourmand's language: "the creaminess of the quenelles brought out the dark, deep flavor of the truffles: not too overpowering, but mingling with the tender flesh of the fish . . . just as the deep notes of the cello . . . harmonized with the sound of the piano" (199). The opening pages fill in his character: wanting above all "to lead a peaceful, quiet life," he is accustomed to being admired for his taste, his wealth, and his collection of porcelain; he firmly believes that "in a world of mad, brutal men and their stupid victims, the only harmless people were egoists like him" (200, 201). People who love others more than themselves and demand acknowledgment of their love cause all human misery; it is far better to "think of life as an interesting theatrical production . . . [which] acquire[s] great beauty" for those who contemplate its details (201). Indeed, if his lunch reminds him of music, a Europe threatened by Nazis "has the charm of those who are about to die," which he had experienced the previous year, listening to Mozart in Salzburg, just before the Anschluss (203).

This is a man devoted to art, as Némirovsky was, but in whom a preference for objective, apparently apolitical art becomes pure aestheticism, which treats history and food and an "anemic child" viewed in the street as if they were already works of art, rather than elements of life that make moral demands on him (201). It would not occur to him that he might lunch on bread and cheese rather than truffles and donate the money saved to feed the hungry. Further, his aesthetic sensibilities entitle him to special treatment: "he had worries on a spiritual plane that the mass of humanity could not grasp. . . . a night spent in an ugly hotel room overwhelmed him with sadness" (202). His great wealth has encouraged this view, but so has his rootlessness: though he possessed "one of the greatest fortunes in Uruguay," he was born in America of a Scandinavian mother and an Italian father and considers himself "a citizen of no man's land" (205, 206). He leaves on a ship bound for America in early September, his assumption leaving "that he could do nothing to help" Europeans if he stayed unexamined.

Of course, for this is a story with a lesson, the ship will be torpedoed on its second night at sea, and Hugo will injure himself jumping into the water. And although he takes the precaution of wearing a life preserver, the stress of hearing sirens makes it impossible for him to add a jacket. So he ends up shivering on a raft with some other passengers, including two little Jewish refugee girls who do not respond when he speaks; perhaps they are already dead. As the night goes on, his pain grows worse; soon he is unable to move his head and is vomiting over himself. His first thought is rage at the unfairness that he, a neutral, should be caught in the war and shame at the indignity of being "reduced to the level of a savage" (213). But rage and shame are not all; a passage from the Gospels—"Is not the body more than clothing?"—emerges from buried memories.[4] When a woman next to him offers comfort, he says, "Thank you," but he "wanted to do better" (218).

Hugo lacks time to formulate a new philosophy of life, but he recognizes the inadequacy of his old one. The sea that always looked so beautiful from a French beach is now ready to kill him, while the pity others offer touches him but has no practical value. He imagines people reading about the "neutral ship torpedoed" in the newspapers without letting the information alter "their fastidious scruples" any more than he had allowed the announcement of the pact between the Soviet Union and Germany to alter his. They will behave "like chickens that allow their mothers and sisters to have their throats cut while . . . pecking at their food. They did not understand that it was this passivity, this silent acquiescence, that would, when the time came, also deliver them up to a strong, merciless hand" (220). This last sentence might well have come out of a Marxist editorial denouncing the novel of manners and writers who failed to take political actions as fascism spread.

"Brotherhood"

We seldom find Némirovsky, with her commitments to irony and complexity, offering an unequivocal message of the kind seen in "The Spectator." "Brotherhood," begun in 1936 and published in 1937, is more typical, set in the consciousness of a highly assimilated French Jew who encounters an impoverished refugee at an isolated train station. Philipponnat sees the germ of the story in a conversation between Némirovsky and Pierre Loewel, a lawyer and man of letters who had consistently reviewed her novels enthusiastically. Like Némirovsky, Loewel was a highly assimilated Jew; when she asked him if did not feel that he had something in common with her David Golder, he replied, "not more than with an oriental merchant of glasses" (*OC* 1: 1620–21). She saw the limits of this response of a "poor imbecile of an intelligent man," and in "Brotherhood" she created in Christian Rabinovitch a man pondering the same question with more painful consequences, as his barely suppressed fears undermine his brief impulse to identify with an uneducated Russian Jew.

Because the story dramatizes an issue over which Némirovsky struggled and because it refuses moral simplicities, "Brotherhood" raises the specter of anti-Semitism, though more subtly than *David Golder* did. Since even the most assimilated Jew is acutely aware of the traits stereotyped as Jewish, we may have trouble reading his anxiety about them. Does he see these stereotypes as unjust to all Jews, or does he see himself as an exception? Like Némirovsky herself, Christian Rabinovitch shows no signs of Jewish religious education and feels no nostalgia for the lost world of the *shtetl,* its language, customs, and diet, with which he has little experience. The drive not to seem Jewish shapes Christian Rabinovitch's response to the auto accident that forces him to complete his journey by rail. Knowing that Jews are stereotyped as prone to dramatic emotional expression, he has cultivated a reputation for being "self-possessed . . . calm" (127). Although accompanied by his driver, Florent, he was behind the wheel, "worn out . . . his reflexes . . . slow," when the car crashed; as he waits for the train, he feels proud to have concealed his fear from Florent, "at least he hoped so!" (124).

As she wrote "Brotherhood," her most probing examination of whether an assimilated French Jew is morally obligated to claim brotherhood with an eastern European Jew, she was surprised herself at the degree to which she was "demonstrating . . . inassimilability" (PL 251). As Susan Suleiman documents in "Irène Némirovsky and the 'Jewish Question,'" the notes Némirovsky kept while drafting "Brotherhood" suggest internal conflict. At one point Némirovsky comments that the bond between the two Rabinovitches is not religion but "race," and she even adds, "Oh, Hitler, you're not wrong." The thought is all the more shocking because she had always resisted racial essentialism, whether promoted by romantic nationalists, Zionists, or fascists. The Enlightenment tradition, the belief that people are capable of making lucid choices about their values and behavior, undergirds the novel of manners; if we simply act out the impulses heredity lays down for us, we are back in the bloody realm of the national epic. Almost everything she had written was premised on choice; if Hélène Karol and Antoinette Kampf were doomed to be as vulgar and appetitive as their mothers, neither *The Ball* nor *The Wine of Solitude* would have a plot. Yet having noted the irony of affirming Hitler, she immediately seems to backtrack, saying, "I have scruples," which Suleiman interprets as meaning, "I may be wrong." But then her thought seems to contradict itself again: "above and before all is the inalienable right to truth." A few lines later, however, Némirovsky implies that the brotherhood of the Rabinovitches is "a matter of history, not biology" (29).[5]

These notes prepare us to see in "Brotherhood" a highly nuanced but indubitably critical portrayal of a smug, "self-hating" Jew—that is, the very figure Némirovsky's detractors see in the writer herself. Its publishing history, moreover, reinforces the observation that even raising the question of how an assimilated French Jew saw desperate refugees carries risks. The author's handwritten notes on the manuscript report that it was "rejected for anti-Semitism" by René Doumic, the editor of *Revue des Deux Mondes* (Suleiman, "Jewish Question" 30). In the end, *Gringoire,* the literary and political newspaper that grew increasingly anti-Semitic after 1936, published "Brotherhood," earning Némirovsky further criticism.[6] We should be prepared, then, for the story to make us uncomfortable.

The narrative of "Brotherhood" is largely set in the consciousness of Christian Rabinovitch, whose name encapsulates his cultural aspirations: a rich Frenchman, eager to minimize his connections to a Jewish heritage he frames as a genetic liability: "My nose, my mouth, the only specifically Jewish traits I've kept" (124). But the story is poised from the beginning to undermine the reader's confidence in him, to underscore his inconsistencies, his wishful thinking, and his habit of deflecting ill-suppressed fears. Christian wishes to be perfectly at home with the native aristocracy, a wish that loses none of its force for being illusory. The story finds him at a vulnerable moment when, en route to a hunting weekend and shaken by a crash that has disabled his car, he faces a long wait at a rural train station. There he meets another Rabinovitch, an impoverished refugee, and the encounter sets off changes in his already troubled consciousness, without provoking an epiphany or altering his actions.

More fearful of appearing frightened than of actually dying and never sure of his status in the eyes of others, Christian is the classic Jamesian narrator, a point Némirovsky underscores with an English phrase: "he was . . . too clear-headed—*self-conscious*—he said—to believe in happiness" (124). Along with hiding his distress from others, Christian, whenever wounded, is "slow to admit what truly hurt him, what really pained him" (129). Némirovsky figures this move in clinical terms early on, describing nights when Christian suffers from insomnia until "toward morning, it would be as if an invisible dam deep in his heart had finally given way" (129). This classically Freudian breakthrough does not operate on a political and historical level because Christian only imperfectly senses that his anxiety connects to public events.

Part of the story's historical context must be recovered from Christian's mind, where it is half-buried; the encounter with the other Rabinovitch, which confronts him with the fate of foreign Jews, must supply the rest. Némirovsky provides a month, October, but no date. A few markers point to current affairs: Hitler is in power; refugees in France anticipate losing permission to work or being expelled; established and assimilated Jews still retain their civic status.

The story makes few references to public history, though we learn that Christian is a World War I veteran who had served conscientiously but without distinction, since after a few months his weak heart sent him behind the lines. As we already know, Léon Blum, a Jewish socialist prime minister, was in and out of power from mid-1936 through April 1938; yet on November 12, 1938, a government decree provided the basis that would be used in 1939 for interning refugees and enemy aliens. Christian may block out politics on this level, but his anxieties accurately track the public's growing resentment of refugees and a resurgence of the same Action Française movement responsible for the anti-Jewish hysteria around the Dreyfus Affair.

Thus, as he waits for his train, the entirely private and psychological torments to which Christian most easily recurs acquire a political edge. From worries over his son's marriage he turns to "the financial crisis and ever-increasing taxes" and "political uncertainties" (128). Now he admits that "after every speech given by this or . . . that dictator, [he] would visualize war not in the next month or the following year, but tomorrow, immediately" (128). Other rich members of the bourgeoisie retain their health and good humor even while prophesying the worst disasters: "He was the only one who was eaten up inside and worried sick" (128). And why is he different? The answer suggests itself when he moves on to his anxieties over the forthcoming weekend, which he will spend with the Count of Sestres, father of his son's fiancée: "How difficult. His race" (129). He reflects that the marriage will inevitably be miserable, that the couple will never understand each other; yet he finds no solace in speculating that Sestres may forbid it, which would "insult Jean-Claude, and himself" (129). But his objections are brutally earnest: "he would cut off his own two hands to prevent the marriage!" (129).

"Race" must mean "Jewish" in the language of the time and is consistent with Christian's earlier reference to his facial features. Oddly, however, "race" is a word he uses to characterize his deepest impulses. For example, he has mourned his wife for ten years; though he married her "without love . . . he was the kind of man who was faithful" (125). In the original French "the kind of" is literally "of the race of men"; similarly, a phrase Patterson translates as "one of those men who aged early" is more literally "of the race of men who aged early" in French (130).

Do these evocations of a race of faithful men born mature beyond their years correspond to Jewish stereotype? One can just manage the argument: he is faithful, the text says, because his profoundest desire was for "a home, with its warmth and lamplight, that feeling of stability and peace in and around him" (125). His wife had given him this feeling, which he lost when she died; now he is only happy at home "alone or with his children . . . safe from human beings" (126). This domesticity fits a philo-Semitic vision of the Jewish home but hardly conjures up *Mein Kampf* or *L'Action française*. "He didn't like people. He didn't like society," we are told (126). Does this make him slightly inhuman? The context however, suggests other possibilities, such as a dislike for cocktail chatter or sports: "He knew equally well that he hated country walks, sports, riding, cars, and hunting" (126).

Just at this point, when Christian has almost admitted to himself that he dreads spending the upcoming weekend doing things he detests with people from whom he feels entirely alienated, he looks up to see the other Rabinovitch. This Rabinovitch looks openly miserable; he is thin, badly dressed, ill-shaven; he clutches a little boy whose red wrists protrude from a too-small jacket. Seeing Christian glance at the child, the poor Rabinovitch asks to share his first-class waiting room; the boy has a cough and their third-class waiting room is unheated. This Rabinovitch has no inhibitions about self-expression and without encouragement embarks on the history of his family's migrations. Born in Ukraine, where five of his children died young, Rabinovitch migrated to Paris after the revolution; his older son, the child's father, became a photographer in Germany, but then, "Along comes Hitler!" (136). Now he is en route to Liverpool; a younger son, worn down by hard labor, died of tuberculosis in Palestine. The poor Rabinovitch works in a hat shop but plans to take up peddling if he loses his work permit.

His story accurately documents the miseries of the stateless: the constant scramble for papers, "passport, visa, work permits," and the recurrent crises, "a war, a revolution, a pogrom" that lead to packing everything up and moving on to another place where one must learn yet another language (136). Of course his high anxiety level, his catastrophic sense of history, and his fixation on his children will instantly recall Christian's, though Christian is determined to deny any affinity: "What did he have in common with this poor Jew"? (134). But when he nonetheless admits to the refugee that they share the name, "Rabinovitch," the other assumes that they also share a history, a language, and a fate. Christian rebuffs his Yiddish overtures and his attempts to discover which of Christian's ancestors had migrated from Russia or Ukraine; a cold "possibly" is his only response to the observation that all the Rabinovitches come from "over there" (133). Undiscouraged, the refugee draws from Christian's fine appearance the hope that his own grandson might prosper some day: "your grandfather would have been a poor man," he insists. "Those who were rich or happy didn't leave" (137).

Happy people do not emigrate. The immediate, emotional bond between the two Rabinovitches is their unhappiness. The refugee with his poverty and his dead children is, if anything, too obviously the embodiment of the rich widower's suppressed anxieties about his son's marriage and his night terrors about a war that will strip him of everything. If there is anti-Semitism in this story, it lies in Christian's unwillingness to identify with the refugee, his sense of embarrassment at the other man's heavily accented French, his dirty hands, his volubility as he spontaneously spills out a painful history to a listener so reticent about his own. For the refugee, Jewishness is fate, not only an excuse for his persecution but something more essential, a restless discontent: "that's how Jews are" (135). Such reductive and essentialist notions are as repellant to Christian as they would be to poststructural theory, and he rejects them out of hand: "By education and by culture, I'm closer to a man like Sestres"; and "I'm much further away from that Jew than I am from an oriental peddler" (139).[7] Again he recurs to his Jewish features but argues that they have no meaning: "Only the soul matters!" (139).

Though unwilling from long habit to share confidences, Christian treats the refugee courteously, inviting him to warm himself in the first-class waiting room and giving him twenty francs for carrying his bag and hunting rifle. Nor are his thoughts entirely unsympathetic: "wretched creature . . . He touched me because he was quaint, a relic of a bygone age" (138). Repeating the question about what he might have in common with the refugee, he tells himself that they are separated by an "abyss." As he uses the word "nothing" four times in two sentences, any reader of Flaubert or James will understand that Christian is protesting too much. We hardly need the narrative intervention that follows: even as he argues with himself, Christian is swaying back and forth, exactly as generations of rabbis, money changers, and tailors have done. "He did not realize it," but the narrator and the reader do. Then Christian begins to notice what we have already seen: "That's what I'm suffering from" (139). "That" is his Jewishness, the familial history of "misery, sickness, oppression," and its disquiet ferments in his blood: "Yes, for the moment, at any rate, he was free from exile, poverty, and need, but their indelible mark remained" (140).

Doubtless the same people who talk about how easily Némirovsky might have emigrated would advise Christian to do so. But we cannot advise a character in a story, any more than we can know that, had we lived in France in 1936, when Léon Blum was prime minister, we would have predicted that a few years later he would be in Buchenwald and that by the end of the war over 75,000 other Jews living in France would have been deported and killed. What we know of Christian's tendency to suppress fear, his resistance to racial theories of identity, and his need to be a modern Frenchman suggests, however, that he will push aside his insight that any respite from the fate of the other Rabinovitches will be short-lived. "No, no! It was humiliating, impossible" (140). When the train journey ends and Sestres and his friends meet him, he is happier, free from the painful impression provoked by his encounter with "the Jew" (140). He and they speak the same language, dress in the same way, have the same habits and tastes.

So the story ends with Christian reinserted into a milieu with which his ideas and ambitions are at home. But not his body: "Only his body, shivering with cold in spite of his warm English clothes, and his oversensitive nerves acknowledged their ancient inheritance" (140). Nazi discourse not only rendered Jewishness racial but also marked Jewish bodies as unattractive, unfit, and disease-ridden. The narrator of "Brotherhood" comes closest to anti-Semitism in descriptions of characters that sound authoritative; in the worst case, the refugee's excessively mobile, expressive face and body make him "look almost like a monkey" (131). He and his grandson are too thin; they both have feverish black eyes (131). On rereading, one notes that Christian is initially described at greater length but in similar terms: "a thin, frail, hunched man with silver hair; his narrow face had a yellowish tinge; his dry skin looked starved of nourishment; his nose was excessively long and pointed; his lips, also dry, seemed parched by a thousand-year-old thirst, an affliction passed on from one generation to the next" (124). In spite of Christian's pampered life, his body, too, is unattractive and unhealthy. His aversion to golf and hunting is probably overdetermined, but physical vulnerability plays a role: "Golf? He imagined feeling the wind stinging his face on a day like today, on a golf course. . . . Of course he'd hate it" (126).

In appropriating the language of anti-Semitism, Némirovsky risks suggesting that she shares Christian's discomfort with Jewish identity. Certainly he feels cold as he moves toward Sestre's car, and hears the aristocrat's exclamation, "What fine weather!" How can Christian argue with him? "'Isn't it? Isn't it? A bit cold but so bracing.' And surreptitiously he covered his icy ears with his hands and got into the car" (141). We cannot sort out all the nuances at play or explain why a family history of oppression leaves one shivering in weather an aristocrat finds bracing. But we can say that nothing in this story disposes us to value the athleticism of the idle rich over the vulnerability of this Jewish body. It is the only body we can inhabit in this story, and the cold wind that slaps Christian's cheek slaps our own. His ears do not just feel cold: they are icy, and when he covers them, the gesture refuses more than the October wind.

When last seen, Christian is a troubled figure, not only shivering from cold but making the classic gesture of Kikazuru, the monkey who hears no evil. He has blocked out history, cutting himself off from his voluble kinsman to join men with whom he cannot talk candidly, even about the weather. In his English wool, with his English rifle in its fine suede case, Christian Rabinovitch is dressed to play a country gentleman, another *bourgeois gentilhomme* in a literature that has been mocking them for centuries. Yet although the story sees his self-deception ironically, it does not invite laughter. The phrase in the story that captures its tone most succinctly is spoken by the other Rabinovitch, who meets Christian's incomprehension of Yiddish with "an inimitable expression of disbelief and mockery, mixed with affection and some tenderness, as if were thinking, 'If he wants to show off, he can please himself . . . but to be called Rabinovitch and not understand Yiddish'" (133). This tender mockery from a poor man suggests pity for a fate he knows that they face together.

Alert to the difficulties of understanding oneself in history, "Brotherhood" leaves us balancing the desire to define oneself by one's tastes, education, and decisions against the disturbing possibility that something else might determine them. Indeed, in its alternation between biology and history, the story comes close to collapsing the two. In effect, it resolves the question of whether the Jewish problem is race, religion, or history by metaphorical conflation, as the Biblical writer did when he said that the sour grapes eaten by their fathers will set their sons' teeth on edge. Genetics can tell us why men resemble their ancestors and cousins, and psychoanalysis can explain how anxieties are passed from parents to children.

But neither quite explains why people so often use race (biological heredity) to explain history. Perhaps "race" is an apt metaphor for the persistence of the irrational. Walter Benjamin, who was to commit suicide at the Spanish border in 1940 after being denied passage from France, saw the modern belief in progress as false. "The tradition of the oppressed teaches us that the 'emergency situation' in which we live is the rule," he wrote, echoing the Eastern European Rabinovitch's sense of Jewish history. That is why he criticized people who express astonishment that barbarity is "still possible" in the twentieth century. "The beginning of knowledge" lies, Benjamin argued, in realizing that "the conception of history" on which the expectation of progress depends "is untenable." In "Brotherhood," Némirovsky contemplates the perfectibility of human beings as another such untenable idea. To discover that there is something "inassimilable" in us is to understand that something in human nature that is savage, barbaric, and resistant to reason is also intractable.

The Dogs and the Wolves

On January 19, 2016, the *New York Times* reported on the difficulties "canine scientists" encounter as they investigate the common assumption that dogs evolved from wolves. In fact, "there is no stretch of [DNA] code that says 'wolf' or 'dog' any more than there is a single skull feature that defines a category." Whether dogs evolved from wolves attracted to human settlements or from wolf puppies tamed by people remains unclear. Moreover, it is possible that dogs did not evolve from wolves once, but twice, in widely separated locations. The Victorian obsession with creating new breeds of dogs, as well as random breeding among dogs or between dogs and wolves, observed the Oxford biologist Greger Larsen, "created a 'tomato soup' of dog genetics, for which the ingredients are very hard to identify." "Some scientists are not convinced that the two are even different species," the article states, reflecting "broader debates about how to define a species, and how much the category is a fact of nature as opposed to an arbitrary line drawn by humans" (Gorman).

Of course, Némirovsky's 1940 novel *The Dogs and the Wolves* makes no contributions to canine genetics, but we benefit from a reminder that she chose for her title two species whose underlying similarities are as striking as their differences. A book called *The Dogs and the Cats* or, to use a theological metaphor, *The Sheep and the Goats,* would have evoked opposites. In French, moreover, as Sandra Smith explains, "'*entre chien et loup*' [between dog and wolf] means 'dusk,' the time of day when it is difficult to distinguish clearly between similar shapes" (*Dogs* v). Nor are the moral implications of comparing a person to a dog clear: is the author thinking of "man's best friend" or the secondary definition of dog as a person regarded as "unpleasant, contemptible, or wicked" (Dictionary.com)?[8] Certainly we would not wish to forget "it's a dog's life," a cliché with the same meaning in both languages, which Israel Sinner's career of working long hours for limited rewards seems to illustrate. His efforts to labor under oppressive social and economic circumstances could easily be contrasted with the wild freedom of the wolf. Perhaps as a result of these shifting connotations, reviewers of the English translation disagree on the intended meaning: are anti-Semitic wolves harrying Jewish "dogs," or are the "dogs" assimilated Jews and the "wolves" their struggling, unassimilated Jewish counterparts, whose behavior seems savage in comparison?[9]

The novel opens with a description of a Ukrainian town "beyond the Pale" where both Jews and Christians live. Among Jews, the poorest and most stigmatized live at the bottom; at the top are the richest and most privileged; the "mortals" live in the middle. As the first paragraph explains, the hill is a literal one. What matters is not just that rich people live in good neighborhoods but that under the czars most Jews were not allowed to live in Christian areas "beyond the Pale." However, people in some professions were exempt from that requirement and "it was unheard of for a bribe not to circumvent even the most severe laws" (1, 2). The first pages, then, mark Jews as people who face special restrictions, whose literal place in the world depends on their ability to adapt to injustice. And since paying bribes is illegal, the man who pays one is easily stereotyped as underhanded. "Everyone thought money a good thing," the narrator later tells us, but the Jews needed it more, for without it, "How could they get their children into school when there were already too many students enrolled? How could they buy permission to go here or there, to sell this or that?" (16).

The Dogs and the Wolves is a longer, more complicated version of a theme "Brotherhood" introduces: the relationship of successful, assimilated Jews to their struggling counterparts. In this novel the Jews are part of the same family, the Sinners—the author's fluent English suggests that the name is no accident—who start out at opposite ends of the Ukrainian hill. Israel Sinner is a poor widower who supports his daughter, his father, his sister-in-law, and her two children on the meager commissions he earns as a *makler,* a go-between who buys and sells on behalf of other people: "you could tell who they were by their rapid speech, their gestures, the way they hurried (at a time and in a country where no one hurried) . . . and by the many other qualities unique to them" (3). In other words, they have some of the behaviors stereotyped as Jewish, but the nature of their work determines them, not moral flaws or bad genes. The novel often takes this tack, speaking of distinctive Jewish traits, even flaws, but explaining them in sociological or historical terms.

At the very top of the hill lives Israel Sinner's grandmother's first cousin, Salomon Sinner, the richest man in town, with mansions in London and Vienna as well. He shares his elegant house with an extended family that includes his cosseted grandson, Harry. Israel Sinner is much too modest to take advantage of this family connection, but his stronger-willed sister-in-law Raissa has no such scruples, and her constant allusions fascinate the child Ada. The first time she sets her eyes on Harry Sinner, a schoolboy the same age as her cousin Ben, she becomes obsessed with him. Though he has "the same black curls, fine nose, long delicate neck" as Ben, he is dressed like no other boy she has seen, in "a suit of light beige silk and a large fine linen collar" (22). The rich Sinners have no interest in seeking out their poor relatives and have distanced themselves culturally as well: while old Salomon has a Yiddish accent, his daughter prefers Russian or French, and his "disagreeable" sisters-in-law "knew no Yiddish, thank God" (97). After the revolution, when the Sinners move to Paris, Harry is destined to be almost perfectly assimilated into French society, so much so that he eventually marries a French Catholic woman.

Ada's obsession with Harry keeps the two branches of the family connected, if only loosely. The sixth, seventh, and eighth chapters of the novel describe a pogrom in the lower town, which prompts Ada and Harry's first face-to-face meeting. Pogroms were of course a regular feature of life in czarist Russia, one the author experienced as a two-year-old. The sound of whistles and shouting draws Ada to the window, but Aunt Raissa pulls her away roughly, shouting, in her own fear and anger, "You horrible child!" (36). The children are hustled off to bed with instructions to remain half-dressed and the hasty reassurance that "nothing will happen tonight" (36). For a few days they hear nothing more serious than a few breaking windows and curses but are forbidden to leave the house. Then suddenly they hear a "savage unearthly clamor," and then "someone they didn't recognize . . . because the face was so disfigured by fear" rushes in, grabs them roughly, and drags them up a ladder "to a junk room in the eaves" (39). The stranger is Ada's usually gentle father, who orders them not to move and to be quiet, paying no attention when they ask for food. For hours the children wait in the freezing attic, hearing crowds roaring "like wild animals" and hurling "themselves like rams against the walls, hitting . . . backing off, furious battering . . . striking them again and again" (40). In their terror they open an old trunk and snuggle into it, and soon are playing out a frantic fantasy of being pirates struggling through a terrible storm, dodging icebergs, the "screams and cries" in the streets transformed into crashing waves and roaring wind (41).

The next morning Aunt Raissa comes up with a change of clothing and a bit of black bread, urging them out into the street with the Christian cook, Nastasia, who can take them safely to a Ukrainian friend's house. The street looks "as if there had been a cyclone or a flood"; debris and the smell of smoke are everywhere. Frightened, Nastasia is as incapable of comforting them as Aunt Raissa was. When a group of women standing in front of a church warn her against taking the street where they expected safety, she panics, running from one person to another asking what to do. Cossacks on horseback enter the street, and in the ensuing panic, the children are separated from the cook.

Running blindly, the children eventually find themselves in a peaceful, wealthy neighborhood; perhaps, thinks Ada, its residents "looked upon the horror and confusion of the ghetto as if they were at the theater," reassuring themselves "that would never happen to *me*" (48, 49). "And yet," as Ada realizes, "they were Jewish too" (49). At her insistence, they ring Salomon Sinner's doorbell and march into the room where his family are having breakfast. The contrast between the disheveled children with their torn clothes and the luxurious Sinners in their silks and lace strikes everyone; even after Ben has blurted out the whole terrible story, a female relative warns them not to get close: "They might be dirty. They might be diseased" (54). But Ada does not go to the kitchen for her bread and tea without talking back: "If you'd spent the whole night hiding in a trunk, your faces would be all dusty and your beautiful dresses would get all torn, too" (54).

But in a deeper sense, she understands: "The famished children stood before these wealthy Jews as an eternal reminder . . . of what they themselves had once been. . . . No one dared to add: 'what they could become again someday'" (55). We saw the theater metaphor in "The Spectator" and in "Brotherhood" saw Christian Rabinovitch's half-acknowledged fear of being reduced to the condition of a refugee. Here, however, the point of view is that of the poor and persecuted. Fortunately, the familiar misery prompts old Salomon Sinner, who looks like Ada's grandfather, to offer help. He praises Ada's father as an "honest Jew" and promises to find some work for him. The Sinners contact her father, and the children are taken to safety. By the time of Salomon's death two years later, the poor Sinners have become comfortably well off and move "higher up, halfway between the top of the hill and the ghetto" (59). Their ambitious Aunt Raissa finds the children an elderly Parisian to teach them French, which gives them access to the Alliance Française, which sponsors the dance where Ada and Harry will meet again, when he is thirteen and she a little younger.

In the years since they appeared at their rich relatives' doorstep as fugitives from a pogrom, Ada has remained infatuated with Harry, while Ben on the contrary has become obsessively jealous. Ben is used to Christian privilege as being "in the natural order of things"; Harry, however, "could be me, and I could be him" (65). He wishes Harry to suffer as he has and imagines himself in Harry's place, "well fed, well dressed, loved . . . rich" (66). For just as Christian Rabinovitch's wealth inspired in the other Rabinovitch a hope that his grandson might prosper, the wealthy Sinners inspire hope as much as they arouse envy. As for Harry, he will refuse to dance with Ada at the Alliance Française party, which crushes her with disappointment. But both sense a deep bond: Harry because he is "dying of shame," knowing he would be "sick with remorse over his behavior," aware that he fears her because "she represented unhappiness . . . strangely, terrifyingly contagious" (71). For Ada, Harry's rebuff awakens "extreme hatred and extreme love . . . so contradictory . . . that she felt . . . wrenched in two" (71). But then, when he apologizes and she sees his tears, "Ada no longer felt anything but love" (71).

Socially ambitious Aunt Raissa decides that it is time to move to Paris: knowing her brother-in-law's devotion to Ada, who already shows promise as an artist, she argues that the girl and her cousin Lilla, an aspiring actress, need the best possible instruction. Némirovsky frames Israel's assent as typically Jewish: "if it had been a case of sending Lilla and Ada away to be educated . . . [for] a safe, ordinary profession," he would never have permitted it. But training in the arts? "It was not a question of logic, but of a dream"; and where dreams are concerned, Jewish parents will take any risk. Why this is so the novel does not explain, but it indicates that Israel "always wanted to ask Ada's forgiveness for bringing her into the world" (77). This guilt is better understood historically, in terms of the children's experience during the pogrom, than as a genetic imperative. So, "since Russia was not the ideal country for a little Jewish boy," he packs all three children off to Paris with Raissa and the French teacher (78).

The family arrive in Paris in the spring of 1914. For two years Israel sends them money, but "then the Revolution swept through Russia . . . destroying . . . the life, the destiny, and even the memory of Israel Sinner" (78). Left penniless, Aunt Raissa shows her true mettle by setting up a dressmaking business. Lilla is dispatched to work in a music hall; Ben delivers dresses; and Ada's artistic talents are either channeled into copying stolen dress patterns or suppressed in favor of menial labor in the shop. Aunt Raissa becomes no warmer when forced to earn her own money; as Ada grows prettier, the tension between them escalates. Ada's artistic temperament comes into play: although she always stands up for herself, "her imagination was so fertile and strange that nothing could really hurt or offend her" (80). Ada sees her "aunt's harsh, intelligent, bitter face not as an ill-treated young girl would, but with the eye of a painter" (80).

In time the family learns that the rich Sinners have emigrated as well and are living in an upper-middle-class neighborhood nearby. Events move quickly once Ada ventures near their house and catches a glimpse of Harry, struck again "by his resemblance to Ben"—that is, "the classic Jewish man . . . slight, intelligent, and sad" (85). She slips into a reverie, imagining how strange it would seem to other people if she compared her love for Ben to Dante's for Beatrice. She pauses to wonder, for example, whether other people have such "mad dreams" or whether they are exclusive to Jews because "we are such a hungry race, starving for so long that reality is not enough to satisfy us" (86). This recalls Christian Rabinovitch inheriting his ancestor's ill ease. In her preoccupation, she loses the eight hundred francs a customer has paid her for a dress; Aunt Raissa slaps her and orders her out of the house.

Ben follows Ada down the street and proposes that they marry, even though he knows her infatuation with Harry keeps her from loving him. His argument is an entirely practical one: she is too young to live alone, and he doesn't "give a damn about the future" in which, she says, she will be sure to leave him (93). She agrees to marry after they debate about her claim that he always does everything the hard way and always chooses the road "where each step forward is earned by shady, shameful deals" (92). He retorts that he has never come across any other road. No one will ever help them, but he is determined to survive "by trafficking, scheming, buying and selling, always being on the move, by lying" (92). In other words, he will do the things anti-Semites accuse Jews of doing but only because he has no alternative after a life of hardship, rejection, and mockery. Ada, he argues, is just as mad, dreaming of Harry at seventeen as she did when she was eight: "We're not logical, we're not philosophers, we're not French, not us!" (92).

At chapter 15 the narrative switches abruptly to Harry Sinner's perspective. Always rich and always loved, he nonetheless resembles his poor cousins in his attraction to what is forbidden—in his case, love for Laurence, the blonde daughter of a French banker. Again, we are reminded of Christian Rabinovitch, whose son is engaged to the daughter of a French count. Harry's mother also fears her son's wish to marry among the native French: "she always felt that people were going to harm Harry, hurt him, humiliate him" (98). And yet again the alternative, that the French family may reject the marriage, is enough to make her heart bleed "at the thought of Harry's humiliation" (99). As she approaches Laurence with an expression she intends as welcoming, "she contorted her face into a fixed, sickly smile that made her look like an old street hawker approaching . . . a client" (99). Laurence reacts with possibly unconscious anti-Semitism, thinking Harry's mother is trying to "judge what I was worth" (99). And as the narrator comments, she is partly right: Mrs. Sinner is not trying to estimate income but "just the possibility of happiness, and her heart was breaking" (99).

Harry's marriage will be forbidden for two years because of the overt anti-Semitism of Laurence's father, M. Delarcher, in whom "everything that came from the East aroused insurmountable mistrust. Slavonic, Levantine, Jewish—he didn't know which of these terms disgusted him the most" (105). Knowledge of the fine reputation of the Sinners' bank does not prevent him from believing that it "had its roots in some money-lender's shop . . . some small-time usurer" (106). His anti-Semitic stereotypes extend to "physical impressions": he sees the Sinners as having "greasy skin, sharp features, anxious eyes," while Harry's mother is "that fat Jewess covered in jewelry!" (106). He finds evidence of the racial taint in Harry himself: "you could tell that the boy had to do everything in his power to straighten his hair every morning"; his eyes "shone . . . as if they were burning in hot oil"; and his complexion is "pale, yellowish" (107).

We have often seen sallow skin, frizzy hair, or some other apparently unattractive physical trait linked to Jewishness in Némirovsky, usually by a third-person narrator or a Jewish character embedded in the narrative. What makes *The Dogs and the Wolves* distinctive is the deliberate ascription of such sentiments to a French character explicitly marked as xenophobic and anti-Semitic. As Sandra Smith has argued, Delarcher's diatribe "is meant to fill us with revulsion," to remove the ambiguity that allows questions about self-hatred to be raised in *David Golder* or "Brotherhood" (Smith, "In Defence"). Sadly, as we see in Naomi Price's claim that "a Nazi publishing house" that had "commissioned the novel stipulating the perpetuation of racial stereotype would not have been disappointed," this attempt to put distance between the narrator and anti-Semitism can be overlooked. Perhaps Némirovsky's insistence on showing a redeeming side even in M. Delarcher, who eventually consents to the marriage, blurs that intention. But we need to remember that Mrs. Sinner shares his apprehensions about this intercultural marriage. Its failure will prove their parental fears justified but will not justify the social and political ramifications of his xenophobia.

Nonetheless, Némirovsky has raised questions about Jewish identity, even while emphasizing its social construction through experiences of exclusion and persecution. We know that Ada and Harry are fated to have a love affair as soon as Némirovsky creates her triangle, and the premise of some transcendental Jewishness, some element of the inassimilable, will be suggested, as it was in "Brotherhood." Just as Christian Rabinovitch is shown to have more in common with a poor refugee than with Frenchmen who share his income and cultural sophistication, Harry must come to feel a bond with Ada that he does not feel with his wife, in spite of the romantic fervor that kept him devoted to Laurence during the years her father forbade their marriage.

Ada is an artist endowed with a romantic temperament and an intense fixation on her goals; she feels compelled to paint people like those who lived in the Ukrainian ghetto of her childhood. She herself wonders why she does not want to draw sunny portraits of happy mothers or fashionable people at the seaside but "was driven to seek out, cruelly, tirelessly, the secrets concealed in sad faces, beneath dark skies" (115). She also obsesses over Harry, shadowing him and Laurence as they browse in neighborhood shops. On one occasion, she observes that Harry yearns for a rare book, which costs so much that Laurence calls his desire for it "madness" (116). Poor as she is, Ada manages to buy it and leave it for him as an anonymous gift, an act at once generous and manipulative. Harry will wonder who the giver is and be driven to wonder about her, and thus she will "insinuate herself between" him and Laurence. It is the first time she has ever bought anyone an expensive gift, and she thinks that Ben is too "Spartan" to appreciate one, "offering him a gift seemed as strange as tying a ribbon around a wolf" (116).

But Ada, for all her ardent prayers, her demands that God "make him mine," never campaigns to take Harry away from his wife and child. She becomes an occasion of their quarreling, however, after he finds himself deeply moved by a painting displayed in the same bookstore where Ada purchased his gift. The painting witnesses to "a distant reality, one destroyed . . . long ago" (119). Soon he is recalling snowstorms that raged, teachers and friends he had forgotten, and his grandmother holding him close, stroking her grandson's hair and "murmuring words . . . in Yiddish, which the others found scandalous" (119). When he inquires about the painter, the salesman identifies Ada and adds that she once bought him a rare book. Harry is annoyed, assuming she intended to cultivate the Sinners for their money. Her doing so bothers him all the more because "like all Jews, he was more sharply, more sadly scandalized than a Christian by faults that were specifically Jewish." For him "that tenacious energy, that almost savage need to get what one wants" is "Jewish arrogance," and he wants no contact with it (121). So he buys two of Ada's paintings but makes the salesman promise not to identify him as the buyer.

But the mischief is done. Harry cannot stop talking about the paintings or displaying them to his friends, and Laurence becomes jealous, especially when she hears a friend remark that Harry "adores" Ada's "wild, dark side" (123). When the same friends insist on being taken to Ada's studio, Laurence is offended by the confidence she believes Ada conceals behind her "ridiculous shyness" and turns "colder toward her [and] hostile" (124). When Harry steps aside to talk to Ada, their conversation moves immediately into dangerous territory. Recalling the time of the pogrom, he confides that the appearance of the wild-looking children was a signal event in his childhood and that "I dream about you, very often" (127). Soon Ada is underscoring their ethnic bond: "our roots are there." "In Russia?" he asks, but she says no, "Before that . . . further back" (127). And Harry knows exactly what she means, not "just some climate or . . . place . . . but a specific way of loving, of desiring" (127). When she asks him what he has desired most, he answers "Laurence"; when she replies that her greatest desire is "to know" Harry himself, he says he pities her if she desires him as "passionately, as hopelessly, as I desired . . . Laurence" (127). Ada immediately challenges the word "hopeless," but he explains that he only has his wife "like an object seen in a mirror" that one cannot grasp (127).

As in "Brotherhood," Némirovsky seems to suggest that candor emerges when a Jewish person speaks to another, even if they are strangers. In the next chapter, when Harry tells Laurence that Ada's paintings help him "rediscover myself, the true me," we can see how far from appealing she finds the idea of a "real Harry" revealed in paintings of the ghetto. If he is discovering "within me, the sadness from which I was so carefully protected" and realizing that it is "true . . . in its immortal essence," she is finding her inner anti-Semite just as rapidly. His proposal that they host a reception for Ada repels her to the point that Harry accuses Laurence of imagining that his cousin will "run off with the silverware" (133). She in turn accuses him of displaying "a hysterical side" that she finds "extremely unpleasant" and which, even worse, she has detected in their son, "without realizing that he got it from you" (135). In pointing to their son's tendency to "display excessive joy or anger," which he himself sees as an alarming sign of "emotional instability," she has "struck upon the thing that would hurt Harry the most" (135).

Afterward nothing is hidden. She says that encouraging Ben, of whom Harry knows nothing, means introducing an "opportunist" who will take advantage of her family and Harry himself. When he tells her that assuming his cousin is an opportunist only makes him feel like a brother, Laurence retorts that it also makes him see his own wife "as a foreigner" (136). The dispute over the reception for Ada reveals "a deeper, more serious conflict" in their marriage, and she confesses to never having understood him. "I thought you were happy," she says, and he shouts back, "No, I have never been happy." Harry's voice sounds "shrill," even to himself, and he runs out of the room (136). Since Laurence will not have the reception in their home, he asks his mother to hold it.

Mrs. Sinner's reception for Ada sets in motion the rest of the plot. Harry and Ada eventually begin an affair, and Ben, exactly the opportunist Laurence feared, renews his ties to the rich Sinners. While explicitly disavowing genetic explanations about "race or blood," Ben believes a history of persecution has created "a bond" that the Sinners can never forget (139). In his view this bond imposes no obligation on him; recognizing their instinctive sympathy merely provides an angle to exploit. Although Harry warns his uncles against placing "all your trust in a petty opportunist we know nothing about," they take Ben's advice and loan their money recklessly to unstable governments "in the Orient" (162). They scoff at Harry's fears that the family business will come crashing down and dismiss his warning that "the air of secrecy around you is the cause of much hatred" (162). Hatred? As Salomon says, he has known hatred all his life and fears it no more than "fish . . . fear water" (163). The upshot is that Ben schemes and plots, making risky deals in places so chaotic that their industries cannot be developed or their resources safely exported. When matters become desperate, Ben commits forgery and flees France a wanted criminal.

Thus Ben's business practices conform to most of the anti-Semitic stereotypes of the 1930s, although, contrary to stereotype, his first victims are his Jewish family. Moreover, his equally Jewish wife and cousin oppose everything he stands for, and his Jewish aunt is as fearful as his French sister-in-law that "those opportunists are going to drag us down with them" (168). "You," Ada tells him, "are the person I distrust and detest most in the world, the most evil" (179). Yet, does all this talk of financial scheming manage to reinforce some of the period's anti-Semitism, even as the novel insists that other Jewish characters have very different attitudes towards money and morality? When Ben says that the older Sinners had become aware of his plots and did nothing to stop them, he explains that "I appealed to something in them that was older than they were" (178). At this point we may find Némirovsky appearing to conflate the old "bond of tears" with race, as she seems to do when she describes Christian Rabinovitch as prematurely aged and instinctively fearful.

Although Ada's obsession with Harry is tracked for years, their actual love affair takes up less space in the novel than one might expect. Any sexual attraction between them seems to be reduced to fatalism, which Laurence perceives as "an obscure blood tie against which she was powerless" (168). As for Harry's feelings, "the bond of tears" is hard to distinguish from a genetic imperative. Harry and Ada, like the two Rabinovitches, are united by their shared unhappiness: "with Ada," Harry thinks, "words . . . were pointless . . . subtleties in her voice, her eyes, revealed to him the very essence of her soul" (141). But as for Ada, she shares Harry's mother's fear that she will "drag him down," and her compulsion to protect him overcomes her need for his physical presence. (173)

The curious anachronism imposed by Némirovsky's publication (and translation) history intrudes on our reading of *The Dogs and the Wolves.* Since it came out on the cusp of the German invasion, there was no time for the usual series of reviews or even the tallying of sales. Most of the people who read and reviewed the novel encountered it more than six decades after the war, when everyone knew the fate of the Jews. In *The Dogs and the Wolves,* it is Ben, the least lovable Sinner, who takes satisfaction from knowing that Harry's money, manners, and European acculturation cannot save him from anti-Semitism: "Just wait! You'll be considered part of that scum again one day. You'll be back into it [even though] . . . you . . . thought you'd escaped" (152). That is, Ben articulates the thought Ada suppressed when she first realized how much her rich relatives feared the contagion of poverty and oppression their ghetto cousins represented. In "Brotherhood" the poor Rabinovitch may mock Christian softly for denying his family's history under the czars, but he is much too kind to confront him. But Ben rationalizes his crimes by making a Marxist argument that the upper-class values Harry embodies, whether they are manifested in clean collars or in financial honesty, are just disguises for class privilege: "What you call success, victory, love . . . is what I call money" (152). This message is not the intended moral of Ben's story, but it is fully credible as the belief of someone who survived a harsh childhood.

But we cannot ignore our historical knowledge. When Ben takes off for South America with his formidable mother, Raissa, the reader is probably meant to judge him ignoble, finding survival at a moral price a more honorable man would disdain. But in real life, as we know, his flight would have saved him from Auschwitz—that is, from the author's fate and the probable one of the more admirable Sinners, who not only are Jews but under fascist law aliens.[10]

This same knowledge intrudes as we follow the Harry-Ada subplot to its conclusion. Harry, as we recall, warns his uncles against Ben but is rebuffed. When Ben's crimes are exposed, the Sinners go bankrupt, and Ada and Harry see his own social standing and reputation as irretrievably lost. Harry broods over his losses and his undeniable Jewishness: "He had been born feeling guilty of a crime he had not committed, knowing that no one . . . would save him" (192). And then, as Némirovsky reproduces the scene from "Brotherhood," we watch him: "Thin and frail, rubbing his beautiful hands together, he swayed gently in the darkness, just as so many moneychangers standing behind their counters . . . as countless rabbis . . . as a multitude of immigrants . . . had done before him. . . . Like them, he felt like an outsider, lost and alone" (193).

This passage strikes a contemporary reader as historically just: in a period of rising anti-Semitism, an assimilated Jew whose family's name appeared in headlines about financial fraud could expect to lose the protection his cultivated speech and his Christian wife had once offered. But in the novel, Ada thinks of a way to sacrifice herself for Harry. She begs Laurence to take Harry back; the two women agree that M. Delarcher will be able to protect Harry and that Laurence will drop her plans for a divorce if Ada ends the affair. Ada sends Harry a note saying that she is leaving Paris with her husband. A few days later, the wife of a wanted criminal, she receives a deportation notice and finds refuge in "a small country in eastern Europe" (195).

What the text seems to intend and what history tells us about probability are again at odds. The text says that Harry's father-in-law managed to hush up the connection between his son-in-law and the Sinner bankruptcy, apparently allowing Harry to resume his comfortable life. He looks weak because the text acknowledges that Harry "could find Ada if he really wanted to" and makes no effort to do so, but we are meant to think him safe (194). Ada, on the other hand, goes off to a new life; she will give birth to their son, about whom Harry knows nothing, in the unnamed country. She finds a job as a sales assistant, resumes her painting when she has a day off, and makes friends in the shabby hotel where she lives, mostly with Jewish refugees whose relatives are in concentration camps. So many doctors and midwives live in the hotel that she does not lack for care when her son is born, a redemptive event. Childbirth has "split" her "into a thousand Adas . . . with not a thought for . . . the real Ada and her past" (211). Ada has "given up a part of her life for her newborn child, but he was giving her . . . the gift of forgetfulness" (211).

How much of this tentative fairy-tale ending Irène Némirovsky expected her readers to believe in the spring of 1940 is unclear. The book never directly addresses political anti-Semitism in France, though it makes much of social prejudices. When Ada returns to the East, the anti-Semitism is as political and as immediately threatening as it was during the pogrom. Pierre Loewel is not the only reader to imagine Ada and her baby being dragged off by sinister men in uniforms, and we of course construct a similar fate for Harry. But all of this is speculation. What the novel does show us is that Irène Némirovsky, in the last novel she published in the French Republic, clearly understood what was happening to European Jews. She clearly understood that assimilated Jews in France, like their affluent ancestors under the czars, feared persecuted Jews who embodied a fate that could strike them next. She was not willing to depict a gallery of noble Jews. Ben and his crimes and the venality of the older Sinners uncles cannot be denied, and their flaws are stereotypical ones. But when she faced up to Jewish identity, like Christian Rabinovitch or Harry Sinner, she could not deny its reality nor that it was the product of a violent history that showed no signs of ending.

The title metaphor of dogs and wolves is not reiterated often in the novel. There is the reference to Ben as a wolf already cited, and then later, after arguing with Ada about what he and Harry have in common, Ben says they are similar "the way dogs and wolves are similar" (181). It may be possible to imagine Harry as a pampered German shepherd settling down by the fire in his beautiful house, but the text never makes the comparison explicit. But even scientists have trouble distinguishing between dogs and wolves because their historical origins are so complicated. The metaphor of dogs and wolves as Jews of different classes with different behaviors, as used in this book, seems to suggest traits shared at a time before animals were anthropomorphized. "Man's best friend" and "the howling beast," with their moral connotations of loyalty and frightening rapacity, tell us more about human fears and needs than they do about canines. Of course, after anti-Semites have constructed Jews so negatively over so many centuries and after a whole pseudoscience has been concocted to prove that duplicity and greed are hardwired into the Jewish genome, anyone whose ideas of reason were shaped by the Enlightenment, as Irène Némirovsky's were, resists the idea of an innate Jewish identity. She did associate any claim of something essential and "inassimilable" in Jews with Hitler, but she also saw that as the power of persecutors to limit Jewish rights became as undisguised as it had been under the Inquisition or the czars, Jewish people were forced to claim their common history and speculate about how it had shaped them.

Thus, when Ada receives her deportation order, her harsh aunt Raissa receives one too. And though they have been estranged for years, Ada flees first to Raissa; and though she and her friends are no more attractive than they ever were, Ada is forced to acknowledge that "these are my people . . . my family" (205). She is ready to accept the friendship of her fellow refugees in Eastern Europe and to experience her bond with her new son as the strongest of her life.

Naomi Price is not altogether wrong when she finds "crude anti-Semitism" in *The Dogs and the Wolves,* but she is wrong in failing to notice how carefully the novel defines the worst behaviors corresponding to stereotype as understandable responses to persecution, which many Jewish characters who have experienced the same persecution reject. The traits the book links most explicitly to Jewishness, the ones shared by both its dogs and its wolves, are morally neutral. The most persistent are intensity, a will to improve one's life, intelligence, emotional sensitivity, a bond to family, and a propensity to unhappiness. These can make one an artist or a con man, a loving and self-sacrificing father like Isaac or a harsh mother like Raissa, who ensures her children's survival but never recognizes their need for gentleness. Many of the qualities that an anti-Semite like M. Delarcher finds repellant, like curly hair and liquid eyes, are from another perspective as "beautiful" as Harry's hands (193). As long as people inherit their genes from their families and their prejudices from a social world that reproduces them by means of segregated housing and education, and through the stereotypes embedded in familiar narratives and even colloquial usage, Jewishness will remain distinctive. But what matters more about these characters, as their family name constantly reminds us, is that Isaac and Raissa, Ben and Harry and Ada are all human, all Sinners.

Chapter 6

The "Vichy" Novels

We have seen that, in the narrowly racist sense in which the right wing used the term in the 1930s, the "French" novels of Irène Némirovsky are impure: haunted by the repressed life of the Jewish or métèque other. Némirovsky wrote two more novels focused on the native French, *All Our Worldly Goods* and *The Fires of Autumn,* before beginning *Suite Française.* Jonathan Weiss was the first to characterize these novels as "showing a point of view that fits in well with the Vichy regime," an observation reviewers occasionally paraphrase to suggest political sympathies Weiss carefully avoids attributing to Némirovsky. "These novels do not really reveal Irène's attitude at the time," he adds, but "she was undoubtedly hoping that her publishers would take them" (132). We need to understand publishing conditions in Vichy France before we hope to make sense of Némirovsky's wartime writing.

But first let us note that "Vichy France" is the usual term for what was officially the collaborationist "État français" headed by Maréchal Pétain after the Armistice. The National Assembly of the Third Republic in effect committed suicide, passing over authority to Pétain on July 10, 1944, giving Vichy a debatable but real claim to legitimacy. Militarists and conservatives in France had advocated many of its authoritarian policies for years, and although socialists and Jews recognized its dangers immediately, many conservatives and the apolitical accepted its legitimacy early on. Certainly we should not think of Vichy France as a Nazi military government like the General Government imposed on much of Poland and Ukraine after German victories there.

Vichy itself is an old spa, or resort town, which gave its name not only to a water but to a cold soup, vichyssoise, long associated with luxurious dining. Located in central France and having in 1936 a population of about 25,000, it was chosen as the capital of the new state because of its accessibility to Paris by train and its large number of hotels, convenient for an influx of government officials and their departments. Although the state was in theory sovereign over all of France, in reality its power was limited to the Free Zone, roughly the southern half of the country. The Germans directly occupied Paris and the northern half of France, which also included strategic "exclusion zones" barred to ordinary citizens. Alsace-Lorraine was incorporated into the Reich.

When the Maréchal took over in 1940, he claimed that he was offering himself to France as a protector, a "shield" between its people and the German victor. He used the argument again during his postwar trial for treason. Although at first his claim sounded plausible to many, deteriorating conditions, exacerbated by German demands that food and then laborers be shipped to the Reich, proved this protection illusory. How free was the Free Zone? Certainly it was free of German soldiers, and Jewish refugees flocked there; many escaped over the Pyrenees to Spain or eventually sailed from Marseille—some 2,500, thanks to the aid of the American consulate. Vichy France, however, interned Jews in wretched conditions, and began abolishing their civil liberties in the summer of 1940. In November 1942, in response to the Allied invasion of North Africa, the Germans marched into the Free Zone, effectively abolishing the distinction between Occupied France and the Free Zone. By July of that year the deportation of Jews to Auschwitz had already moved into high gear, to continue into the summer of 1944.[1]

Writing in France While Jewish: 1940–1942

All Our Worldly Goods began life entitled "Jeunes et Vieux" ("The Young and the Old"), under a contract to Jean Fayard signed in April 1940. By October 8 Fayard, who was "riding roughshod over the contract, . . . informed [Némirovsky] that he was no longer prepared to publish her next novel and he graciously relinquished the 30,000 francs already agreed before war broke out" (PL 316). Subsequently the novel was serialized by the anti-Semitic weekly *Gringoire,* the last installment appearing in June 1942, a month before Némirovsky's arrest. Though this novel's origins precede the Vichy state and its first appearance in book form was delayed until 1947, *All Our Worldly Goods* is in some sense a "Vichy" novel, written with a view to publication under censorship and to some extent reflecting state ideology. In both *All Our Worldly Goods* and *The Fires of Autumn,* we can see a tension between that public ideology and the author's own understanding that she was one of the ideology's targets. In both books we may see the damage done by concessions to anticipated censorship, but we also see ironic resistance to ideological demands.

Angela Kershaw's *Before Auschwitz: Irène Némirovsky and the Cultural Landscape of Inter-war France* (2010) uses Pierre Bourdieu's social theory of literature to analyze Némirovsky's novels as a negotiation between the writer and the France she experienced as an immigrant in the 1920s and 1930s. For Bourdieu such a negotiation is no "simple chain of causality leading back to some point of origin," but a "web of interrelations" (Kershaw 50). Bourdieu sketches out two extremes between which an author's relationship to the social world develops: in one, we have something like the popular vision of Emily Dickinson, largely unpublished in her own time, writing her poems in solitude and then tucking them away in a drawer. In the other, we have our worst vision of the Hollywood hack, writing solely to sell scripts for the highest dollar, shamelessly catering to the worst prejudices of the market. Most writers, as Kershaw says, occupy some middle position between these extremes, negotiating between their sense of the "market" and their vision of art and truth. That is, as people who must pay the rent, they wish to write good books that sell, and as artists who wish to produce great art, they value the opinions of at least some of their peers.

Irène Némirovsky makes an excellent subject for Kershaw because she clearly cared about art but always saw herself as a professional writer who needed to support herself and her family. Kershaw's analysis, then, is rich in details of Némirovsky's relationship to the world: the influence of her professors at the Sorbonne, who were shaping the new discipline of comparative literature; her contract negotiations with publishers; her interviews; and her friendships with other writers and with literary editors. Throughout the 1930s, according to Kershaw, "[Némirovsky's] writing was focused toward the goal of cultural assimilation, and she adopted traditional, rather than experimental models of cultural expression which were easily recognizable within the French literary field" (75).

But once the Armistice was signed in June 1940, Némirovsky was forced to deal with official censorship, something quite different from subtle pressure to conform to cultural expectations. The publication history of *All Our Worldly Goods* encapsulates the fate of Jewish writers under Vichy: the breaking of the prewar contract justified as a case of *force majeure*. "It would be inconceivable for us to pay for a novel we are not allowed to publish," Fayard explained (Weiss 151). Fayard was referring to the Statute of Jews (October 3, 1940), which excluded Jews "from a large number of jobs in public office, in teaching, in journalism and in the cinema," while authorizing the internment of foreign Jews in "special camps" (PL 315). The following day the first version of the "Otto list," enumerating writers "proscribed by the occupying power," was published. Némirovsky's name did not appear on the original list or on the second, but it did appear on the third in an appendix of "Jewish writers in French" (Weiss 146). A more general law banned the selling of any Jewish writer's work "except scientific works on certain subjects" (145). The net occasionally permitted a text to slip through: Némirovsky's novel *Deux* ("Two," 1939) was actually reprinted several times before January 1942, and Julie Dumot bought a copy of *The Dogs and the Wolves* in Paris in April of that year (PL 316).

Némirovsky attempted to parse the statute with Fayard, arguing that "writers for newspapers" applied only to journalists, not fiction writers serializing "extracts" from their work (316). She was not to know that the legal advisor to the Society of People of Letters unequivocally agreed with her: "We cannot compare a great writer such as Irène Némirovsky . . . to a journalist who is [an] employee" (PL 316). It hardly mattered. Fayard rejected this advice, urging that government officials be consulted; later, under pressure, the society's president, Jean Vignaud, also repudiated it. In a letter to Némirovsky, he reported that even well-known novelists who contribute to newspapers must prove themselves "neither foreigners, nor Jews" (PL 317).

The only workable ruse was to publish under a pseudonym, which required a sympathetic editor willing to run risks. It is deeply ironic that the anti-Semitic editor of *Gringoire,* Horace de Carbuccia, proved to be the most generous. Or perhaps more troubling is how unimportant Némirovsky's need for income seems to contemporary critics who express horror at her willingness to publish in such a revolting venue. Her husband, Michael Epstein, lost his bank job after the Armistice on the grounds that he had abandoned his post during the German invasion; in truth, all the bank's employees joined the exodus. But this injustice, while galling, had little practical effect: Jews caught outside Paris in June 1940 were forbidden to return to their homes. A decree published on April 26, 1941, canceled all Jewish bank accounts, making Jews legally destitute.

Recognizing this situation, Albin Michel allowed Julie Dumot, a family friend, to sign a book contract for Némirovsky in 1941. Everyone involved in the transaction knew who the real writer and intended beneficiary of the contract was. Albin Michel had published six of Némirovsky's novels during the 1930s and would publish two more, as well as her biography of Chekhov, after the war; they did not, however, publish her, even pseudonymously, during the war. But the contract was honored with fortunate results, for Julie Dumot became the guardian of the Némirovsky children after their parents' deportation. The amount originally agreed upon was three thousand francs but was raised to five thousand in the spring of 1942 and, at the urging of her friend at Albin Michel, André Sabatier, to six thousand for 1943 (PL 366).

Sabatier, her most loyal defender, visited the Némirovskys in Issy-l'Évêque in April 1942, knowing the author was forbidden to travel; after her arrest, he kept up a correspondence with her husband and others documenting real efforts to intervene on her behalf. Yet he was hardly a hero of the Resistance. Having been captured by the Germans in Beirut while serving in the French Navy, Sabatier returned from a German POW camp to join the Vichy government. First assigned as a liaison to the Germans, Sabatier became Vichy's ambassador to Turkey and was sentenced to death by the Allies in 1945. The sentence was eventually commuted; Sabatier returned to Albin Michel and oversaw the posthumous publication of three more of Irène Némirovsky's books. Sometimes the Samaritan is the real friend.

Since Vichy quickly, without waiting for German orders, banned all literary publication by Jews, any direct negotiation between a Jewish writer and the censorship was impossible. A Jewish writer intending to publish under a pseudonym was above all obliged to hide any Jewish sympathies or any specialized knowledge of Jewish culture, so a focus on native Christian French characters was advisable; beyond that a writer could only imagine what the Vichy censor would accept. Certainly Némirovsky rejected any idea of actively playing to the new political masters. Her novels of 1940 and 1941 do not endorse anti-Semitism and authoritarian government; they do not justify concentration camps; and they do not glamorize militarism or its trappings—the parades, uniforms, and stirring anthems that fascism admired.

Némirovsky, however, was well aware that Vichy had replaced the French Revolution's slogan, "liberty, equality, fraternity," with its own trinity of "family, homeland, and work." Vichy rhetoric blamed the French defeat on the Popular Front and the corruption of government officials (not all of them leftists) by foreigners and corporations, encouraging a penitential attitude toward the hardships of the occupation. Most famously, in the spring of 1942 it conducted a show trial of highly placed generals and government officials from the previous decade. Both *All Our Worldly Goods* and *The Fires of Autumn* are centered on families of impeccably native, French, Christian origin; *All Our Worldly Goods* in particular appears to celebrate hard work, traditional communities, and faithful marriage. *The Fires of Autumn* betrays more irony about work and families but explores the question of blame for the collapse of France in some of the same terms used at the trial in Riom. In this respect, its vision of political corruption and bribery in the Third Republic is similar to the one in *The Prey.*

All Our Worldly Goods

All Our Worldly Goods begins early in the twentieth century at a seaside resort where, after several summers, two families have developed an uneasy friendship. The Hardelot family come from the small town of Saint-Elme in the north of France, where they have owned a stationery factory for generations; they are therefore thoroughly upper middle class and eminently respectable. Brewers from Flanders, the Florents are outsiders, and villagers express surprise that Mme. Gabrielle Florent remains in Saint-Elme three years after her husband's death. Though the Hardelots' twenty-four-year-old son, Pierre, has been friendly with Agnès Florent since childhood, it is inconceivable to them that he might marry her.

Mme. Florent is vaguely disreputable: her taste in clothing runs to the flashy and fashionable; she had to work for her living before her marriage; she taught music; and it is possible she knew actresses. Though she observes the outward formalities prescribed by the Hardelots—wearing dress shoes to go walking in the dunes, swimming in a black wool costume "designed to hide a woman's natural shape as much as possible"—nothing removes the whiff of vulgarity that accompanies her everywhere (18). Nonetheless she and Agnès are invited guests in September, when the Hardelots host a dinner party to celebrate Pierre's engagement to Simone Renaudin, a rich heiress.

The reader quickly learns that this marriage was arranged by Pierre's tyrannical grandfather and does not need to be told twice that Simone, whose sight makes Pierre "feel nauseous, like a meal that is too heavy," is not the love of his life (2). Agnès, a slender, gentle, imaginative young woman who mercifully bears no resemblance to her own mother, is obviously perfect for the role. We know that this Romeo and Juliet will be united: only a short time, an innocent tryst, some village gossip, and the interference of Agnès's pushy mother will be required to bring about their marriage. It is a pity that sullen Simone will never lose her obsession with this early rejection.

The tension Némirovsky usually describes between the French and immigrants is reproduced in social divisions that might be invisible to a stranger in the village. But if we look closely, we will catch sight of the David Golders and Dario Asfars: "Further down the coast, a luxury hotel had been built. . . . Down there, they danced and gambled until dawn. But no one envied those outsiders . . . [who] deserved neither interest nor consideration" (9). "The people of Saint-Elme," observes the narrator, "had a remarkable talent for ignoring whatever they didn't wish to know" (6). But these unflattering descriptions suggest another distance, the narrator's own: "It was like horses and cows, who can live side by side in the same field for their entire lives without seeming to notice each other" (23). When money and matrimony mix, as of course they always do in the novel of manners, the simile is equally unflattering: "All introductions of this kind were arranged at someone's marriage or engagement . . . such solemn occasions were like county fairs, where everyone brought along the thing they wanted to sell" (18). If a certain intimacy creeps into negative characterizations of Jewish and Russian outsiders in Némirovsky's other novels, here insiders are held at an arm's length. This narrator does not identify with farmers, and comparing the Hardelots and Renaudins to them injects irony.

Némirovsky always emphasizes the instability of Jewish life, a history of fleeing persecution in one place only to encounter a new version in a new land; her dispossessed Russian aristocrats learn that revolutions turn the world upside down. The people of Saint-Elme, at the beginning of this novel, have no such experiences: "Until the end of time, the Hardelots would continue to furnish the businesses of Pas-de-Calais and the north with their stationery. . . . They would buy land, see their children marry, save their money, and die in their beds" (24). Such ironic certainties are familiar enough in novels about the Great War, but *All Our Worldly Goods* is inclined to indulge them, to take seriously the possibility that middle-class families like the Hardelots have a special purchase on property and stability.

The Hardelots of course cannot remain unscathed by the war. At its onset "even Saint-Elme was in a state," and "the world . . . seemed as shaky and vulnerable to collapse as the scenery in a theatre" (45). People like Charles Hardelot are unprepared for the invasion and occupation of northern France: "Laws, agreements, traditions had always defended his person, his freedom and his possessions. He refused to believe they had been abolished" (67). But they have been, at least temporarily: the village is overrun and then destroyed, including the Hardelot houses and factory. Pierre goes into combat and feels his identity disappearing in the general chaos and ruin: "He became anonymous, to some extent, lost, just as he might be tomorrow and forever" (86). In the end he is badly wounded, taken prisoner in Germany, returning home pale and unrecognizable, with a hip wound that will cause a lifetime of pain (105, 121).

The Hardelot parents go to Paris, where they share a small flat with Agnès and her formidable mother; everyone is uncomfortable and querulous. Charles Hardelot's death there is attributed to an actual historical event, the German shelling of a church in the Marais district, Saint-Gervais-et-Saint-Protais, on March 29, 1918, which killed eighty-eight people attending Good Friday services. Charles Hardelot is depicted as a gentle, patient man, the opposite of his forbidding father, Julien. One difference is that although Julien believes that "the teachings of Jesus didn't apply to his century," Charles dies praying that God will take his life and spare Pierre, "the best of our line" (92, 94). Although death in a bombed church might to some suggest that faith is futile, the narrator underscores Charles Hardelot's selflessness: "He found himself face to face with Christ, and God was listening to him" (93).

So Némirovsky does not flinch from the massive French death toll or from the destruction of the devastated North, where the "gutted earth spewed forth its insides . . . yellowish slimy mud mixed with scrap iron, boots, tins of food, wood, steel debris" (100). Nor does she evade the bitterness of the survivors: describing a victory parade on Bastille Day 1919, the day her own family had arrived in France, Némirovsky notes, "there was no real joy on their faces. . . . France was weary and wanted . . . to stop thinking about the war" (104). As in *The Prey,* these understandable responses leave veterans clamoring for comfort and pleasure, ready to "leave politics to the schemers, the profiteers, the braggarts, the thieves" (104). Still limping and bandaged, Pierre is jostled by the crowd, "not maliciously, but because no one really noticed the wounded anymore." Pierre believes that civilians "pity us . . . because we make them feel uncomfortable," but "their pity will disappear long before our wounds heal" (105). Still, "it was the final war. There would never be another" (106).

Yet where suicide stalked the damaged heroes of *The Pawn on the Chessboard* and *The Prey,* Pierre embodies the strong survival instincts of the French upper middle class; on this point, the novel concedes to the Vichy ideal. His father's death and his own distinguished war record persuade his grandfather to welcome him back to Saint-Elme and the factory. Town and factory are rebuilt; only the old shade trees cannot be replicated so quickly. One threat develops: Simone Renaudin, now married to a veteran named Roland Burgères, invests her money in the factory; old Julien, who always had his eyes on her fortune, welcomes her as a partner. Between them Simone and Julien will manage to make life difficult for Pierre, Agnès, and their growing family, but Pierre is determined to persevere and Agnès's fidelity is unquestioned. The two are "totally one entity," in her view "a great mystery and a great blessing" (112). A dearth of intimate evenings at home, of the kind found in the Bohun family or, for that matter, with Bella and Boris Karol, helps sustain this mystery.

Yet the outside world undermines this secure ideal. A third of the fortune Julien Hardelot left his grandson vanishes in 1936, when a regional bank collapses. By then Pierre has spent all of his cash on the factory; years of economizing and borrowing have left him in debt. Simone, however, now grossly fat, dresses in perpetual black for innumerable relatives who die childless, making her their heir. After the birth of a daughter, Rose, she and Roland lead largely separate lives; absorbed in the Hardelot factory, she keeps Roland's profligacy and extravagance in check in Saint-Elme so that her fortune and the Hardelot name remain largely intact.

Guy, Agnès and Pierre's oldest son, is initially a disappointment. Echoing the disillusion of the postwar generation, he lectures his father that "everything will inevitably end in a series of violent clashes . . . it will be catastrophic" (135). Moreover, he rejects familial assumptions: "It's . . . not the Hardelot companies that are the issue, but a vast complex machine of which . . . we are only a tiny cog" (147). Rather than choose a career, he plunges into a passionate, self-destructive affair with a beautiful Parisian blonde named Nadine Laurent.

A melodramatic event, however, forces Guy to reconsider. The affair ends when the reprobate Roland Renaudin is killed in a car accident. Rushing to the hospital with Pierre, Guy bribes a nurse into talking about the other occupant of the car, who fled the hospital. The nurse's description of a blonde woman wearing "a red necklace, dark garnets in the shape of stars," and a "dark-red felt hat" confirms his terrible suspicion: Nadine was also Renaudin's mistress. Guy comes home for the funeral and then returns to Paris to attempt suicide.

Though he eventually pulls through, his parents spend months with him in Paris, leaving Simone to run the factory. When Pierre returns to Saint Elme, Simone reveals that she has paid all the bills for the past two months and that Pierre's only alternative to bankruptcy is letting her buy him out. The rejected fiancée becomes the sole proprietor of the Hardelot's factory.

What was once unthinkable has become fact: the family saga makes a miniature anticipatory sketch for the fall of France. Pierre and Agnès take a flat in Paris, having just enough income to support a modest life; a sobered Guy finds employment as an engineer in a factory and "leads an ordered, gloomy life" (169). But public events shatter whatever private peace and order the Hardelots find. Returning home for the funeral of an elderly maiden aunt, Guy hears a radio broadcast bringing "the clatter of swords, the tramping of boots, and the distant rumble of marching armies" into "even . . . this peaceful Saint-Elme sitting room" (174).

The melodramatic interplay between the novel's personal and historical themes once more erupts. Though the author takes little time to establish probability, Guy's brief trip to Saint-Elme provides time for him and Simone's daughter Rose to fall in love. If Guy must learn not to resent Rose because of her father, Rose's mother, Simone, must overcome her desire to spite the Hardelots at every turn. In a comic interlude, Agnès's dreadful mother, Gabrielle Florent, having survived the rest of her generation, makes a confidante of Rose. She tells her a story about how Agnès and Pierre overcame the obstacles to their marriage, heavily edited to make her own role more attractive. Casting herself as the friend of young lovers everywhere, she lends Rose train fare to join the Hardelots in Paris. Since it is 1938 and Hitler has invaded the Sudetenland, Guy has been called up in a general mobilization of French troops. Pierre honorably returns to Saint-Elme to persuade Simone to drop her opposition to the marriage, though not her refusal to help support the young couple. Though associating the marriage of Rose and Guy to the Munich Pact is hardly propitious, the novel leaves the implications unexplored.

French troops were mobilized again when war was declared in September 1939, although most were not drawn into combat until the German *Blitzkrieg* began early in May. The newlyweds, separated for most of the so-called Phony War, take hope from the baby they are expecting in June. Meanwhile, with most of her workers in the army, Simone suffers a heart attack and summons Pierre to take over the factory. The Germans are marching into Belgium, but Pierre has a new lease on life: "he would work again, have problems to resolve, orders to give, responsibility" (224). Rose must return to her mother, but the two are soon headed south as part of the exodus. Agnès joins her daughter-in-law when Simone proves too ill to go on.

The tone of Némirovsky's narrative of the Hardelot's return to Saint-Elme is all but unreadable. The novel did pass the censorship; we can imagine readers of *Gringoire* finding nothing suggesting dissent from the Vichy line. The Hardelots know that a terrible war is beginning and initially expect it to last as long as the previous one. Pierre expresses the view, generally compatible with Vichy ideology, that his generation's war makes fighting this new one more difficult: the young soldiers "know all our sacrifices were useless, that victory conquered no one. . . . How often have we told them how stupid it all was, how pointless?" (213).

What he does not say, and could not say if the novel were to be published, is that losing the war would put France at Hitler's mercy and ensure the deaths of thousands of people who had sought refuge there. So what Pierre expresses instead is an optimism that the narrator defines as childish yet takes care not to label outrageous. A child building a house of cards, she says, "understands that the house is fragile, while these middle-class people were certain they knew what tomorrow would bring. . . . They had inherited a sense of security; it was passed down through their blood" (225). We can add parenthetically, "unlike the Jews," but of course *Gringoire*'s readers did not know the author's name.

So the narrative demonstrates that the Hardelots' confident plans for the future will not all bear fruit but never fundamentally questions their worldview. In the circumstances it is pointless for Rose to arrange the linen closet for her baby's layette and slightly comic that Agnès frets about the details of moving from Paris as if no German troops needed to be taken into account. The account of the exodus south in *All Our Worldly Goods* suggests some of the chaos of the actual event, including the impediment that bumper-to-bumper traffic presented to French troops. Yet in general the French refugees are depicted less ironically than they will be in *Suite Française,* and conditions are less harsh. Agnès improbably manages to buy gasoline at a point when supplies should already have been exhausted, and she and Rose are welcomed to rest in a rural miller's home, even though it overflows with refugees. When Rose goes into labor, an attractive blonde gives up her room so the Hardelot heir can be born in decent privacy, if hardly in ideal conditions. We may cringe when the blonde identifies herself as Nadine Laurent, former mistress of Rose's husband *and* her father, but perhaps readers of *Gringoire* took for granted that the nation's ordeal would ennoble its fallen women.

Meanwhile, back in Saint-Elme, Pierre has full scope for displaying his hereditary loyalty to the workers and capacity for heroic leadership. Located in the vulnerable North, Saint-Elme is once more attacked and burned. The narrative concedes what *Suite Française* will analyze and illustrate in detail: "their way of life was buckling and collapsing. . . . people who had been considered pillars of society . . . revealed themselves incompetent and cowardly" (236). But the Hardelot exception is stressed; they "alone thought of others throughout those days of blood and battle when so many could think of nothing but themselves" (237). Pierre dashes through the burning village, rescuing babies abandoned by drunken mothers, leading people to safety in an abandoned quarry and, above all, giving sage advice: "We must go back to our homes. Salvage what we can and wait for better times" (248).

Agnès exhibits similar determination: she organizes the birth of her grandson, down to the boiling of water and the locating of diapers, and sends the recovered mother and child south to stay with Renaudin family members. Then she struggles to get home; Saint-Elme is in the Exclusion Zone, to which French refugees are forbidden to return.[2] But Agnès's struggles are meant to be rewarded. Soon after she learns of her son's survival by finding his name on a list of prisoners of war, a German army truck takes her home. Pierre, of course, is alive and well, reassuring her, "We'll rebuild. We'll survive" (263). Agnès echoes his thoughts, adding biblical imagery: "all she had left to do was eat the bread made from grain she had milled herself, drink the wine from grapes she had pressed. . . . They would live out the rest of their days together" (264).

One can understand how this novel made it through Vichy censorship, but then censors are seldom skilled at detecting irony. Reading it two generations later, we still see a celebration of work, community, and family, all Vichy values. Pierre and Agnès are heroic in ways that suggest admirable qualities in the traditions of the French upper bourgeoisie; they are the best of their line, as old Charles Hardelot believed. Némirovsky admired the qualities of persistence, loyalty, and selflessness they embody, and she makes them credible. That Pierre and Agnès are as blind to outsiders as anyone else in their community is not a point the novel stresses, but the early comparison between grazing livestock and unobservant human beings is far from flattering. Ignorance is no excuse. Old Julien Hardelot thought the nineteenth century had outgrown Jesus, and no one except his son, Charles, applies any conception of Christian teaching to everyday life. Guy's marriage to Rose ensures that the factory will stay in the family, but the proximity of Pierre and Simone's marriage negotiations for their children to the date of the Munich Pact hardly seems propitious. One concludes that the Hardelots and their factory will survive the war without believing that the French property-owning classes are the only people who matter.

The Fires of Autumn

Némirovsky completed *The Fires of Autumn* in the spring of 1942; the manuscript was published by Albin Michel in 1957 and translated into English by Sandra Smith in 2015. As Smith explains, two typescripts of the novel survive: the first was used for the 1957 edition, while the second, containing "cuts, additions and modifications that were sometimes quite significant," was the basis for a new French edition (2011) edited by Olivier Philipponnat and Teresa Lussone (viii). The English translation is based on this second edition, which also includes three chapters from the first that Némirovsky intended to cut; the editors found their descriptions of "the ravages of the 1914–1918 war" important for "the contemporary reader" (viii). Certainly it is true that a contemporary audience is much less familiar with World War I than a French audience would have been in 1942; still, we do not quite have the text Némirovsky planned.

Apparently Némirovsky had hopes of publishing this novel under the censorship; certainly its title, referring to the "purifying fires" that farmers traditionally lit after the harvest, fits in well with the Vichy regime's penitential rhetoric. *The Fires of Autumn* explores the question of fixing blame for the defeat far more exhaustively than *All Our Worldly Goods* did, taking us back to the corrupt politics of *The Prey.* We know that Némirovsky followed the progress of the trials of government officials that Vichy conducted at Riom in 1942, and her novel's view of political corruption in the 1930s harmonizes with Vichy's. She does not allude to Léon Blum's courageous self-defense at Riom, and it is unclear how much she knew about it.[3]

The Fires of Autumn is less melodramatic than its immediate predecessor, and with the exception of long-suffering Thérèse Jacquelain, its characters are realer and its vision of the French bourgeoisie much less idealized. Most characters are lower middle class or rich arrivistes who resemble the Golders and the Karols far more than the admirable Agnès and Pierre Hardelot. The book begins with the lower-middle-class Bruns family at their Sunday dinner; although these families have high aspirations for their sons' educations and future professional careers, their pleasures are modest. As in *All Our Worldly Goods,* Némirovsky distances herself from her character's milieu. When she describes a flat decorated "with drawings bought in the large department stores" of "girls playing with kittens" or tells us that his neighbors attribute Monsieur Humbert's early death to vanity, believing that his insistence on a weekly bath led to his fatal chill, we can reasonably assume that she and her readers have better taste in art and more up-to-date standards of personal hygiene (5, 10).

The Fires of Autumn, from its first sentence, continually evokes the dates and events of French history. As the Bruns family are introduced at their table, we notice a salt cellar, a souvenir of the 1900 World's Fair, and learn that its inscription has faded in the twelve years since. With its Henry II sideboard and its sentimental engraving of a woman abandoned by a Hussar in the Napoleonic Army, their small flat resonates with a conventional version of the nation's history. The Bruns couple's emphasis on educating their nephew Martial as a doctor, and ensuring their son Bernard's admission to the *polytechnique* indicates their commitment to upward mobility, but their pleasure in spending a Sunday afternoon on rented chairs watching "foreign princes, millionaires . . . courtesans" stroll down the Champs-Élysées also proves them at home in their time and place (13).

The war will destroy the young people's confidence that they live in "the century of science, of progress" (17). Bernard Jacquelain, who is only seventeen, hopes at the outset to experience "heroic times like Austerlitz and Waterloo" and longs to identity with a regiment, "like a drop of blood that is part of the red river that flows through my heart" (26). His older cousin Martial, who marries Thérèse Bruns twenty-four hours before reporting back to duty as an army surgeon, already knows that it is a "filthy war" and that Bernard will be its "perfect prey" (38). But it is Martial, with his lack of illusions, who is destined to die heroically after he returns to a flooded house to rescue a double amputee medics have accidentally left behind.

Bernard serves his four years in the army faithfully. He fights at the front, where he is wounded twice; when Raymond Détang, a childhood friend, offers to find him a safe office job, he angrily refuses. But though he is physically strong, "mentally . . . he had been wounded in a way that nothing in future could ever heal" (54). When he comes home, his parents do not recognize him; he is cynical about the war's aim and finds the values of fidelity and frugality he was taught to respect "almost laughable" (61). When he asks his father to pay a five-thousand-franc gambling debt, his mother says he is "undermining the principles" of his family (68). The intense sensations of life at the front have left him dissatisfied with the bland pleasures of a petit bourgeois who accepted his place in the world; after the equality of suffering at the front he will not sit on a rented chair to watch celebrities parade by in expensive clothes. Worst of all, he seems to believe the sufferings of war have entitled him to a future of compensatory pleasures; he will absolutely not return to school, a decision his father labels "lazy" (79).

The only member of his family who understands is widowed Thérèse, who tries to tell his mother that soldiers who have seen "so many horrible things" need entertainment to help them forget (68). As she continues her quiet domestic life at the old flat, Thérèse falls in love with Bernard, who is too easily distracted to notice. When his father dies, Bernard's efforts to ensure a pension for his mother bring him back to Raymond Détang. Raymond invites him to a party at his home; though Raymond does not use the term, Bernard is invited as a handsome extra man, what Némirovsky calls a "gigolo." But when he meets Raymond's wife, Renée, he recognizes the beautiful daughter of Mme. Humbert, the milliner friend of his parents. They become lovers, and Bernard takes a job with Raymond quite similar to the one he refused during the war. Bernard is soon Raymond's "front man," handling the behind-the-scenes negotiating—and the bribes—needed to get French contracts for American machinery and resources; as a politician, Raymond needs to preserve a distance between himself and such matters. Soon American oil is on its way to colonial Syria and Cilicia, a Turkish region France administered from 1915 to October 1921.

But simmering in the background is another plot, driven by Thérèse's devotion and Bernard's better self. In one of the novel's best-realized scenes, Mme. Jacquelain and Thérèse go to Bernard's luxurious new apartment, where they have been invited for dinner. But Bernard does not appear; a servant periodically reports that his master has been detained and finally invites them to begin eating without him. Mme. Jacquelain is tempted to think that she and her husband had been wrong to live at such a reduced scale, so taken is she with the ambient luxury. Thérèse, meanwhile, realizes that while she might compete with Renée for Bernard's affections, she cannot compete with the luxury he craves: "you can't tear a man away from the seductive charm of a car, a bathroom with green floor tiles and a Siamese cat" (125). Thérèse goes home miserable, humiliated by Bernard's indifference.

In the course of a long, wakeful night, Thérèse decides that it is time to abandon her scruples. She, too, must be reckless; she determines to meet Bernard when he returns home in the morning and to offer herself to him. Even if their affair is brief, it will offer her the "sensuality and pleasure" that everyone else seems to be enjoying (133). But Bernard is still not home, so she must wait for him in a café across the street until it is nearly noon. But she does not have to compromise her principles. Having just learned that René has taken a lover, Bernard returns devastated, filled with resolve to abandon his new milieu, where people who "aren't human beings" but "wild beasts" are doing more damage than they realize: "I don't want to become a complacent gigolo, then a crook, or a shark, and end up a complete and utter bastard" (139). He pleads with her to marry him and help him free himself of their horrible influence.

For a few years, Bernard returns to his family's values. He has a modest but steady job in a bank, and Thérèse becomes a devoted mother to their son Yves. But she cannot compete with the excitement he felt in the Détang's circle, and he feels trapped as their family grows to include two daughters. He drifts back to Renée and soon is buying airplane parts in America for the French Air Ministry. The couple separate, with Thérèse warning that Bernard's business and government associates "are evil and dangerous and will cause our downfall" (161).

Two Vichy themes that barely surfaced in *All Their Worldly Goods* shape the novel's remaining chapters. One is political corruption in the 1930s as an explanation for France's defeat, and the other is rather naïvely Catholic redemption. France's rapid collapse between the German invasion on May 10, 1940, and the Armistice of June 22 shocked everyone at the time, including the German generals. A conventional explanation formed in the Anglo-Saxon world, which is wonderfully encapsulated in William Faulkner's *The Mansion:* "It was 1940 now. The Nibelung maniac had destroyed Poland and turned back west where Paris, the civilized world's eternal and splendid courtesan, had been sold to him like any whore and only the English national character turned him east again" (233). This poetic and moralized view, in which the sensuous, frivolous French fail because they lack stern Saxon discipline, is still visible in some popular accounts of the French defeat.[4]

As we have seen, Marshal Pétain's Vichy developed a related narrative, according to which the French had been betrayed by leftist and Jewish politicians, such as Léon Blum, who had failed to live up to the strong military tradition espoused by the Right and the army. As noted earlier, in February 1942 the government put seven men on trial, accusing them of responsibility for the defeat: three former prime ministers, Blum, Édouard Daladier, and Paul Reynaud; the former minister of the interior, Georges Mandel; the commander-in-chief of the French Army in May–June 1940, Maurice Gamelin; the former minister for the French Air Force, Guy La Chambre; and the former comptroller-general of the army, Robert Jacomet. A good deal of self-contradiction was built into this narrative and into the Riom Trials, named for the small town in central France where they took place. For one thing, Jews and the Left had much more to fear from Germany than did French fascists, whose hereditary anti-German sentiment was tempered by their sympathy for large military budgets, racism, and authoritarian government. That is why people on the Left criticized the Popular Front for doing "more for guns than butter" (Jackson 13). As Robert Young demonstrates, the Popular Front "did allow . . . the rapid acceleration of production in 1938, 1939, and 1940 without which the military imbalance between France and Germany would have been as decisively adverse in fact as it has been made out to have been in fiction" (191). For another, spending too much time brooding publicly about the defeat ran the risk of offending the new German authorities with whom Vichy collaborated.

Though lucidity is not a word one associates with Adolf Hitler, no one could have pointed up the paradox more clearly than he did after the international press gave favorable coverage to the defendants, who had much more latitude for introducing evidence and arguing than they would have had in Moscow or Berlin that year. "If you read between the lines," observed the Führer, "they would be covering them with flowers if they had won" (Pottecher 163). He gave orders, and the trial was stopped. The part of the aborted trial that Némirovsky followed most closely was the examination of Guy La Chambre, and the allegation that the failure to build an effective air force resulted partly from corruption in the procurement process.

Was that accusation true? Many people, including Némirovsky, have thought so. Certainly the frequent changes of administration in France during the 1930s were not conducive to efficient planning. After noting that in the early 1930s the aircraft industry was "artisanal and underequipped" and "procurement . . . medieval," Eugen Weber compiles a detailed indictment: "Aircraft programs were incoherent, inefficient, based largely on spreading orders among as many manufacturers as possible. Prototypes swarmed. In 1928 the Navy used 400 planes of eight different makes: twenty-seven models, forty-four types, powered by eleven kinds of engine. In January 1930 the Air Ministry placed orders for 115 planes of thirty-seven different models. Mass production only came in with Pierre Cot, and by then it was too late. The Germans started to rearm their air force in 1934, the British in 1935; the French only really got going in 1938, by which time the Germans had three times as many hands at work in aircraft industry as France" (*Hollow Years* 173).

Weber's facts accord reasonably well with Némirovsky's argument that orders for parts were won through bribery, with no testing to ensure they would prove compatible when assembled together into airplanes. The scandal of buying parts in the United States, as Bernard is commissioned to do in the novel, was not that they were of poor quality but that they did not fit French planes. Némirovsky focuses more on Bernard's qualms of conscience, which are sharpest when he loses Renée the first time and after the defeat of France, when she also follows the details. These include political maneuverings, such as Raymond Détang's plan to put a questionable appropriation up for a vote "one morning when the benches are empty" in order to circumvent "those trouble-makers" in parliament who want to "prevent us from making a pretty packet" (171). But they also include the issue of whether the engineering is compatible. On this point, Détang says experts disagree; he rationalizes that some parts will work for some planes and some for others. But although Bernard also wishes to rationalize that "he is just a broker," he can only hope that Détang "won't find anyone who will consciously sabotage our country's Air Force" (173).

When Bernard expresses the view that the purchases are "nothing to do with me," the reader can already see Némirovsky planning the domestic novel's most basic political strategy. The engineering problems, the political maneuvering, and the public debate must be brought home; it must all become personal. Bernard's eighteen-year-old son is the obvious conduit for the message that the safety of French aircraft is a matter of life and death. Although Yves's role in the novel is only too ideological, his harsh adolescent criticisms of his father are psychologically credible to the extent that they reflect his identification with his mother. He goes so far as to tell Thérèse he would have preferred that Martial, her first husband, had been his father: "He has an honest face. . . . what he did was good, it was brave" (166). In the circumstances, Thérèse can probably be forgiven for assuring him that "in a certain way, you are his son, just as you are the son of all the men who died in the war" (166).

When, in the winter of 1938–39, Bernard invites Yves to accompany him on a skiing trip, the scene is already set for an open rupture. Yves instantly dislikes the people he meets at a lunch given by the wife "of a well-known Member of Parliament" (177). He dislikes them for being middle-aged and pot-bellied, for trafficking in armaments, and for displaying fascist sentiments the author takes care not to label as such: "What we need is someone with a firm hand, a real leader" (177). Again, his aversion is grounded in a recognizable psychology, but it quickly turns into an ideological diatribe. His father, though "not an evil man," is "part of an evil set that out of spinelessness, blindness or deliberate treason is causing the downfall of France" (180). Scorning his father for wanting "to stay alive" and as a result refusing to commit himself totally to anything, he yearns to dedicate himself absolutely to a high cause, "something austere, harsh, and strong" (181, 182). Were he a believer, he would "become a priest," but in the circumstances he chooses "being a pilot" because it "requires you to offer yourself up entirely" (182, 183).

At this point in the novel, the ideological machinery creaks too audibly. Bernard must lose all his money, which he had entrusted to one of those Némirovsky villains, like Abel Sarlat, who commit suicide when their extensive histories of fraud become public. He must go home to Thérèse and be called up to fight in a second world war: "father and son left together the day the war was declared" (190). Two months later, stationed in Lorraine, he must learn that Yves is dead, killed in a training accident. Nor is the moral point made subtly: "He knew better than anyone why some aircraft were lost in accidents that seemed inexplicable" (195). Any reader who misses the moral will hear it repeated as an officer explains to a barmaid: "there's a group of old crates that have a fatal tendency to crash to the ground the first time they try to take off. Apparently some of the parts were bought from America and didn't fit our planes" (198).

The ideological message of the novel's ending also acquires a Catholic dimension. As we will explore Irène Némirovsky's 1938 conversion to Catholicism in a later chapter, we will only note it briefly here. In the last five years of her life, Némirovsky's fiction began to sprout allusions to the Catholic Church and to the New Testament, reflecting an interest that we also see in her journals and letters. In *The Fires of Autumn* these are no subtler than the argument about American aircraft parts and have the additional disadvantage of being imposed near the end rather than developed throughout the narrative. As noted, Yves equates becoming a pilot with being a priest; he also cites a line from the Gospels Némirovsky ponders elsewhere: "Anyone who wants to save his own life ends up losing it" (181). As soon as he hears of Yves's death, Bernard concedes that there must be a God "because He is punishing me." Taken prisoner after the fall of France, he develops respect for priests in the POW camp because they "were the only ones who felt peace, certainty; suffering was a gift from God" (215). At the end of the chapter set in the camp, Bernard "felt like crying and begging forgiveness," emotions not limited to Catholics but consistent with the idea that Bernard might be internalizing the Christian message.

The last two chapters of the novel bring us back to Thérèse, struggling to keep herself, her mother-in-law, and her two young daughters alive in wartime. Thérèse has always been self-sacrificing and virtuous but not noticeably religious; by the end she is a devout Catholic. This too-hastily-acquired religion is much less real than her day-to-day struggles with wartime austerity. After the second hard winter, her two daughters develop whooping cough, and Thérèse sells her old fur coat to get enough money to rent a small cottage in the country. Making this fictional transition allows Némirovsky to draw closely on her own wartime experience in Issy-L'Évêque and gives the final chapters a sharp domestic realism that the father-son chapters lack. Anyone who knows her biography will recognize details from the author's experience: the child recovering from serious illness, the modest meals centered on fresh eggs and fruit, an idyllic setting with a wood bordering the farmer's fields.

But of course our knowledge of the biography also includes Némirovsky's arrest by French police in July 1942. Even lacking it, a reader would probably find the wish-fulfilling, moralizing ending unsatisfactory. We have never seen Bernard and Thérèse living together happily, and Némirovsky does not take (did not have) the time to show the couple finding a way to live more harmoniously. Instead, we get ideology: Bernard participated in political corruption that killed his son; Thérèse was faithful and sacrificed for her children. Thérèse is allowed a brief spiritual crisis, recognizing that her son "died for nothing because France had been beaten" and fearing that even if he did come home, Bernard would reject her because she has aged so much. So she quotes Matthew 12:39 and asks Jesus, if he has not abandoned her, to "give me a sign" (227). And since we are reading rather weak ideological fiction at this point, we are not surprised when she returns to find a telegram announcing Bernard's release and imminent homecoming. Nor are we surprised later when one glimpse of Bernard is enough to tell Thérèse "that he had changed, he had come back more mature, a better man and, at last, he was hers, and hers alone" (229).

So the second of Némirovsky's wartime novels, which would not be published until its author had been dead for fifteen years, ends with a moment of badly contrived marital redemption. Was this what she believed a Vichy censor wanted? Or did she end the novel hastily, having given up on the possibility of publication? Both are possibilities, but we need to consider a third. In the

Gospel that Némirovsky quotes, Jesus characterizes the people who "seek after a sign" as "an evil and adulterous generation." And he adds, "No sign shall be given it, but the sign of the prophet Jonah."[5] A similar passage appears later in Matthew 16:4 and in Luke 11:29; the trope of the generation that asks for a sign they will not be given also appears in Mark 8:12 without the reference to Jonah or the phrase "evil and adulterous."

What is the "sign of the prophet Jonah"? Doubtless much theological ink has been spilled over this question, but Jesus explains its most literal sense: "As Jonah was three days and three nights in the whale's belly, so will the Son of Man be three days and three nights in the heart of the earth." That is, Jesus refuses to offer a magical solution to the problem of death, which he tells his hearers they must face. The biblical numerology, "three days and three nights," implies that in some dimension death may have a term; Jonah and the Son of Man are released in three days. Is something similar available to ordinary people? Traditional Christianity would say yes, but the immediate context offers no such consolation.

A Jewish writer in Vichy France, if she hoped for publication, could only tell her story between the lines. Like the references to the French bourgeoisie's blindness or to the all-night gambling in the casinos they can barely make out from their beach house windows, the sign of Jonah might be seen to lurk beneath the waters as Bernard and Thérèse celebrate their reconciliation. All around them unseen are other people, many of them descendants of the authors of the Hebrew Bible, for whom only the sign of Jonah appears. We cannot prove that Némirovsky intended us to retrieve this allusion, but if we want an image for a Jewish writer trapped in fascist France in 1942, we will find nothing better than Jonah in the belly of his whale.

Chapter 7

The "Catholic Némirovsky"

It will seem strange to speak of a Catholic Némirovsky after exploring the Jewish Némirovsky so exhaustively: her early and late representations of Jewish characters, her problematic family, her lack of positive associations with Jewish spirituality, and then the accusations of anti-Semitism hurled decades after her death. Yet on February 2, 1939, as she was drafting her last Jewish novel, *The Dogs and the Wolves,* in what Jonathan Weiss calls "one of the great ironies" of her life, Irène Némirovsky was received into the Catholic Church (96). For a hostile critic, this conversion proves her self-hatred, while even sympathetic readers often assume her motives were more prudential than spiritual. Others speculate that stress had overwhelmed her; Philipponnat and Lienhardt cite a credulous 1939 article about astrology in *Marie-Claire* as an instance of people turning to "superstition" in periods of crisis (277). Others, also assuming that the conversion should not be taken seriously, cite her daughter Denise's statement that she could not remember her family practicing Catholicism. Némirovsky left no sustained account of her conversion, though religious allusions, mainly to the New Testament, are scattered through her late journals. Critics often note a pattern of increasing attention to Catholicism and the New Testament in the last novels; her earlier fiction is relentlessly secular. The death of Charles Hardelot in a German bombing as he attended church services in Paris on Good Friday 1918, which we have already discussed, has no parallel in accounts of World War I she wrote before 1938.

So we cannot speak of a Catholic Némirovsky as we might of a Catholic Joyce, of someone brought up in a family and nation so saturated with Catholicism that it pervades his choice of subject matter, the psychologies of his characters, and even his aesthetic long after he ceased to believe. Nor, since she never wrote a book celebrating Catholicism, can we speak of a Catholic Némirovsky as we might speak of a Catholic Franz Werfel. A Jewish refugee trapped in France by the German invasion, Werfel spent five anxious weeks in

Lourdes in the summer of 1940. He vowed that if he and his wife were permitted to escape to America, he would write a book about the Virgin Mary's appearances at Lourdes in the mid-nineteenth century. Though Werfel always identified as Jewish, his *The Song of Bernadette* (1941) recounts the apparitions in a manner consistent with Catholic belief.[1] The novel and its Hollywood adaption (1943), which resulted in an Oscar for Jennifer Jones, were enthusiastically received by Catholics; Cardinal Francis Spellman, the middlebrow spokesman of American Catholicism in the 1950s, called *The Song of Bernadette* "an inspiration and a consolation" (Steiman 151). When Werfel died in 1945, still unconverted, the Archbishop of Los Angeles–Monterey, John Cantwell, authorized a full Catholic funeral.

On the other hand, we can speak of Némirovsky as a Catholic novelist if we follow the definition proposed by Conor Cruise O'Brien (writing under the pseudonym Donat O'Donnell), who in his 1952 *Maria Cross* defined Catholic writers not as orthodox believers but as persons whose "exceptionally vivid imaginations . . . are permeated by Catholicism" (vii).[2] Catholic writers going back at least as far as Dante, whose Inferno is well-populated with clergy, have been vigorously critical of their church. Their books have been accused of heresy and their authors of most of the mortal sins, often on reliable evidence. Outsiders offer a valued perspective; in England it is almost a requirement for Catholic writers to be converts: Gerard Manley Hopkins, John Cardinal Newman, Evelyn Waugh, Graham Greene, and Muriel Spark are the first who come to mind. And while Catholicism has its share of orthodox churchmen insisting on assent to a whole range of doctrines, it also has a tradition of "negative theology" and of honoring the "dark night of the soul" wracked with fundamental doubt. A Thomas Aquinas who insists on how impossible it is for humans to define divinity and a Saint John of the Cross who sees intense despair in the face of doubt as proof of the soul's innate craving for God leave ample room for imaginative exploration, even excess.

The Blasphemous Convert

It would be impertinent to speculate about whether a deathbed utterance at Auschwitz might have settled the question of the sincerity or at least literalness of Némirovsky's belief for all time. We have also been told what is or is not possible or credible "after Auschwitz" so often that it would seem insolent to hypothesize what someone who actually died there might have thought if she had survived.[3] Given how little place religious formulas had in Némirovsky's upbringing or in her early letters, the evocation of God's protection in her two last letters to her family seems worth noting but hardly dispositive. What we can more reasonably say is that a rather literal reading of the Gospels creates a moral compass for judging the characters satirized in *Suite Française*.

We can also add that since Némirovsky's own death, Auschwitz has become a metonym not only for the systematic murder of millions but also for the crisis of faith it engenders for those who look at it unflinchingly. As the German theologian Dorothee Soelle wrote, Auschwitz made it impossible for her to believe in God as "the father, begetter, ruler, and controller of history" (26). Auschwitz can prompt one to declare God guilty or even dead; it raises doubts about whether God can be both omnipotent and loving; and it certainly casts a shadow over churches and their members. If every baptized person had refused to work in a concentration camp, the system would have failed. And although obviously Némirovsky did not live to read such theology, we know that in the summer of her arrest she created an uncanny figure who anticipates some part of it, the blasphemous Jewish convert.

In her journal she wrote, "For *Captivity* [the projected, unwritten third volume of the *Suite Française*]: for the concentration camp the blasphemy of baptized Jews, 'May God forgive us our trespasses as we forgive you yours'" (*Suite Française,* appendix 1, 381). This entry, the only one entirely capitalized, is followed by an ironic observation: "Obviously, the martyrs would not have said that" (381). Perhaps they would not have, but the rabbi in Elie Wiesel's *The Gates of the Forest* would: "Yes, He (God) is guilty" (Cohn-Sherbok 95). That Némirovsky so accurately intuited how the concentration camps would loom over theology underscores both her historical awareness and the seriousness with which she took religion.

Storm in June

In *Storm in June,* the first volume of *Suite Française,* the French Republic surrenders after a chaotic exodus in which hundreds of thousands of civilians are displaced. Settled lives are radically troubled, and disoriented people struggle to survive in a world without familiar authority figures, where old rules no longer apply. Catholic institutions, Catholic religious, and Catholic rituals and symbols continually remind us that we are a world the church has shaped, where its values are frequently evoked, and where, more important, they are being tested. Sometimes, Némirovsky's satire is quite straightforward, directed at hypocrisy and blind spots. But in other cases she raises questions about more fundamental beliefs, as we see in the case of a young priest murdered by the orphans he was helping to evacuate from a Paris orphanage. In the end we can speculate about what vision of Christianity attracted the convert in the first place or how she thought it might have changed the world if only Christians had taken it to heart.

For satire that ranges from light comedy to something much more corrosive, we need look no further than that incarnation of Catholic haute-bourgeois respectability, the Péricand family. At its head is the formidable

Madame Charlotte, mother of five children, mistress of a prosperous household who watches over its elderly patriarch's final years with "terrifying tenderness" (11). Although the virtues of a Catholic mother keep her from the sexual excesses of several wicked mothers, the "Jezebels" of Némirovsky's earlier fiction, the confidence and rapacity of her commitment to riches matches their own. She has, it is true, suffered for her faith, enduring eight pregnancies, including three stillbirths that nearly killed her. Indeed, she has given her oldest son, Philippe, to God, though she believes, "It's such a waste" that he has chosen to work in a poor parish (21).

We can be sure that Madame and her family observe every fast and that her children progress smoothly through the sacraments, with their mother prompt to remind them of the catechism, as she does on the flight from Paris: "you know very well you should share with those who are less fortunate than you" (51). Two pages later, discovering that the shops have run out of food, she stops them from handing chocolates out to strangers: "I forbid you to touch the food." As the narrator observes, "Christian charity, the compassion of centuries of civilization, fell from her like useless ornaments, revealing her bare, arid soul. She needed to feed . . . her own children. Nothing else mattered any more" (53). When a bomb falls on the house where Madame and the children found refuge, she rejoices: "The most precious things have been saved! Thank you God!" The narrator drily explains that her jewelry is safely sewn into a pouch pinned in her blouse and that she had the presence of mind to grab her fur coat and some silverware before she ran out of the burning house. And finally, "She had her three children!" (109).

Madame Péricand draws on all the managerial skills and confidence her class affords to arrange the next stage of their evacuation. As the mother of a large family she feels entitled to all the best places; as a rich person she always knows where and when something is for sale. She quickly hires a donkey cart to take her youngest children and their nurse to the nearest functioning railway station and surveys the countryside with the air of a conqueror. Within a few hours they are all on the train to Nîmes, where she cries out in alarm. What is wrong? She has just realized that in her haste, "We forgot my father-in-law!" (112).

His portrait, as the older Monsieur Péricand faces death among strangers, in a Catholic hospice, is even more savage. A local priest is summoned to administer Extreme Unction and pronounces that the old man "had made his peace with God and would die a very Christian death" (122). Of course he does not know that Monsieur Péricand owes the foundations of his wealth to profiteering from the last world war, which "had taken two sons from him and tripled his fortune" (126). To honor his dead sons, the old man founded an institution, "The Penitent Children of the 16th Arrondissement," whose orphans will play a key role in a later episode (126). The family is inordinately proud of this charity, which includes workshops in which orphaned boys learn woodworking and shoe repair, and on occasion Madame personally entertains them by playing classical music on the piano. As readers learn when they accompany Philip to the orphanage, the children are pale and too small for their age, and they wear garments "made by charitable persons using leftover wool" (22). The director's account of how much the children enjoyed a three months' evacuation at the beginning of the war, in a borrowed château where "we didn't have any heating at all" and the water in jugs turned to ice overnight, corresponds to no reality the boys themselves would recognize (23).

It is to this Dotheboys Hall that Monsieur Péricand's imagination returns fondly as he lies on his deathbed, urgently requesting that a notary be summoned after the priest. For the past decade, he has been a helpless old man, dressed and washed by others, but at the center of a long-imagined deathbed scene he intends to regain his power: "To punish, reward, disappoint, delight, distribute his worldly goods according to his own wishes. To control everyone. To influence everyone. To come first" (125). Given the Gospels' insistence that "the first shall be last and the last first" (Matthew 20:16), this is a strange ambition for a dying Christian. And so he dictates a new will, commanding his heirs to pour another five million into the orphanage, ordering them to commission a portrait or bust of himself to be placed in its vestibule, and specifying that Bléoville, his château, be converted into an asylum for wounded soldiers. There three thousand francs must be spent on a monument to the war dead on which his older sons' names will be written in large gold letters, "then all the other names in small letters" (127). Grandiosely, he commands that his American stocks be sold and converted into French holdings and that all of his great-grandchildren be given his Christian names as gender dictates, Louis-August or Louise-Augustine. Only one detail escapes his control: he draws his last breath just as he reaches for the pen to sign his will.

Even if we did not know that the creator of Charlotte and Louis-August Péricand would die in Auschwitz before she turned forty, we would conclude that she was unsentimental about actual Catholics and their institutions. But it is equally clear that her satire is directed at human failings rather than at the figure and teachings of Christ. It is also clear that her satire of the Péricands recapitulates some of the themes of her novels set among equally rich Jewish arrivistes. From the aging grandmother who greedily laps down a second cup of chocolate before going to a memorial mass for two grandsons to the aesthete who safeguards his porcelains while reflecting that a single stone of a château on the Loire "was worth more than a thousand human lives," most of the French haute-bourgeoisie in the novel could be characterized as "miserly and cautious" (184, 79). Compared to Charlotte Péricand abandoning her father-in-law or the old man using his last breaths to reduce his children's inheritance, David Golder's desperate familial and tribal loyalties seem positively admirable. And while few could match her fictional novelist Gabriel Corte for sheer egotism as he happily agrees with a flatterer that his own life is a national treasure ("you owe it to mankind"), nearly all upper-middle-class characters despise the masses for their poverty, vulgarity, and inability to cope (158).

"There was nothing human left in this miserable mob," thinks Madame Péricand as she looks at the streams of refugees, and the squeamish Charles Langelet, finding in the same crowds "ugliness" and "vulgarity," would agree, as would Corte, trapped in a mob whose "sadness . . . had nothing human about it anymore, for it lacked both courage and hope" (50, 66, 46). Mentally comparing his "handsome pale face ravaged by an expression of suffering" to Byron's, the great writer finds the "atmosphere of tragedy" spoiled by "these filthy people with their whining" (66). Satire so broad allows us to construct an ideal behavior as its mirror image: selflessness, compassion, recognition of one's mortality as an antidote to hoarding, empathy sufficient to see a shared humanity in the poor and the suffering. This ideal is by no means limited to Christians, but it corresponds to some of the most familiar Gospel precepts, such as laying up treasures in heaven where neither "moth, nor rust doth corrupt" (Matthew 6:20). Some allusions are more direct: Langelet's satisfaction that he "wasn't like ordinary men" inevitably recalls the Pharisee whom Jesus, in Luke 18:11, cites thanking God for the same thing in a public prayer (38). When Maurice Michaud tells his wife, who mistakes every weary soldier for her son—"You see your son everywhere, my poor Jeanne"—one may be reminded of the story of the king, in Matthew 25:40, who tells his followers that when they served "the least of these my brethren" they served him (56). Where Corte and Langelet see "a herd of frightened animals," good people see human beings like themselves, but the spiritual ideal is finding the face of Christ, something divine, in everyone (50).

An ethic of self-sacrificing love, however, comes into question in the disturbing death of Philippe Péricand. Philippe discovered his vocation while recuperating from tuberculosis in a sanitarium, a circumstance that may or may not carry warning echoes of *The Magic Mountain,* a novel in which consumption is to some degree a metaphor for the sickness of Western civilization, and its treatment is associated with leisure, a high-calorie diet, and for many, sensual indulgence. An idealistic and ascetic Catholic, Philippe lacks practical experience of the world and the self-knowledge that can come from facing up to one's sexuality. It is clear, however, that his self-awareness greatly exceeds that of his mother or grandfather, and his desires, unlike theirs, extend beyond preserving his own comfort or power. As noted earlier, he takes in realities of orphanage life that elude the others—the pale complexions, the scent of boiled cabbage.

On the other hand, he is too wrapped up in his own feelings of inadequacy to take actions that might actually improve the orphan's conditions.

Unlike the famous writer Gabriel Corte and the porcelain collector Charles Langelet, he believes that he should love the poor, even when they look sullen and repellent. The distance he perceives between himself and them is a source of self-reproach rather than satisfaction: "His face took on an expression of harshness and sadness as he looked into his heart. He disliked these unfortunate children" (24). He knows that he is too much estranged from their lives and experience to speak to them as they speak to each other; his pious words about everyone being members of the same body and speaking to God as to a father evoke no answering warmth. And how could they, when his real emotions on looking at them are aversion and fear? "They were children of Satan," he thinks, "without even enough spirituality to . . . [desire] divine light" (24).

To believe in an ethic of love and to feel it are entirely different matters. How disastrously the children's experiences and Philippe's naiveté collude becomes apparent later, after the orphanage's truck has been requisitioned for wounded soldiers and he is left marching wearily through the woods with his charges. Noticing that one boy's too-small shoes make walking painful, Philippe "took his hand to help him" and then "placed two fingers round his neck and pulled him up straight" (137). The child "didn't resist" but on the contrary "leaned his neck against the hand that held it," and "this strange, ambiguous caress (or rather this expectation of a caress) made the priest blush" (214). In response he tips up the boy's chin to look into his eyes, but "his eyelids were lowered and he couldn't see into them" (137).

Philippe quickens his step, attempting to pray. He feels his failure anew, reproaching himself for "a kind of impatience to be holy, the desire to gather liberated souls around him. . . . He recognized something similar in the way a greedy man hoards his gold" (138). Philippe's insight into the connection between his spiritual heroics and the familial avarice is probably accurate, but the reader cannot easily push aside the subtext of his exchange with the boy, especially the charged words "did not resist" and "ambiguous caress." The child's submissive response to his touch suggests a history of sexual abuse, possibly by priests, a suspicion that lurks around the text without entering Philippe's consciousness. We see no signs that he recognizes the emotion that summoned the blush to his cheeks.

A brief lull follows as Philippe takes the boys to the deserted grounds of an isolated chateau, where he encourages them to pick strawberries before organizing them into teams to set up camp. As they follow his directions, Philippe becomes sympathetic: "What they really liked . . . what really touched their hearts was . . . this intoxicating scent of fresh air and freedom they were breathing in, so new to them" (139). Philippe realizes, quite correctly, that the boys are unaccustomed to freedom and liberty, words with political and historical resonances in a France they do not know. Indeed the Third Republic's imminent defeat will hardly change conditions in the comfortless authoritarian institution, virtually a model of the Vichy state, to which they are already inured. But Philippe's idealization of nature, his scrupulous self-preoccupations, even his sexualized yearning for "my cherished Friend" to whom he is nothing more than "dust beneath your dear feet," blind him to the what is really going on, to the dangerous impulses untried liberty can set off.[4] The sleeping boys, among whom he fondly wanders, occasionally adjusting a blanket or bestowing a kiss, are only pretending to sleep, and as soon as he is distracted, they storm the chateau.

What follows is a scene out of William Golding. The boys shatter the windows and, once inside, turn "wild, as if possessed" (143). Although they find the liquor cabinet empty, their frenzy suggests intoxication: "the carnage was enough for them" (144). They turn on Philippe "like wolves" and "one of them bit him, drew blood" (143). Bashing his head in with a side table, they stumble over his body as they pillage the rest of the elegant furnishings, which they "rip apart and throw on the grass" (144). The language suggests medieval warfare or more topically the fictional pogrom in Némirovsky's *The Dogs and the Wolves* (1940) or the historical ones of Kristallnacht in November 1938. They drag Philippe's body to the chateau's lovely pond; two swing it back and forth over the water "like a bundle" as the rest urge them on, shouting out, "Kill him!" in "high-pitched, hoarse voices, some of which still sounded childlike" (144). To their surprise, Philippe is still alive and tries to pull himself up on a tree branch, displaying "his battered face, red, swollen and grotesque." The branch cracks under his weight as volleys of stones strike him; he does not drown, but the mud at the bottom of the shallow pond traps him: "and that was how he died, in water up to his waist, head thrown back, one eye gouged out by a stone " (144).

This horrible scene might seem better suited to an account of Nazi atrocities in Ukraine than to *Suite Française,* which for long stretches is essentially a novel of manners, although one by a particularly mordant observer of power struggles and emotional cruelty. Most of the war's violence occurs at the margins of the text; the British bombing of the French Navy's *Bretagne,* for example, which killed 1,297 of England's recent allies, is mentioned twice. Doubtless the novel needs this carefully evoked scene of brutality to remind us of what Némirovsky's more self-obsessed and purblind characters refuse to face: the defeat of France will license powerful people, not all of them foreigners, to act out the most brutal impulses of human nature on other people, who will be defenseless. But what does it mean that she chose a Catholic priest as the victim? Surely the historical victims were more likely to be Jewish? And why should she hint at Philippe's attraction to young boys? After all, the text does not summon its readers to stop child sexual abuse in orphanages, a sociological fact for which there is abundant evidence, but limits itself to oblique suggestions of clerical perversity. These are difficult questions, though they will vex us less if we value what Gustavo Gutiérrez calls "the critical function of theology with respect to the presence and activity of humankind in history" (xiv).

Liberation theology, according to Gutiérrez, argues that Christians should be committed to social justice in the actual historical world and that this commitment should be "radical, total, and efficacious."(xiii) Christians should reconsider "the great themes of the Christian life within this radically changed perspective and with regard to the new questions posed by this commitment."(xiii) Doing so requires us "to let ourselves be judged by the word of the Lord, to think through our faith, [and] strengthen our love" (xiii). Némirovsky hardly needed to read theology to recognize that the French defeat stripped the nation of its justice system, its free elections, and its confidence in cultural traditions assumed to define civilization. All around her she saw rich people like the Péricands finding new ways to maintain their property and comfort, or writers who modified their morals depending on circumstances like Gabriel Corte and mentally edit their old books and lectures to "to win favour with the new government" (161–65).[5] The text puts the New Testament's stress on finding the image of God in the poorest sinners, on the necessity not only of loving others but meeting their basic needs, at sharp odds not only with its worldly characters but also with an institutional church too closely bound to their values.

Philippe's death at the hands of a vicious mob is probably not an allegory of the church in France, although the boys' behavior might alternatively illustrate the doctrine of Original Sin or the claims of attachment theory. His family's grudging support, "cold as charity," has formed the orphanage and these pitiless children, and one may attribute to the same source whatever mix of sexual repression, dishonesty, and self-preoccupation makes him such a disastrous choice for shepherding thirty of them singlehandedly through a countryside at war. But the novel offers a handful of other characters to suggest what an ethic of love might lead one to do in a national crisis.[6]

The Michaud family—Jeanne, Maurice, and their son Jean-Marie—are portrayed much more sympathetically than other major figures in *Storm in June*. Jean-Marie is a soldier, wounded in the German invasion and separated from his regiment during a bombing. A family in the remote countryside nurses him back to health, but since communications are cut off, his parents spend weeks fearing for his life. Maurice is a bookkeeper in a Paris bank; Jeanne, a music teacher who lost most of her pupils when their parents sent them to the country in September 1939, is secretary to the bank's director, Joseph Corbin.

They love each other as no other married people in the novel do, even rising at dawn the morning of their exodus to clean the small apartment where they have lived for sixteen years, "a supreme proof of love to those we hold dear" (40). When Corbin decides to evacuate the bank to Tours, he insists that they accompany him, and when his mistress, Arlette, and her dog take the places in his car promised to them, he orders them to find an alternative. As he is obviously prepared to fire Maurice on the slightest pretext, they comply, leaving Paris on foot.

Of course, the Michauds initially fare worse than the evacuees in cars, but his philosophical stoicism and her Christian charity avert the selfish greed of the others and keep them focused on the humanity of their fellow refugees. Maurice "had a unique way of thinking . . . in his own eyes he was not that rare and irreplaceable creature most people imagine when they think about themselves" (55). The exodus from Paris is another of those great "mass displacements . . . necessary to humans, just as the migration of livestock was to animals" (55). Countless human beings have left their cities in flames, clutching their children to their hearts; to their "descendants they were no more important than chickens who'd had their throats slit" (55). When he overhears a woman groaning, "There's never been anything as horrible as this," he responds quietly, "On the contrary, Madame, on the contrary" (55).

As noted earlier, Jeanne, desperate to find the son who is her greatest joy and hope, keeps imagining that she sees him on the road. Surrounded by frustrated drivers in stalled cars, the refugees realize that they are moving just as quickly on foot, "enjoying the feeling of shared misfortune" (57). When Jeanne sees the first bombing casualties, she notices how "stunned" their faces look in their astonishment at death. But immediately she recognizes that to others she and Maurice must look equally insignificant: "But what do I know? Perhaps there was a wealth of intelligence and tenderness behind their low brows" (58). She and Maurice would look like "two miserable employees" to a stranger, which in one way is true but "in another . . . we are precious and unique" (58). Their journey by now clearly pointless, they can only keep walking and "place themselves in the hand of God" (58).

Jeanne Michaud, then, illustrates a lively sensibility whose ability to empathize with others depends on a spiritual sense of every human life as rare and precious. She has few heroic acts to perform, although when another bombing separates small children from their mothers, she takes the time to gather them near the porch of a cathedral, calling out their location to passers-by. Several emotional reunions ensue, although "no one of them thought to thank Jeanne" (60). As she and another mother with a missing son crane their necks to see wounded soldiers being hastily transferred from a disabled train to civilian vehicles, she takes comfort from realizing their shared humanity: "There was no reason at all why it should be her son rather than another woman's who appeared" (61). For the first time she allows herself to think that he may be safe. Good deeds are not necessarily met with rewards, but a generous spirit seems to calm the one who possesses it.

We know that Némirovsky intended Jean-Marie to survive the invasion and fall in love with Lucile Angellier, the young woman at the center of the second volume, *Dolce,* though whether she intended them to survive the war is unclear. Certainly Némirovsky is too sophisticated a writer for us to assess her beliefs by noting which characters she rewards and which she punishes. Still, since Philippe's horrible death has been read as a satire on Christian hope, we may be interested to follow the Michauds back to Paris. In the confusion of the evacuation, Corbin's wife had discovered a photo of his mistress, wearing only a beautiful necklace. Afterward, angrily rejecting his contention that the jewels were synthetic, she refused to return to Paris with him; in the meantime, Arlette has been seen in the company of German officers. Already in a dudgeon over his marital troubles, Corbin leaps to the conclusion that the Michauds had failed to join him in Tours because they were enjoying a pleasant vacation in Paris. When he receives a letter from them asking for further instructions and their previous month's salary, Corbin accuses them of desertion and dismisses them both with only two months' salary.[7]

Maurice, ever the stoic, is inclined to bear this trouble without protest. Jeanne, however, is enraged by the injustice and demands to know why it is always the petit bourgeoisie who suffer the most in a national crisis. Maurice's argument that economic laws are as immutable as natural ones and "they're neither for nor against us" fails to persuade her: "what we're going through is down to people . . . alone" (177). He counters with the view that Corbin is "a harmful specimen, like scorpions, snakes, poison mushrooms" (178). While the metaphor is acute and the text hardly refutes it, we notice that Maurice is dehumanizing the bank director in much the same way that Gabriel Corte dehumanized his fellow refugees. The consolation Maurice claims is abstract: "my certainty that deep down I'm a free man" (178). Jeanne, however, tells him that God helps those who help themselves and heads back to the bank to call on its other director, Furières, who has always been kind to her and, she suspects, may welcome an opportunity to contradict Corbin. Jeanne succeeds, returning home with a commitment to six months' full salary and a belief that "heaven helped me" (179).

The text gives us no hint of divine intention; we note only that it portrays the faith of a competent and likeable human being, rather than attributing belief solely to emotionally troubled clergy or hapless victims. Jeanne's willingness to imagine the humanity of everyone she encounters may or may not be rewarded by God, but it helps her gauge the relationship between Furières and Corbin justly; in a scene she does not witness, Furières tells his codirector that he frightens him. Possibly, too, it gives her the courage to risk a painful confrontation.

Dolce

Storm in June focuses on the exodus of late May and June 1940; only its three final chapters are set during the German occupation. *Dolce*'s great topic is the German occupation: in particular, the relationships between soldiers and French civilians and the extent to which a relationship between two human beings can be free of their national origins and the loyalties they shape. Although the village church is a landmark mentioned numerous times and although the Angellier women attend Mass regularly, *Dolce* evokes religion less often than *Storm in June* and, when it does, with a different emphasis. The first volume evokes Catholic institutions, priests, and nuns to remind us that France is still pervaded by Catholicism but makes little reference to the church's political affiliations. The emphasis is on evocative passages from the Gospels and the often ironic contrast between stated belief and actual behavior.

But of course the question of how the institutional church and the government relate to each other has been a perennial issue in French politics since 1789, when the revolution overthrew the King, who had always ruled by divine right and traditionally with the full support of the Catholic hierarchy. The revolution zealously closed churches, destroyed crosses and other religious images, and by 1793 a priest who refused to swear loyalty was under a sentence of death. Anyone sheltering a priest was to die as well. Some thirty thousand priests fled France, and most Catholics lacked access to the sacraments. Jacques-Louis David's painting of Napoleon being crowned by the Pope in 1804 marks an iconic moment: the revolution was dead and the Catholic Church restored.

Given this history of outright antagonism between church and state, it is hardly surprising that the Third Republic formulated the principal of laicity —a rigid separation of church and state not balanced, as it is in the U.S. Constitution, by the right to "free exercise" of one's religion. Outside France, many people question a law passed in 2004 banning the wearing of religious symbols in state schools or in private schools receiving state funding. While a similar law would clearly be unconstitutional in the United States, it is defended in France as a logical extension of laicity, the principle that the public sphere should be purely secular. Nonetheless, the assumption that the republic, or democracy more generally, was an antagonist of the Catholic Church remained, as we saw in the 1930s when the Right, including fascists, defined the "real France" as Catholic. Franco's Spain and Mussolini's Italy, with their close alliances between fascism and Catholicism, were much more congenial models to the French Right than Nazi Germany, which in spite of its concordat with the Vatican regularly shut down Catholic schools, newspapers, and youth organizations.

So when Maréchal Pétain formed his government in June 1940, everyone took for granted that laicity, like other republican principles, would quickly be abandoned. The Archbishop of Bordeaux, preaching at the Cathedral of Notre Dame on June 25, called for a "new social order": France had been defeated because its people had failed to support the triple ideal of God, nation, and family (Duquesne 17). This penitential theme was adopted by Vichy officials, who counted on church support to restore order. Most historians conclude that "in 1940–41 the Church was hand in glove with the regime," citing as proof the declaration by the French Assembly of Archbishops and Cardinals of its "sincere and complete loyalty to the established power," that is, to Vichy (Halls 62).

It should be noted that much of this loyalty was personal, focused on the aging Maréchal Pétain, the hero of Verdun who claimed to have assumed the burden of office to make himself a "shield" between the occupiers and the native French. As Jacques Duquesne notes, a cult of personality, almost of sainthood, became associated with Pétain, the "providential and venerable man" (48). On November 11, 1940, the Bishop of Clermont-Ferrand thanked God that he had "blessed" France with the Maréchal and his "courageous and magnificent" outline for the "renewal of France" (49). This enthusiasm faded as conditions deteriorated: Hitler's decision to occupy the previously unoccupied zone in November 1942 and to conscript young men to work in Germany proved that Pétain could not protect France. However, the cult of the Maréchal was also supplemented with the kind of popular penitential enthusiasm one associates with the Black Death, and this passion had more staying power. "The Great Return," a procession of pilgrims accompanying a statue of Our Lady of Boulogne from Lourdes to towns throughout France, continued until June 1946, at one point crossing battle lines under protection of the Resistance (Duquesne 29). Popular superstitions, including texts of dubious prophecies by Malachi, St. Odile, and Nostradamus, circulated from hand to hand, often as clergy warned the faithful against them (27).

The strain of Catholicism that sanctified Pétain and saw the defeat of 1940 as an occasion for spiritual renewal is represented in *Dolce* by one of its least lovable characters, the Viscountess Montmort. In her, religious and political fanaticism are indistinguishable, both being tied explicitly to sexual frustration: "she had a passionate nature that was troubled by certain stirring images" but "no hope of the Viscount satisfying her, since he had little interest in women in general and her in particular" (166). At nights she cannot sleep for all her worries about "the future of the white race" or "the threat posed by Freemasons and Communism." By day she is zealous about her good works among the villagers, who detest her. She herself, as she organizes a village library, gives informative talks, and even invites young people to her home to view "edifying films," must struggle in a "spirit of mortification" because the village children, "fat and pink, overfed and with dirty faces, like little pigs," repel her (245, 266). The narrative continually points out her hypocrisy: it tells us, while she is urging poor villagers to donate food for prisoners, that her shoes cost 850 francs, and it depicts her bargaining with Madame Angellier to get contraband wheat for her chickens and refusing food from her estate to local farmers even when they offer to pay.

Before the war the Viscountess had been rabidly anti-German as well as anti-Semitic: "there was something wonderfully dramatic" about these hatreds, as there later would be in the "devotion to Maréchal Pétain" that "sent shivers down her spine" (262). In 1939 she lectured against Hitler, depicting all Germans as "madmen, sadists, and criminal"; during this time she also distributed "the famous prophecies of Sainte-Odile, who predicted the extermination of the Germans at the end of 1941" (262). Although she preaches to the villagers that the Maréchal is their "only consolation," by the summer of 1941 the viscountess is clearly on her way from sympathy with Vichy to a full embrace of collaboration with Nazi Germany (243). The viscount is appointed mayor of the village and soon is entertaining the occupiers, with whom he goes hunting; his attentiveness keeps the Germans from quartering their officers on his estate.

Like many conservatives, the viscountess thinks of Communism as the ultimate political evil and worries that the peasants are "becoming Bolsheviks" (312). Thus even in her anti-German phase she saw the Nazis as a lesser evil, and when she discovers that the German officers are "cultured men," she prefers them to her boorish tenants: "What separates or unites people is not their language, their laws, their customs, their principles, but the way they hold their knife and fork" (315). Her penitential take on the defeat, the hope of its prompting the regeneration of France, soon evolves into wondering "if she shouldn't thank the Good Lord for the German occupation of France" (312). When she catches a local farmer, Benoît, with his hands full of vegetables from her garden, "château and farm" are already waging "interminable guerilla warfare against each other" (313). He taunts her about her collaboration; in return, she reports him to German headquarters, grateful that "the Germans know how to bring people into line" (317). Thus she provokes the most disastrous local consequences of the occupation: the German discovery of Benoît's gun, his rapid killing of a German junior officer and his dog, and a regional manhunt after his escape.

The Viscountess Montmort—in her devotion to Sainte-Odile, in the consolation she finds in the Maréchal, and in her easy acceptance of local German headquarters as a substitute for legal authority—shows how closely Némirovsky observed the behavior of the institutional church and many of its followers during the first two years of the occupation. The Gospel is quoted only twice in *Dolce*, both times by the viscountess and both times with a sense of something like blasphemy. There is the time she justifies collaboration because "Jesus wanted us to love our enemies, didn't he?" and the time, quoting Matthew 10:34, she tells her husband to take action against local poachers because "our Lord Himself said: 'I have not come to bring peace but the sword'" (262, 310). Her husband snaps back, "You're not Jesus Christ," but the point is lost on her.

The viscountess, in short, is the embodiment of everything about the French church during the occupation that its critics condemn, just as Jeanne Michaud is the embodiment of a French women whose ethical values are those of the Gospel. In the event, as Némirovsky is already aware, the Catholic Church in Vichy France had many faces. The official one was repugnant, although even it evolved as conditions in France worsened and as German defeats multiplied. After the summer of 1942, when Némirovsky was deported, six Catholic bishops denounced the rounding up of Jews and "thousands of the clergy and faithful performed acts of charity." As René Bédarida summarized, "If a majority of the Jews in France, aliens and citizens alike, survived the genocide it was to a very great extent thanks to the help they received from Catholics and Protestants—sometimes as individuals, more often through their institutions (convents, boarding schools, presbyteries, associations, families)—where the potential victims were hidden and protected." Among those whose survival was entirely due to Catholic people and schools were Denise and Élisabeth Némirovsky, as their mother had hoped when she appointed Julie Dumot their guardian. The Jewish convert might truly be blasphemous but also expect some Christians to act decently.

A portrait of another angry and unsentimental Christian that may help us connect the contradictory perspectives offered in *Dolce* can be found in James Baldwin's "Stranger in the Village." Baldwin's father, an evangelical minister, literally died of paranoia, starving to death under the delusion that his wife and then the staff of the hospital where he was a patient meant to poison him. Encountering Swiss children collecting money for missions in Africa, Baldwin said that he avoided thinking about "these so lately baptized kinsmen, or of the price paid for them, or the peculiar price they themselves would pay, and said nothing about my father, who having taken his own conversion too literally never, at bottom, forgave the white world (which he described as heathen) for having saddled him with a Christ in whom, to judge at least from their treatment of him, they themselves no longer believed" (120).

Where a Charlotte Péricand hears a commandment to share with those who have nothing as a soothing formula easily abandoned in a crisis, the blasphemous convert imagines it as a call to action. One after another in *Storm in*

June, Némirovsky's characters imagine the world in May and June 1940 as a jungle, and in such a world the command to love others is a radical imperative, at odds with human nature. Moreover, as the case of Philippe Péricand illustrates, admiring that ethic, even passionately wishing to obey it, does not automatically bestow the deep clarity about one's own nature that makes recognizing and loving the humanity of the other possible. In the last months of her life, the "blasphemous convert," Irène Némirovsky, weighed the hypocrisy and inhumanity of Vichy France against the words and precepts of a religion in which, judging from their treatment of her, its natives no longer believed. In its sense that the fundamental words and beliefs of its established religion could be shaped into a powerful ethical and psychological critique of Vichy France's behavior, *Suite Française* is a Catholic novel.

Chapter 8

Dolce and the Unfinished *Suite Française*

Most of the surviving manuscripts, letters, and journals of Irène Némirovsky are assembled in the archives of IMEC (L'Institut mémoires de l'édition contemporaine), since 1995 housed in the Ardenne Abbey near Caen in Normandy. Some of this material is collected and translated in two appendices to Sandra Smith's translation of *Suite Française;* critics including Patrick Lienhardt and Olivier Philipponnat, Susan Suleiman, and Angela Kershaw quote from the archives liberally. Still, the scholar may occasionally stumble on something new, as this one did when reading the journal the author purchased as a newly arrived refugee from the Soviet Union and resumed in the war years, when, presumably, paper shortages made its blank pages useful. Over the years her handwriting, once sprawling, becomes microscopic; the early passages are occasionally written in impeccable English as well as in Russian and French. The unpaginated notebook is not a diary, and she records dates only infrequently. It is a collection of short poems, random thoughts, ideas for novels, and observations on art.

On a page dated November 4 that must have been written in 1940, she lists topics of "novels for a better time" ("Carnet" n.p.). She lists several topics and then begins a brief outline of the projected five volumes of *Suite Française.* It was striking to find the single word "Juifs" occupying the left-hand corner of a page. Unexplained and all the more striking for being the only word on the top line of a closely written page, this topic seems from its context to belong in *Suite Française.* As noted earlier, the projected third volume was to be called *Captivity;* the reference to a Jewish convert in a concentration camp was intended for that volume. Both fragments of evidence suggest that the complaint made about *Suite Française* when it was first published in English, that it lacked Jewish characters, may have more to do with Némirovsky's early deportation and death than with her conception of the whole work.

The notebook with its ambiguous reference to Jews is one more reminder that when we come to the final volume of the *Suite Française, Dolce,* we are reading a draft version of the second part of an unfinished work. We know that the author feared that her last novel would be posthumous; whether she also considered the possibility of surviving the camps and thus adding an autobiographical dimension to *Captivity* is unknowable.[1] But we can be sure that she did not think of *Dolce,* which covers the period from Easter 1941 to the German invasion of the Soviet Union on June 22, 1941, as her final word on Nazi Germany, the Second World War, or any other grand historical topic. We also know the autobiographical sources of its description of a village in occupied France.

Issy-L'Évêque, the Burgundian village where she and her husband lived after June 1940 until they were deported at separate times in 1942, was in the Occupied Zone.[2] To keep her daughters safe, Némirovsky sent them to board with Marie-Louise Mitaine, the mother of their nurse Cécile, after the declaration of war in 1939; in June 1940 their parents joined them. After the defeat Jews who were living outside of Paris at the time of the Armistice were forbidden to return to their homes in the city. At first the Némirovskys stayed at an inn where their fellow guests included German soldiers. Michel Epstein had served as a liaison with German customers at Banque du Nord, and he proved to be the only fluent speaker of both German and French in the village. As a result, he "served as an interpreter and even began to get along with two noncommissioned officers, Feldwebel (Sergeant) Ewald Hammberger and Lieutenant Franz Hohmann"; little Élisabeth was so fond of a soldier named Paul Spiegel that she called him *"mon petit chéri"* (PL 308). Only after the Germans left for the Eastern Front were the family able, in September 1941, to rent the fourteen-room house directly across from the police station where Denise and Elisabeth remained until their father was arrested in October 1942.

The apparent congeniality between Némirovsky's family and the Germans has been a source of contention for her critics. The fact that Michel Epstein sent a testimonial from Feldwebel Hammberger calling the family *"anstände"* and *"zuvorkommende"* (decent and obliging) to the German Ambassador, Otto Abetz, when he was seeking his wife's release earns Ruth Franklin's contempt, although it might arouse someone else's pity. Edward Rothstein seconded her point and complained in the *New York Times* that Némirovsky's ability to "sense the deepest moral flaws" in her French characters, while finding "virtue" in the Germans finally "become[s] a perversion."[3] In Rothstein's view, she avoided writing about Jews because she did not see how to make their plight fit into the war: she "thought she was writing a historical novel," but *Suite Française* lacks a "context" and "has no sense of history." Anyone so confident that in similar circumstances he or she would not have corresponded with fascists is welcome to that certainty. But the question of how German soldiers and French civilians actually interacted before July 1941 requires exploration.

Nazi ideology described Slavs, Jews, Roma, and others as "subhuman," a fact that doubtless contributed to the brutality of German soldiers' behavior in Poland and the Soviet Union. On the other hand, the English, the Dutch, and the Scandinavians, as Germanic peoples, were considered "fully human" and eligible for membership in the Nazi Party. The French were Germany's traditional enemy but in the racial mythology allied to the Spanish and Italians with their friendly fascist governments. Hitler also admired French culture and understood that his forces were spread thin over the continent. Thus Allan Mitchell, in his book on the occupation of France, writes of an early "German charm offensive" that included strenuous efforts to encourage Parisians to enjoy German music (28).

Mitchell argued "that German restraint" was a "common denominator in the first phase of the Occupation," which ended with the invasion of the Soviet Union (34). During the next year, 1942, the Germans executed some five hundred hostages in Paris alone (54). There is a correlation between the withdrawal of German forces in France and the increased harshness of the occupation; paradoxically, because fewer Germans were available, punitive regulations were more zealously enforced. But relations would probably have soured in any case, as Ambassador Abetz claimed they had by mid-September 1941, when French "passive resistance" had increased. A Professor Friedrich Grimm who toured France giving lectures intended to build solidarity with the natives had a similar complaint at the same time: initial French "stupor" had been replaced by "bitter recriminations," and in his view "a genuine reconciliation with France [was] not possible" (19). A year later the situation had deteriorated further. On November 10, 1942, after the Allies had landed in North Africa, Hitler's soldiers marched into Vichy territory in France. The Vichy secretary of the navy defected to join the Free French and De Gaulle in London, and his successor, Admiral Auphan, gave orders to scuttle the remaining French fleet at Toulon on November 27 to prevent its falling into German hands. By this point the idea of Vichy as an independent French state was all but indefensible.

Thus, although the German occupation always eventually led to atrocities, we should not expect daily life in a French village in spring 1941 to have been as harsh it was in Warsaw.[4] Irène Némirovsky did not portray the Nazi occupation positively, but she found it important to distinguish between official ideology and the young soldiers she lived among. A journal entry written soon after the troops departed for the Eastern Front reflects this distinction. After speaking briefly about her realistic "worries . . . threat of a concentration camp . . . the status of Jews," she goes on to describe the departing soldiers. Depressed at first by their new orders, they had become "cheerful" by the time they sent "their packages home" and went off "admirably disciplined and, I think, no rebellion in their hearts." Then she adds, "I swear here and now never again to take out my bitterness, no matter how justifiable, on a group of people, whatever their race, religion, convictions, prejudices, errors. I feel sorry for these poor children." But then she goes on to add that "I cannot forgive . . . those who reject me, who coldly abandon us, those who are prepared to stab you in the back" (*Suite Française,* appendix 1: 374). Many of those, doubtless, were former friends, and French.

Dolce begins with Easter 1941 in Bussy, a fictional version of Issy-L'Évêque, as the widowed Madame Angellier and her young daughter-in-law Lucile lock away the family's documents and silver in anticipation of German troops, the third contingent to have occupied their small village since the defeat the previous spring. Lucile's husband Gaston is a prisoner in Germany, and we quickly understand that Lucile "never loved" this "heavy, bored man, interested only in land, money, and local politics" (217). Although his mother adores Gaston, Lucile had married him only on her father's advice, after he "lost his fortune," and feels trapped under her mother-in-law's disapproving scrutiny. Though the Angellier house is the most beautiful in the neighborhood, frequent descriptions of its "iron bars," its "thick railings whose high spikes in the shape of a fleur-de-lis impaled any cat who wandered by," and its door with "the kind of lock you find on prisons and an enormous key that creaked dolefully" gives it a forbidding atmosphere; even the pear trees in the back yard "stretch out their arms, crucified on wires" (222). In this musty house kept cold to save on fuel, Lucile has no visitors and few pleasures other than reading or walking in her garden.

The long lines of soldiers who march in, accompanied by tanks, trucks, motorcycles, and cavalry horses, at first seem intimidating, but as they settle down in the village, they acquire names and individual characters. An old-fashioned convention, dating back to 1870, expects patriotic French people to close their windows when German soldiers march by and speak to them only when absolutely necessary. But as French and Germans live cheek to jowl, with soldiers billeted on civilians and everyone sharing the few stores and bistros, fraternization becomes inevitable. Relatively pleasant conditions, adequate food supplies, abundant sunshine, and fine weather promote good will. Merchants sell their goods to soldiers at inflated prices; mothers send their children to play in the ramshackle households where soldiers replaced owners who fled south; girls flirt with the only young men available; and almost everyone laughs sympathetically with "poor Johann who had lost his whole family in an air raid, 'except for my mother-in-law . . . because I've never had much luck'" (366). Some cultural misunderstandings, such as German contempt for white bread and the French view of the superiority of their own cuisine, are simply comic. "Germans more or less inherited the social status of their landlords" and become known as "the La Forges' Ewald, the Angelliers' Bruno" (236).

Yet this positive impression is balanced by a reminder that the soldiers, however ordinary and human, are enforcers of Nazi ideology. Their propaganda posters feature pictures of handsome soldiers giving French children slices of buttered bread but also include caricatures illustrating world domination by "the English and the detestable tyranny of the Jews." Long lists of activities are *verboten,* forbidden on pain of death: breaking the curfew, sheltering escaped prisoners or English soldiers, listening to the BBC, refusing to accept German currency (212). The locals never entirely forget that "Willy who asked permission to kiss my kid, saying he had one the same age in Bavaria" would, if "given the order, . . . kill me with his own hands without thinking twice" (333). Passive resistance coexists with cordiality; the local farmers refuse to vaccinate their children because the Germans order them to do so and toss German-issued rat poison in the fire.

Only two of the Germans, Bruno von Falk and Kurt Bonnet, emerge as more developed personalities. Von Falk is billeted in the Angellier house, a handsome young man with a courteous, ironic manner. When he realizes that Madame Angellier has locked both the piano and the library, he requests the keys in a note, adding "his word of honor that he will not remove the instrument or damage the books" (224). Von Falk is a gifted pianist who had planned a career as a composer; he speaks impeccable French and is well acquainted with the nation's culture. Anyone who has read a Gothic romance knows that when a bored but beautiful young woman is left alone in a house occupied by a dashing officer with much leisure on his hands, the two of them will fall in love. We suspect this outcome from Lucile and von Falk's first encounter in the third chapter, but other than an episode in which he asks permission to pick strawberries from the garden for the regimental German shepherd, Bubi, the love story hardly progresses until the tenth chapter. Possibly Némirovsky anticipated the dangers of finding positive qualities in a German officer and took care to evoke the occupation's ideological undergirding before moving into a personal story. For the same reason, she takes the time to introduce us to a Nazi officer of the conventionally evil kind in von Falk's cousin, Kurt Bonnet.

Bonnet is billeted on the Sabarie family, the same farmers who sheltered Jean-Marie Michaud after the defeat in *Storm in June.* The family's foster daughter, now married to their son Benoît, had been in love with Jean-Marie; the stage is set either for Madeleine to fall in love with the German or for her jealous husband to imagine that she has done so. In the version of *Dolce* we are reading, Bonnet's attentions seem unwanted; draft notes for *Captivity,* however, imply that the two are in love. Had Némirovsky wished to develop a love story later, she might have revised passages in this volume that clearly designate him as a war criminal. Herding French soldiers back to Germany "under orders to kill anyone who was flagging," Kurt had "shot the ones he didn't like the look of without remorse, with pleasure even" (230). As it is, an ironic reference to Bonnet as "a cultured man, gifted at all the arts" does not offset the descriptions of him as "more of a machine than a human being," as "leaning towards sadism," and having the "cruelty of adolescence" that cannot pity the sufferings of others because "he saw only himself" (228, 230, 231). He finds the French "barbaric and savage" because they carry chickens to market with their feet tied and their heads down; when the French read a notice banning this practice "beneath another announcement that eight men had been executed as reprisal for an act of sabotage," they are outraged and refuse to comply (231). This man is a Nazi through and through.

But Bruno von Falk is personally attractive and well mannered, and if he and Lucile seem drawn together partly by the conventions of Gothic romance, their shared cultural interests certainly offer a bridge to more personal conversations. However much the Viscountess Montmort's preference for Nazis who know how to "hold their knife and fork" over her own tenant farmers may appall us, we understand that a shared culture is part of Lucile and von Falk's mutual attraction. Madame Angellier, who sees any German as "the personification of cruelty, perversity, and hatred" rather than a human being, is for that reason incapable of "imagining that her daughter-in-law and the German could possibly care for each other" (302). But she has no trouble seeing the treachery of their shared cultural interests; when she finds "the German in his green uniform . . . the enemy" sitting beside Lucile, who is reading out loud to him, she vows to stay in her room until he leaves (307). His beautiful piano playing enrages her not only at Lucile, that "shameless hussy," but at music itself: "anything was better than music" that "can abolish difference of language or culture between two people and evoke something indestructible within them" (334).

As the author demonstrates, art is subversive of nationalism and ideology, and so is the belief in a private life. If the domestic novel sometimes seems to imprison women outside the world of effective social action, it also provides a space in which to isolate, protect, and nourish personal relationships. This space is the natural home of Jane Austen or Henry James, as it is of Irène Némirovsky, and the pathos of Lucile and von Falk's love is that it belongs there too. Even though he realizes that Madame Angellier's house "is like a prison," it is still the space where he and Lucile can speak frankly (273). He can admit that he and his wife married too young, against his mother's advice, that he "feels tied to a child who is still eighteen"; he can talk about his brothers killed in Poland and France. Here Lucile can admit, at least to herself, that she never loved her prisoner-of-war husband and hopes he dies (322).

Both the German officer and the French wife recognize the appeal of an inviolable private space. Von Falk puts it philosophically when he tells Lucile that "the principal problem of our times" is determining whether the individual is more important than the society. He describes Germany as the nation that puts "the communal spirit . . . the spirit of the hive" above everything else, yet he does so regretfully, promising Lucile that he will come back to find her after the war. Lucile more frankly despises the hive, "that evil, grumbling swarm serving some unknown end" (321). At this point she is repeating what Némirovsky wrote in her journal: "Don't talk to me about the spirit of the community" (*Suite Française* appendix 1:378).[5]

Love scenes require such private space, and von Falk and Lucile have only a few of them, usually subdued and undemonstrative. There is the time the power goes out in a rainstorm, silencing the "invisible cursed voices" of the radio news with its talk of "ships . . . sunk, planes crashing, cities destroyed" (287). It is "just blessed forgetfulness . . . time passing slowly, someone beside her . . . long silences. Happiness" (287). These periods of conversation sometimes turn into metaphorical spaces: Lucile's friendship with von Falk becomes "this dark secret, an entire universe hidden in the heart of the hostile house" (321). Enchanted with this space, Lucile defends it: the war is "not our fault . . . leave us in peace" (321). Though von Falk the soldier is constantly aware of the military duty that thwarts "his justifiable desires," he shares her belief that "between them was a harmony of senses that nothing could destroy" (344, 348). The desire for this domestic paradise is one of the world's oldest stories: "In the heart of every man and every woman a kind of Garden of Eden endures, where there is no war, no death, where wild animals and deer live together in peace" (348).

But as we know, the lovely idyll von Falk and Lucile experience for a few brief days in June can no more keep outsiders at bay than it can restore the earthly paradise or enable the lovers to leave the war to other people. The most obvious interruption is a catastrophic plot element involving Kurt Bonnet and the Sabarie family. Although Benoît was a German prisoner of war when his sister and future wife nursed Jean-Marie, he has heard the stories about her infatuation with the educated Parisian. If Benoît is intended as a basically good fellow, he certainly embodies the native peasant, proud of his coarse manners and unbathed body. He has no aspirations to the middle class and is easily provoked to jealousy by Madeleine's "lady's work—when she chose flowers, polished her nails . . . held a book" (247). He worries because he does not know the origins of this former foster child: rather than worry that her parents might have been alcoholics or thieves, he frets that they were middle class. When he pulls her roughly toward him, he senses a "stiffening throughout her body" that indicates "she didn't like him . . . She got no pleasure from him" (248). Kurt Bonnet is immediately the focus of his insecurities, since he believes Madeleine is prone to falling in love with any man whose hands are clean.

Benoît makes one attempt to solve the problem without violence; he goes to the Angelliers and asks them to persuade Bruno von Falk to make Bonnet "see reason" and find another lodging. He may have expected sympathy from them because his cousin Marthe has for decades been a cook for the Angelliers. A sensible solution, but von Falk rejects it, claiming that he has no such power over another officer. Lucile begs him to reconsider, telling him that Benoît is suffering and must not be pushed "over the edge" (271). Von Falk's refusal seems harsh, but he offers Benoît a partial explanation: "that would be letting him [Bonnet] in on the game and I wouldn't be doing you any favors" (271). He explains later to Lucile that "Bonnet is not a simple fellow. Until now, he's been having some innocent fun, but if the husband starts getting frustrated, he's capable of getting really involved. *Schadenfreude,* do you understand?" (286). This potential for taking pleasure in another's distress reinforces the earlier characterization of Bonnet as sadistic.

However, with no relief for his uncomfortable home life forthcoming, Benoît carries his frustrations to the Montmort estate. Class relations in the region are habitually close to a state of war. The only other landowner, Madame Angellier, "considered the food her tenant farmers ate . . . somehow stolen from her," and while the Viscountess de Montmort considers herself "more spiritual" than her bourgeois counterpart, her controlling personality makes her "the more hated" (274). As noted in the last chapter, "château and . . . farm waged silent, interminable guerilla warfare against each other," to the extent that when her tenants offer to buy food from her, the viscountess refuses. (313–14) When she catches Benoît stealing from her garden, she flies into a rage, and they hurl insults at each other. The viscountess returns home and insists that her husband report Benoît to German headquarters; since he boasted about coming back to hunt rabbits, she rightly assumes that he failed to follow German orders that Frenchmen turn in their rifles.

The Germans come to search the Sabarie farm and find a rifle in the cowshed. Denying that it is his, Benoît asks to check it; as soon as it is in his hands, he kills Bonnet and the regimental German shepherd, Bubi. He then jumps out of a window and, knowing the area better than the Germans, finds a temporary hiding place. That evening Madeleine is at the Angellier house, begging Lucile to shelter her husband. He is hiding with the seamstress, she says, but the woman has four small children, and the risk to them all is much too great. Lucile reminds her that a German officer is living in the house, but Madeleine has heard that "he is in love with you and that you can do whatever you like." Besides, she adds, "If we French don't help one another, who will?" (328). An hour later Lucile is letting Benoît in through a side door; three days later Madame Angellier catches Lucile coming back from the wine cellar and learns the truth. For once, her daughter-in-law has done something of which she approves; she insists that Benoît be moved into her own dressing room, where no would ever dare to look.

In the most literal sense, then, the Angellier house has ceased to be a space where Lucile can leave the war to other people, letting "everyone else fight one another, hate one another" (322). Recognizing the irony that in hiding the French peasant she has chosen her mother-in-law's patriotism, Lucile recognizes that "I've already chosen . . . in spite of myself. And I thought I was free" (338). Nor is there any hope that Bruno von Falk might be persuaded to look the other way. Whatever his reservations about Bonnet's character, the motives for his killing appear incomprehensible to him; for him as for Lucile, this incident reveals the depth of his national loyalties. He tells her, "My heart breaks at the thought of this nineteen-year-old boy being murdered. He was a very distant relative of mine. Our families know each other" (346). And what have the Germans "as people" done to the French? Taking refuge in an argument that later became infamous, he says, "we're just following orders; we're soldiers" (346). And even more "stupid and revolting" is the shooting of Bubi, the same strawberry-eating German shepherd that once provided him with an excuse for joining Lucile: "If I ever find that man, I'd happily kill him with my bare hands" (347). She tries to explain how the Frenchman had doubtless also nursed resentments, fantasizing about killing one of the Germans "or even one of their dogs" (347). The speed with which these declarations have sprung to the lovers' lips, "almost against their will," disconcerts them both. But there is no going back. Bruno attempts a bit of cultural relativism, linking his limited empathy for the French to their ascription of bad character to Germans mourning the fleet and colonies they lost in 1918. But he abandons the point, unable to compare "the resentment of a great people with one farmer's blind outburst of hatred" (347).

We can be sure that Némirovsky meant Bruno to pose the paradox of the "good German," the sane and well-meaning person who nonetheless went to war for Hitler. Bruno, she summarizes, "was the most human of men."[6] Although this characterization is an affront to critics who prefer their Germans satanic, it does not whitewash the Nazi party: "human" and "entirely virtuous" are hardly synonymous. Even before Bonnet's death brings the national differences between Lucile and himself into sharp relief, we are beginning to identify Bruno's shortcomings, some of which seem to stem from his Prussian upbringing. Off to requisition horses, for which their owners will be paid only half their value, Bruno "experienced a feeling of joy" because the air "reminded him of eastern Prussia." If he has any qualms, they are eased with a complacent reflection: "The French . . . understood nothing about horses" (320). Where women are concerned, he would hardly go so far as Bonnet, who quoted Nietzsche to Madeleine: "Man is made to be a warrior, just as woman is made to please the warrior" (232). But Bruno von Falk never questions the military ideal of following orders; as he tells Lucile, "Soldiers don't think" (272). He even identifies masculinity as a question of obedience: "Enthusiasm is a term a woman would use. A man does his duty even without enthusiasm. Perhaps that's the way you know he's a . . . real man" (273). Nor can we miss the unpleasantly egotistic fantasy that Lucile would make him a greater composer: "with her . . . I would be inspired" (344).

More troubling still is a passage in which Lucile walks through Bruno's room in his absence, remembering their "strange happiness," the urgency of conversations in which they felt the need to "reveal their hearts to each other . . . the gift of the soul before the body surrenders." But they have never spoken of love: "Words are pointless when your voices falter, when your mouths are trembling, amid such long silences" (324). But in which language will they speak of love? Lucy reaches out to touch the books on Bruno's table and is taken aback by how "bizarre . . . ugly" the Gothic lettering seems to her. The mood switches, and Lucy knows that Bruno has not yet spoken because of his "profound, German patience—the patience of a wild animal waiting for its hypnotized prey to let itself be taken" (324). For he told her that in war "waiting is erotic," and now she realizes that she is waiting. He will return, and she will tell him "in clear, simple French—that the prey he so desired was his" (324). A "sensual smile transformed her expression," as firelight can do: "Lit up by fire the softest features can look demonic; they can both repel and attract" (324). This is a telling passage, since it acknowledges for the first time the possibility that Lucile and Bruno's love is inflected by the circumstance that he is an occupying officer and she a Frenchwoman with few civil rights. Is it possible to confess love in "simple French" if the very letters of the loved one's language strike you as ugly?

Reader and characters, then, have some hints that national differences, nearly instinctive commitments to speakers of one's own language, will keep the characters from achieving their idyll. But it still seems a shock to the characters and perhaps to the reader as well when Bruno, already ordered to the Eastern Front, seizes Lucile in his arms. Suddenly she realizes that they are not in Eden but in wartime France, just outside the house in which she is helping to hide one of her countrymen from Germans who want to kill him. As the cold buckle of his uniform presses against her chest and his metal buttons catch on her dress, Lucile suddenly feels fear and revulsion: "The love that she had welcomed so willingly that she didn't believe it could be shameful, suddenly seemed to her disgraceful madness" (348). The German words he whispers heighten her sense of him as a "foreigner": "forever he would be the enemy, with his green uniform, with his heavenly beautiful hair" (348). They had counted on "the secret movements of blood to unite them," but that same instinctive emotion "now made them enemies" (348).

Bruno, in his usual sympathetic manner, gently helps Lucile detach the "chiffon ties of her dress" from his metal buttons. Then he says sadly, "I thought . . . that you cared for me." "I thought so too," she replies, "[but] it cannot be" (349). Shortly afterward she asks him, in a natural tone and with a plausible pretext, to give her the travel permit and gas coupons that will help Benoît escape; her first political step is to lie to the man who loves her. In a more conventionally political novel, the reader could only applaud her action. But Némirovsky is also writing a novel of manners, sharing its commitments to civilized restraint, to the place where Bruno and Lucile love each other, "an entire world of confused, unexpressed thoughts, like a precious crystal so fragile that a single word could shatter it" (364). Just as the novel tells us that war always sheds the youngest and most ardent blood first, it says war annihilates the world of unexpressed nuances on which Irène Némirovsky's art depends. But then in turn wartime also reveals how complex, multiple, and divided human beings are. In the same moment that she sees "a world of difference between the young man I'm looking at now and the warrior of tomorrow" (363), she realizes that earlier she would have thought herself incapable to lying to Bruno. Such troubling self-knowledge is often imputed to the protagonists of the novel of manners; it is the genre of truth they tell.

Dolce was intended as the second volume of a five-volume series, never completed because its author, having barely finished its last sentence, was deported to Auschwitz. We have a few sketchy ideas of how Némirovsky intended to develop the plot: Bruno would die in Russia; Lucile and Jean-Marie would meet and fall in love. And in any case the ending of the second volume of a five-volume series would have left options open. One possibility, probably inevitable given our knowledge of the author's fate or for that matter the horrors of Stalingrad, is to read pessimistically. If so, we agree with Bruno that "there will surely be much suffering, much heartache and much bloodshed" and "the happy times are over" (362). The last lines of the novel express loss: "Soon the road was empty. All that remained of the German regiment was a little cloud of dust" (367).

Even a more positive alternative will not allow us to forget Lucile's recognition that passion, "the obscure movements of blood" that she had counted on uniting her with Bruno, has met its match in the obscure movements of blood that bind her to France. While protesting that she was "nothing like them," she feels bound to her fellow countrymen "by invisible chains" (323). Yet there is a slight shift of mood when Lucile and Bruno part. Having accepted the loss of her physical desire for the German officer, she is no longer "ashamed of loving him" and feels instead "pity and a profound, almost maternal tenderness" (365). Bruno offers her a farewell gift, a painting of a ship against a threatening sky: "far in the distance, a hint of brightness on the horizon . . . a vague, very faint glimmer of hope" (362). She says she will accept it because "of this hint of brightness"; a moment later, she urges him to "be as careful as possible with your life . . . because it is precious to me" (365). This is the consolation of form, an artistic gesture valued as a faint trace of the civilization the war threatens, along with millions of lives.

Now this is a far cry from the triumphant joy Proust's narrator experiences at the end of *Search for Lost Time,* when he affirms that art transcends history, blotting out even the Dreyfus Affair and the Great War. The consolation *Dolce* offers in affirming that two people whom history separates can share the same appreciation of a painted "hint of brightness" and associate it with the same pale hope is much more modest. We are free to imagine the Angellier house going up in flames when struck by a crippled Spitfire. Nonetheless the painting is as integral to the novel we have just read as Hitler's decision to invade the Soviet Union. Némirovsky did not evade history when she incorporated features of the novel of manners in *Suite Française,* or when she put a love story set in a provincial village at the center of *Dolce,* rather than major battles or crucial political decisions. The novel of manners is well suited for exploring the desire for freedom and the ways the world constrains it. Its scrupulous care for subtle ethical and psychological distinctions, its gentleness toward nuances and shadows, is all the more valuable when its opponents are dictators and tanks, and not just repressive elders like Julien Hardelot or the stifling bourgeois traditions of *All Our Worldly Goods.*

"In my soul," thinks Bruno, "I am free" (344). He longs to love Lucile and to compose music, but of course a German officer ordered to the Eastern Front in 1941 has no such freedom. Lucile had also believed herself free before she realized that the invaders had already forced her to choose her own tribe, her own nationality. What distinguishes *Dolce* from many other stories set during the war is that Némirovsky has shown us why Lucile and Bruno value their personal integrity, their freedom to choose as individuals rather than as members of the hive. When Lucile helps Benoît, she acts courageously, making a choice the novel implicitly endorses. The alternative would be to align herself not only with the Germans but with the Vichy viscountess who informed on him. She acts courageously, for the penalty of hiding a wanted man is death, and she acts in the only way she can if she is to remain the essentially lucid and compassionate character the text shows her to be. Nonetheless, she has lost her personal freedom, compelled to choose sides in a war that is not only murdering people but also trampling on the world that makes and values art. In her last novel, Némirovsky is documenting a real loss, something threatened not only by an ideology of racism but by war itself, as even the just must wage it. It is not the love story, or novel of manners, as a failure to write history but as a history of violence destroying life and art.

Notes

Introduction

1. See Jaillant for a discussion arguing that "the text itself cannot be isolated from its packaging and marketing, on the one hand, and from its reception, on the other" (361).

2. The account provided here is the standard one to be found in PL and numerous other sources. However, Susan Suleiman suspects that while "not completely wrong," this story "simplifies things for greater dramatic effect" (256). Like many Holocaust survivors, Denise found speaking about her wartime experiences difficult. She "often hinted that Julie [Dumot, the wartime guardian of Némirovsky's children] had done something dishonest." There is evidence that Dumot may have kept the suitcase with the manuscript even after her return to France in 1954; Denise may not have received it until Julie's death in 1956 when it was followed by a letter from Catherine Descargues saying the manuscript was "altogether remarkable" and that "as it was unfinished, it could not be published." The evidence for this assertion is an obscure interview with Denise Epstein published in a Swiss newspaper, *Tribune de Lausanne,* in November 1956 (255–56). Unfortunately, Suleiman's excellent book appeared while this book was in press.

3. According to Oleg Budnitskii, "the first Jewish bank outside of the Pale of Settlement . . . was founded in St. Petersburg in 1850" (14). He also noted, "In 1855 there were less than 500 Jews in the capital; by 1910 the number was 35,000" (27).

4. See Budnitskii for a full account of anti-Semitism during the war. Estimates for the number of victims vary widely, presumably because of the era's extraordinary chaos: "Literature on the subject places the total number of victims anywhere in the range of 50,000 to 200,000 killed" (1).

5. The book was serialized in 1939 as *Les Échelles du Levant* but was retitled when published in book form in 2005. *Les Échelles du Levant* could be translated as "Ports of the Levant," but the more familiar meaning of échelles is "scales" or "ladders."

Chapter 1—Monstrous Mothers

1. Both "Poirier" and "Birnbaum" mean "pear tree." Rosine, who knows neither Yiddish nor German, fails to understand this inside joke: she wonders why anyone would choose to share a name with a tree.

2. Fortunately for the children, a group of friends of the family, which included André Sabatier, came together to provide for their care and education. Sabatier subsequently published Némirovsky's *Life of Chekhov* (1946), *All Our Worldly Goods*

(1947), and *The Fires of Autumn* (1957). Fanny Némirovsky lived until 1972. According to Denise Epstein, once the children were settled, "Julie Dumot took off in a hurry for the United States and no one ever heard from her again" (Corpet 40).

Chapter 2—The Russian Fiction

1. In *The Life of Irène Némirovsky,* Philipponnat and Lienhardt use direct quotations from this story to describe an incident in which the fourteen-year-old author watched as the Némirovsky's *dvornik,* Ivan R., was subjected to a mock execution. Undoubtedly the correspondence between life and fiction here is quite close, but it seems reasonable to read the story as fiction, subject to some shaping and rewriting. Their account, for example, suggests that the incident took place in March rather than February (60–64).

2. Ellman scrupulously cites archival evidence made available since the collapse of the Soviet Union and notes that "'victims of Soviet power' are poorly defined and controversial categories, so that differing estimates would be inevitable even if we had perfect statistics" (1162). If we count everyone who was deported or sentenced on political charges during the Soviet era, the figure might well be as high as 12 million (1163).

3. Other comparisons between *The Courilof Affair* and *Under Western Eyes* are briefly evoked in Sorin's "Societies of Misfits" and in "Terror among the Exiles," a review of *The Courilof Affair* that appeared in the *Telegraph of India.*

4. The fictional Victor Haldin kills "Minister de P. . ." in *Under Western Eyes* by throwing a bomb into the carriage in which he is riding. In real life, using the same tactic, Yegor Sazonov killed the czarist minister of the interior Vyacheslav von Plehve on July 28, 1904. As discussed below, the assassination of Courilof is probably based on the shooting of the czarist minister of education, N. P. Bogolepov, on February 14, 1901.

5. In this respect Léon M. resembles Joseph Conrad. Born in 1857 in an area of Ukraine that was once Polish, Conrad in 1862 accompanied his father into exile in Vologda, three hundred miles north of Moscow, after the father's arrest for organizing an insurrection against the Czar. Three years later Conrad's mother died of tuberculosis, which the family blamed on Vologda's miserable climate. In 1869 his father died of the same disease in Cracow. Thus, like Léon M., Conrad was a child and an orphan of revolution.

6. We do know that Némirovsky read Proust's *Swann's Way* and can be tempted to think that she named her revolutionary doctor after Proust's sympathetic Jewish lover, stockbroker, and patron of the arts. "Davidovitch," the name of Léon M.'s father, similarly signals Jewish birth. Although denunciations of Communism as Jewish were a commonplace of the period, *The Courilof Affair* otherwise pays little attention to the ethnic or religious origins of its revolutionaries. Léon M. also confides that he is living in France under the passport of a Latvian Jew who died in Soviet captivity.

7. Courilof and the Prince do speak favorably of Prince Michael (304). As the emperor's fourth daughter, Anastasia, has just been born, the absence of a male heir encourages some monarchists to talk of him as an heir. Léon M. is later freed from a Siberian camp as part of an amnesty following the birth of Prince Nicholas on August 12, 1904.

Chapter 3—David Golder, the Controversy, and One "Revision"

1. "Anti-Semitic" is Franklin's word. She cites Epstein's somewhat milder language earlier—that his wife had "no sympathy, and all her books show this . . . for Judaism."

2. It is understandable that a contemporary critic would expect a Jewish writer to address Jewish issues explicitly. However, it may be anachronistic to expect that Jewish writers in wartime France shared this view; it may have seemed more patriotic or more French to dwell on the fate of France. Jean Azéma makes this argument in his introduction to the journal of Léon Werth, a writer who survived the war in France and published his wartime diary afterward. Werth does not "deny his origins," but "there is no trace of Judeo-centrism" in his diary. In his own introduction, Werth says that it feels "indecent" to him, reading over his journal, to notice how centered it is on his own daily life. But he adds that he was nearly totally ignorant of the "extermination camps." (Azé ma 16–17; Werth 27)

3. For a review article on this subject, see Jeffries, "Truth, Lies, and Anti-Semitism."

4. Those interested in the history of this term should read Paul Reitter's *On the Origins of Jewish-Self Hatred*. He explores Theodor Lessing's popular *Der jüdische Selbsthass*, published in Germany in 1930 but points to its earlier origins in the journalism of Anton Kuh, an Austrian. Perhaps the most surprising fact Reitter uncovered is that the term was originally meant to be opposed to "Jewish anti-Semitism" and therefore to have "affirmative and even redemptive" meanings (122). Kuh "wants to see the aesthetic self-hatred of the prewar era politicized . . . into something that will engender a revolution-inspiring self-awareness" (64). That is, it involves a critical rejection of an older identity in favor of one that a Zionist of the 1920s might embrace. Lessing's book was republished by a Zionist press; the author was assassinated in Prague in 1933, probably by anti-Semites.

5. Martina Stemberger cites this quotation (201). It comes from the eighth chapter, where Hélène realizes that although she speaks French better than Russian, she is still not completely like the French children with whom she plays. She envies them because they were born in these tranquil grey neighborhoods, they are at home, and they have names like "Jeanne Fournier" or "Loulou Massard," which are "so easy to understand, to remember" (OC 1: 1221, 1222).

6. Brasillach was executed for treason after World War II. Louis Rebatet's death sentence was commuted in 1946, and he was released from prison in 1952. Drieu La Rochelle committed suicide in March 1945. That is, some French anti-Semites quickly accommodated themselves to collaboration with the Nazis.

7. "L'expérience juive d'Irène Némirovsky," *L'Univers israélite*, February 28, 1930.

8. When it was first serialized in *Gringoire*, the novel was called *Les Échelles du Levant*. When it was published as a book in 2005, the publisher, Denoël, chose *Master of Souls* to avoid repeating a title used in 1996 for a novel by Amin Maalouf; the English translation of that book is *Ports of Call*. Dario Asfar calls himself "the Master of Souls" in English (297). According to Philipponnat, "échelles" is a pun, meaning both "scales" (as found on a shop counter) and the hard "ladder" of success, which has neither a base nor a summit (OC 2: 205). As for Levantine, on page 218 Némirovsky lists Greece, Italy,

and Asia Minor as places where Asfars have lived. Levantine, however, is a word sometimes applied to Jews or used as a general term for people the French of the period also called "métèques": aliens, people from North Africa, the Middle East, or even southern Europeans. In a notebook she kept while drafting *Maître des âmes,* Némirovsky said, "I cannot say that he belongs to a homeless *(heimatlos)* race, because that is another word for Jews" (*OC* 2: 204). "Heimatlos" is used in the original, otherwise written in French. Recall that Susan Suleiman has observed of Dario Asfar that "although he is not explicitly identified as a Jew, he is clearly portrayed as one" ("Jewish Question" 23).

9. Daniel's negative assessment of his father, which also includes a reference to his brown skin, presents a sharp contrast to the descriptions of, say, David Golder and his friend Soifer. We cannot expect ethnic stereotyping to be rational, but it is curious that Nazi propaganda made so much of the sexually predatory Jew, the cigar-chomping caricature who posed such a threat to blonde German innocence. But Némirovsky often evokes the stereotype of the Jew as "Oriental," particularly when she is hedging about whether someone may really be "Levantine." This stereotype fixates on luxuriousness, effeminate features such as delicate hands, and a propensity for wearing scent and jewelry that more Nordic types disdain. Harry Sinner's father-in-law sees him in these terms.

Chapter 4—France and the Jews in the Thirties

1. As Angela Kershaw's *Before Auschwitz: Irène Némirovsky and the Cultural Landscape of Inter-war France* makes abundantly clear, Némirovsky was a professional writer well attuned to public tastes who managed her relationships with publishers carefully. But had Némirovsky really wished to "pander to the . . . fascist right" by continuing to "traffic in the most sordid anti-Semitic stereotypes," as Franklin asserts, there was little to stop her. Extremely anti-Semitic works like Paul Morand's 1934 *France-la-doulce* (a diatribe against refugees from Hitler) and Louis-Ferdinand Céline's *Bagatelles pour un Massacre* were selling briskly. Often described as untranslatable, the latter is a free-associative rant against Jews; by page 6 the text is already denouncing literary critics as "Jewish cops." *Bagatelles* has not been republished in France since the liberation; Céline's widow, Lucette Destouches, in 2015 still giving interviews at age 103, has said her husband did not want it to be. As a result, the text has become rare; the single copy recently available on Amazon was priced at $332.24. Perhaps we should not be surprised that it is available online from *VHO,* which describes itself "the world's largest site for historical revisionism," or as the unsympathetic might say, "Holocaust denial."

2. An Internet search reveals that most Bohuns are English, though of Norman origin; the search also turns up an occasional Ukrainian or Cossack. It is certainly not a Greek name.

3. They have the same initials, which does not seem like a coincidence. Is there a suggestion that Abel Sarlat is also an outsider? Sarlat, the name of an old medieval town in the south of France, is certainly a native name. On the other hand, "Abel," with its roots in the Hebrew Bible, hardly seems like a name Némirovsky would have chosen if she had wanted to make him unambiguously French.

4. Does Edith have a right to the stocks left to her (and not to her husband) in her father's will? The answer is more difficult than it may seem. That she has a moral right

Jean-Luc himself acknowledges when Cottu first proposes buying them, asking him whether he knows the shares belong to his wife (1719). The Napoleonic Code provided that women could not dispose of their property except in a will. As far as we know, Jean-Luc never discusses the possibility of selling the shares with Edith; he alone decides against the sale. However, when Edith and Jean-Luc are in the process of separating, she reproaches him for having had the means to get money when she was ill and failing to do so: "You think I didn't know about your calculations?" (1773). In principle, French laws in 1938 and 1942 "put an end to the husband's authority and the legal incapacity of married women," although A. Colomer concludes that in practice "the wife's position under the community of practice system had hardly changed" because third parties, lacking sufficient safeguards, "made a point of insisting on the husband's agreement (82)." In Colomer's view, the system did not effectively change until 1965.

5. As the book was serialized before its publication in 1938, the better-remembered Munich Agreement (September 29, 1938) is an unlikely candidate.

Chapter 5—The "Bond of Tears" and Jewishness in the Late Fiction

1. "Le Spectateur" ["The Spectator"] appears in *Dimanche and Other Stories.* Note that Patterson's translation retains original French titles, followed by the bracketed English. Thus the next story analyzed, also contained in that collection, is called "Fraternité" ["Brotherhood"].

2. A lawyer, writer, and literary critic, Loewel (1890–1955), who was Jewish, called *David Golder* "a miracle" in 1930. Philipponnat and Lienhardt characterize him as "one of her most attentive readers" (PL 155, 325). The biographers quote his review of *The Dogs and the Wolves,* which predicted a terrible fate for its heroine, Ada Sinner: "You will learn how the threat of a resounding collapse will condemn her to the holocaust" (PL 304). (The term "holocaust" did not become a familiar shorthand for the destruction of Europe's Jews until the 1960s.) Although Philipponnat quotes from his review of *The Dogs and the Wolves* (1940) in the Parisian journal *L'Ordre,* he also indicates that Loewel left France for Palestine on the "*Champollion* in July 1939" (*OC* 2: 388).

3. Although Hugh Grayer is probably based on Loewel, who also emigrated, Grayer is portrayed as a Gentile, one with sufficient Christian education to recall a passage from the Gospels in a crisis. He is also a rootless wanderer with no real homeland, the historical condition of many European Jews in the 1930s but one for which fascist propaganda frequently attacked them.

4. See Matthew 6:25 and Luke 12:23.

5. Quoted and translated by Suleiman from the Némirovsky archives at L'Institut mémoires de l'édition contemporaine, Caen, France, NMR 14.3, "Fraternité."

6. For more on *Gringoire,* see Suleiman, "Némirovsky in Context." She says it "is misleading to suggest that it was of the same ilk as the extreme right-wing papers *L'Action Française* and *Je Suis Partout* at the time." Suleiman notes that the editor, Horace de Carbuccia, "took risks in publishing Némirovsky's stories under a pseudonym" to evade the law against publishing Jewish writers. Payments from *Gringoire,* along with a monthly stipend from her book publisher, Albin Michel, were crucial to keeping the once-wealthy Némirovsky family modestly comfortable under Vichy restrictions (PL

319). Alice Kaplan ("La Zone Grise") notes that Colette continued to publish in *Gringoire* while hiding her Jewish husband from arrest.

7. Here the literal French is *"plus éloigné de ce Juif que d'un marchand de lunettes oriental,"* the precise phrase Pierre Loewel used.

8. The cliché "man's best friend" is English, but certainly the sense of a dog as a benign pet carries into French. *"Chien"* also has a secondary meaning: "executioner."

9. Because the book was published the same month that the Germans invaded, its original French edition received little notice, other than the Pierre Loewel review already quoted.

10. In July 1940 the Vichy government set up a commission to investigate French citizens naturalized since 1927 and to strip those found undesirable of their French nationality. Six thousand Jews were among the fifteen thousand people thus stripped of their citizenship (Marrus 4, 5).

Chapter 6—The "Vichy" Novels

1. Pétain was sentenced to death for treason, but his sentence was commuted, in part because of his advanced age. He died in 1951 at the age of ninety-five. His successor as head of state, Pierre Laval, was executed by firing squad on October 15, 1944.

2. Although Saint-Elme, being fictional, has no precise location on a map, a village that was part of the "devastated region" of the First World War would likely have been located in the Excluded Zone of the Second. The French were also forbidden to live in the military zone along the Atlantic coast.

3. The trial at Riom was covered by foreign newspapers, including the *New York Times,* so Blum's courageous defense was publicized elsewhere. Someone in Némirovsky's situation, isolated and dependent on a censored press, would have needed to hear the news from someone who listened to the forbidden BBC. Although the practice of listening clandestinely to BBC broadcasts is mentioned in *Suite Française,* we have no way of knowing how familiar she was with their contents.

4. Philip Nord's *France 1940: Defending the Republic* (2015) is framed as a debate between this "moral judgment on France as a nation," which was to have a "long life" and a "more sympathetic understanding" that "sets the French experience in a comparative perspective" (xiii, xvi).

5. I am quoting here from the King James Version but amending that text's reference to the prophet "Jonas" to the more familiar "Jonah."

Chapter 7—The "Catholic Némirovsky"

1. The Catholic Church recognizes apparitions of the Virgin Mary as "private revelations," which the Holy See may or may not declare "worthy of belief," but such "belief is never required by divine faith." According to Father Salvatore M. Perrella of the Marianum Pontifical Institute in Rome, "of the 295 reported apparitions studied by the Holy See through the centuries only 12 have been approved" ("Apparitions"). Lourdes is one of these. Hence the rather sobering name of the website Decent Films does not prevent a contemporary reviewer from giving the film an A+ rating even though its "subtlety and nuance" leave reasonable questions about the apparition's validity unresolved.

Stephen D. Greydanus, who maintains the website, is a critic for the *National Catholic Register* and *Catholic Digest*.

2. Oxford University Press, 1952. The book has been republished several times, most recently, in January 2015, by Faber and Faber.

3. The most famous of such proclamations of course was Theodor Adorno's "To write poetry after Auschwitz is barbaric" ("Cultural Criticism and Society"). This phrase is more familiar to many from a less literal translation, "No poetry after Auschwitz."

4. The French text more literally speaks of an "adored" Christ with "adorable feet." Like the English "to adore," the French "adorer" moves easily between religious and sensual contexts.

5. The wonderful French phrase *"morale selon les circonstances,"* or "as moral as circumstances permit," becomes "moral exhortations" in the published translation.

6. In an unpublished revision of this episode, Némirovsky turned Philippe Péricand into a hero modeled on her friend Father Bréchard, a lieutenant who was killed on June 20, 1940, as he and a handful of men were defending a village in the Vosges Mountains. His fate, like that of his model Bréchard, becomes in the revised version "a signal of his redemption": "He was not killed immediately. He had time to pick up his crucifix and place it on his lips" (Weiss 96).

7. Most of this scenario is based on the experience of Michel Epstein, the author's husband. While most of the bank's personnel were already in Clermont-Ferrand, Michel was ordered to remain in Paris. He remained until June10, when he left for Orléans; according to his doctor, he was "at the end of his tether" (PL 306). Philipponnat and Lienhardt further note, "Joseph Koehl, the managing director, would hear of no excuses, neither a medical certificate, nor the military defeat: by refusing to remain at the bank . . . Michel had signed his own dismissal, after fifteen years of impeccable service." Like Maurice, Michel was offered a minimal "termination payment" of "only 8,027 francs in mid-August, plus a 'bonus' of 5,000 francs at the end of October" (PL 310).

Chapter 8—*Dolce* and the Unfinished *Suite Française*

1. She wrote to her editor about her current writing on July 11, 1941, two days before her arrest, noting that "I suppose they will be posthumous works." See Myriam Anissimov, "Preface to the French Edition," *Suite Française,* trans. Sandra Smith, 421–31, 428.

2. We should note that it was close to the border of notionally independent Vichy France, so that "there was a persistent rumor that the demarcation line could be withdrawn" (PL 310).

3. He further complained that Némirovsky asked for favors from Pétain and that Epstein fraternized with German troops: "In 1940 Némirovsky, accustomed to being championed by the right, wrote a letter to Marshal Pétain, head of the Nazi-aligned Vichy government, objecting to the fact 'that no distinction is made between the undesirable and honorable foreigners'; she humbly requested to be included in the 'latter category.'" Epstein regularly played billiards with German officers. When Némirovsky was arrested, he wrote to the German ambassador, pointing out that while his wife was

"of Jewish origins," her books proved "she has no sympathy for either Judaism or for the Bolshevik regime." The quotations are accurate, but there may be some room for judging the context.

4. Léon Werth, another Jewish writer and intellectual, the person to whom Antoine Saint-Exupéry dedicated *The Little Prince,* kept a journal of the war years that often mirrors Némirovsky in tone and emphasis. He also described the German troops of occupation as at first "very correct, and a major contrast with the shambles of the French forces during the debacle" (Azéma 16, 17).

5. Némirovsky's journal, however, goes on to formulate a thought that does not occur to Lucile, "that dictatorship is built around" the "confusion" of "all men with "one man" (378). To Némirovsky "they're trying to make us believe . . . the individual must perish so that society may live," but what is happening is that "society is dying so the tyrants can live" (378).

6. A literal translation of *"Le plus humain des hommes"* (OC 2: 1817). Smith's translation is "was a sensitive human being" (344).

Bibliography

Adorno, Theodor. "Cultural Criticism and Society." *Prisms*. Trans. Samuel and Shierry Weber. Cambridge, Mass.: MIT Press, 1981. 17–35.

"Apparitions and Appearances." *Catholic Online*. http://www.catholic.org/mary/appear.php. Accessed February 15, 2016.

Armstrong, Nancy. *Desire and Domestic Fiction: A Political History of the Novel*. Oxford, U.K.: Oxford University Press, 1987.

Arnold, Matthew. "Letter to Mrs. Forster." (April 24, 1853). Letter VIP262D1. *Letters of Matthew Arnold: A Digital Edition*. Rotunda, University of Virginia Press. http://rotunda.upress.virginia.edu/arnold/. Accessed April 7, 2016.

Auscher, Janine. "Une interview de l'auteur de *David Golder*" *L'Univers israelite*. 5 July 1935.

Azéma, Jean. "Présentation." Introduction. *Déposition: Journal 1940–1944*. By Léon Werth. Ed. Lucien Febvre. Paris: Viviane Hamy, 1992. 9–19.

Baldwin, James. "Stranger in the Village." *Collected Essays*. New York: Library of America, 1998. 117–29.

Baudrillard, Jean. *The Gulf War Did Not Take Place*. Bloomington: Indiana University Press, 1995.

Bédarida, René. "The Catholic Hierarchy in France during the War and the Persecution of the Jews." Yad Vashem, Shoah Resource Center. http://www.yadvashem.org/odot_pdf/Microsoft%20Word%20-%20686.pdf. Accessed March 3, 2016.

Benjamin, Walter. "On the Concept of History." Thesis 8, 1940. Trans. Dennis Redmond, 2005. https://www.marxists.org/reference/archive/benjamin/1940/history.htm. Accessed January 19, 2016.

Birnbaum, Pierre. *Léon Blum: Prime Minister, Socialist, Zionist*. Trans. Arthur Goldhammer. New Haven, Conn.: Yale University Press, 2015.

Bobo, Jacqueline. "Black Women's Responses to *The Color Purple*." *Jump Cut: A Review of Contemporary Media* 33 (February 1988). https://www.ejumpcut.org/archive/onlinessays/JC33folder/ClPurpleBobo.html. Accessed July 16, 2015.

Bracher, Nathan. *After the Fall: War and Occupation in Irène Némirovsky's* Suite Française. Washington, D.C.: Catholic University of America Press, 2010.

Brontë, Charlotte. "Biographical Notice of Ellis and Acton Bell." 1850. *The Oxford Companion to the Brontës*. Oxford Reference, 2011. http://www.oxfordreference.com/view/10.1093/oi/authority.20110803095506987. Accessed April 25, 2016.

Brown, Frederick. *The Embrace of Unreason: France, 1914–1940*. New York: Random House, 2014.

Budnitskii, Oleg. *Russians Jews between the Reds and the Whites: 1917–1920*. Trans. Timothy Portice. 2005. Philadelphia: University of Pennsylvania Press, 2012.

Burke, Edmund. *Reflections on the Revolution in France*. Ed. Frank M. Turner. 1790. New Haven, Conn.: Yale University Press, 2003.

Céline, Louis-Ferdinand. *Bagatelles pour un massacre*. Paris: Denoël, 1937. Available at *VHO: The World's Largest Website for Historical Revisionism*. http://vho.org/aaargh/fran/livres4/bagat.pdf. Accessed April 21, 2016.

Chartier, Roger. "Histoire des mentalités." *Columbia History of Twentieth-Century French Thought*. New York: Columbia University Press, 2006. 54–58.

Cocteau, Jean. *Le Passé défini II*. Paris: Gallimard, 1985.

Coetzee, J. M. "Irène Némirovsky: The Dogs and the Wolves." *New York Review of Books*, November 2008. http://www.nybooks.com/articles/2008/11/20/irene-nemirovsky-the-dogs-the-wolves/. Accessed April 7, 2015.

Cohen, Patricia. "Assessing Jewish Identity of Author Killed by Nazis." *New York Times*, April 25, 2010. http://www.nytimes.com/2010/04/26/books/26nemirovsky.html. Accessed February 3, 2015.

Cohn-Sherbok, Dan. *Holocaust Theology*. London: Lamp, 1989.

Cointet, Michèle. *L'Église sous Vichy: 1940–1945: La repentance en question*. Paris: Librairie Académique Perrin, 1998.

Colomer, A. "The Modern French Law." *Comparative Law of Matrimonial Property*. Ed. Alfred Kiralfy. Leiden, Netherlands: A. S. Sijthoff, 1972. 80–113.

Conrad, Joseph. *Under Western Eyes*. 1911. New York: Anchor-Doubleday, 1963.

Corpet, Olivier, and Emmanuelle Lambert. "Interview with Denise Epstein." *Woman of Letters: Irène* Némirovsky and Suite Française. Ed. Olivier Corpet and Garrett White. New York: Five Ties, 2008. 33–48.

Davis, Natalie Zemon. "On the Lam." *AHR* Forum on *The Return of Martin Guerre*. *American Historical Review* 93.3 (1988): 572–603.

———. *The Return of Martin Guerre*. Cambridge, Mass.: Harvard University Press, 1983.

"Denise Epstein." *Telegraph*, April 27, 2013.www.telegraph.com.uk Accessed April 25, 2016.

Duquesne, Jacques. *La catholique Français sous l'occupation*. 2nd ed. 1966. Paris: Bernard Grasset, 1986.

Ellman, Michael. "Soviet Repression Statistics." *Europe-Asia Studies* 54.7 (2002): 1151–72.

"Fall Festival Preview." *Indie Wire*, July 8, 2014. http://www.indiewire.com/2014/07/fall-festival-preview-40-films-that-could-debut-in-venice-toronto-telluride-or-new-york-24529/. Accessed September 3, 2014.

Faulkner, William. *The Mansion*. New York: Vintage-Random House, 1965.

Flanner, Janet. *Paris Was Yesterday*. New York: Viking, 1972.

Franklin, Ruth. "Scandale Française: The Nasty Truth about a New Literary Heroine." *New Republic,* January 30, 2008. https://newrepublic.com/article/61151/scandale-francaise. Accessed April 21, 2016.

Gille, Elisabeth. *The Mirador: Dreamed Memories of Irène Némirovsky by her Daughter.* Trans. Marina Harss. 1992. New York: New York Review of Books, 2011.

Gilman, Sander. *Anti-Semitism and the Hidden Language of the Jews.* Baltimore: Johns Hopkins University Press, 1986.

Gorman, James. "The Big Search to Find Out Where Dogs Came From." *New York Times,* January 18, 2016. https://www.nytimes.com/2016/01/19/science/the-big-search-to-find-out-where-dogs-come-from.html?_r=0 m. Accessed January 19, 2016.

Gourfinkel, Nina. "L'expérience juive Irene Némirovsky." *L'Univers israelite.* 28 February 1930.

Greydanus, Stephen D. Rev. of *Song of Bernadette. Decent Films.* http://decentfilms.com/reviews/songofbernadette. Accessed February 15, 2016.

Guéhenno, Jean. *Diary of the Dark Years 1940–1994: Collaboration, Resistance, and Daily Life in Occupied Paris.* Trans. David Bell. 1947. Oxford, U.K.: Oxford University Press, 2014.

Gutiérrez, Gustavo. *A Theology of Liberation.* 15th anniversary edition with a new introduction by the author. Trans. and ed. Sister Caridad Enda and John Eagleton. 1971. Maryknoll, N.Y.: Orbis, 1991.

Halls, W. D. *Politics, Society and Christianity in Vichy France.* Oxford, U.K.: Berg, 1995.

Jackson, Julian. *The Fall of France: The Nazi Invasion of 1940.* Oxford, U.K.: Oxford University Press, 2003.

Jaillant, Lise. "A Masterpiece Ripped from Oblivion: Rediscovered Manuscripts and the Memory of the Holocaust in Contemporary France." *Clio* 39.3 (2010): 359–79.

Jankowski, Paul F. *Stavisky: A Confidence Man in the Republic of Virtue.* Ithaca, N.Y.: Cornell University Press, 2002.

Jeffries, Stuart. "Truth, Lies, and Anti-Semitism." *Guardian,* February 22, 2007, https://www.theguardian.com/world/2007/feb/22/secondworldwar.religion.com. Accessed July 16, 2015.

Kaplan, Alice Yeager. *Reproductions of Banality: Fascism, Literature, and French Intellectual Life.* St. Paul: University of Minnesota Press, 1986.

———. "La Zone Grise." *Nation,* April 3, 2008. https://www.thenation.com/article/la-zone-grise/. Accessed April 22, 2016.

Kassow, Samuel D. *Students, Professors, and the State in Tsarist Russia.* Berkeley: University of California Press, 1989.

Kershaw, Angela. *Before Auschwitz: Irène Némirovsky and the Cultural Landscape of Inter-war France.* New York: Routledge, 2010.

Kritzman, Lawrence T. "Histoire des mentalités." *The Columbia History of Twentieth-Century French Thought.* New York: Columbia University Press, 2006. 54–58.

Malinovich, Nadia. *French and Jewish: Culture and the Politics of Identity in Early*

Twentieth-Century France. Oxford, U.K.: Littman Library of Jewish Civilization, 2012.

Marle, Laurence. "Counter to Cliché, French Translations Sell Better than Ever." *Publishing Perspectives,* January 2, 2014. http://publishingperspectives.com/2014/01/counter-to-cliche-french-translations-sell-better-than-ever/. Accessed September 3, 2014.

Marrus, Michael, and Robert Paxton. *Vichy France and the Jews*. 1981. Stanford, Calif.: Stanford University Press, 1995.

Martin, Benjamin. *France and the Après Guerre, 1918–1924: Illusions and Disillusionment*. Baton Rouge: Louisiana State University Press, 1999.

Mitchell, Allan. *Nazi Paris: The History of an Occupation, 1940–1944*. New York: Berghahn, 2008.

Morand, Paul. *France-la-doulce*. Paris: Gallimard, 1934.

"My Sweet Mother's Voice Lives on in Suite Française." *Sunday Times* (London), February 18, 2007. http://www.thetimes.co.uk/article/my-sweet-mothers-voice-lives-on-in-suite-francaise-82jlgrtgvg7. Accessed February 3, 2015.

Némirovsky, Irène. *All Our Worldly Goods*. Trans. Sandra Smith. New York: Vintage, 2008.

———. "Carnet avec poèmes et notes." NMR 7.1 IMEC. L'Institut mémoires de l'édition contemporaine. Abbaye d'Ardenne. Caen, France. Accessed June 2, 2015.

———. *The Courilof Affair*. Trans. Sandra Smith. Toronto: Vintage Canada, 2008.

———. *David Golder, The Ball, Snow in Autumn, The Courilof Affair*. Trans. Sandra Smith. New York: Knopf, 2008.

———. *Dimanche and Other Stories*. Trans. Bridget Patterson. New York: Vintage, 2010.

———. *The Dogs and the Wolves*. Trans. Sandra Smith. New York: Vintage, 2010.

———. *Fire in the Blood*. Trans. Sandra Smith. New York: Vintage, 2008.

———. *The Fires of Autumn*. Trans. Sandra Smith. New York: Vintage, 2015.

———. *Jezebel*. Trans. Sandra Smith. New York: Vintage, 2012.

———. *A Life of Chekhov*. Trans. Erik de Mauny. London: Grey Walls, 1950.

———. *The Misunderstanding*. Trans. Sandra Smith. New York: Vintage, 2013.

———. *Oeuvres complètes*. 2 vols. Ed. Olivier Philipponnat. Paris: Livre de poche, 2011.

———. *Suite Française*. Ed. Myriam Anissimov. Paris: Denoël, 2004.

———. *Suite Française*. Trans. Sandra Smith. New York: Vintage, 2007.

———. *The Wine of Solitude*. Trans. Sandra Smith. New York: Vintage, 2011.

Nord, Phillip. *France 1940: Defending the Republic*. New Haven, Conn.: Yale University Press, 2015.

O'Donnell, Donat [Conor Cruise O'Brien]. *Maria Cross: Imaginative Patterns in a Group of Modern Catholic Writers*. New York: Oxford University Press, 1952.

Patterson, David. *Open Wounds: The Crisis of Jewish Thought in the Aftermath of Auschwitz*. Seattle: University of Washington Press, 2006.

Perry, Matt. *Memory of War in France, 1914–1945: César Fauxbras*. New York: Palgrave-Macmillan, 2011.

Philipponnat, Olivier, and Patrick Lienhardt. *The Life of Irène Némirovsky: 1903–1942*. Trans. Euan Cameron. New York: Knopf, 2010.

Pottecher, Frédéric. *Le procès de la défaite: Riom Février-Avril 1942*. Paris: Fayard, 1989.

Price, Naomi. "Out of the Ghetto." Review of *The Dogs and the Wolves. Times Literary Supplement*. 30 October 2009, p. 21. https://www.the-tls.co.uk Accessed 3 July 2017.

Prose, Francine. "The Némirovsky Paradox." *New York Times Book Review*. 6 May 2010. https://nytimes.com. Accessed 5 July 2017.

Reitter, Paul. *On the Origins of Jewish Self-Hatred*. Princeton, N.J.: Princeton University Press, 2012.

"Return of the Repressed." *International Dictionary of Psychoanalysis*. Detroit: Thomson Gale, 2005. Encyclopedia.com. http://www.encyclopedia.com/psychology/dictionaries-thesauruses-pictures-and-press-releases/return-repressed. Accessed April 27, 2016.

Rothstein, Edward. "Ambivalence as Part of a Writer's Legacy." *New York Times*, October 20, 2008. http://www.nytimes.com/2008/10/21/arts/design/21nemi.html. Accessed March 25 2016.

Saintsbury, George. Introduction. *Vanity Fair: A Novel without a Hero*. By William Makepeace Thackeray. 1848. Oxford, U.K.: Oxford University Press, 1954. xi–xxii.

"Sandra Smith." Pen America. https://pen.org/user/sandra-smith/. Accessed September 3, 2014.

Smith, Sandra. "In Defence of Irène Némirovsky," *Times Literary Supplement*, Letters (November 2009): 11. *https://www.the-tls.co.uk*. Accessed 3 July 2017.

Soelle, Dorothee. *Theology for Skeptics*. Trans. Joyce L. Irwin. 1992. Minneapolis: Fortress, 1995.

Sorin, Gerald. "Societies of Misfits." *Haaretz*, February 10, 2008. http://www.haaretz.com/news/societies-of-misfits-1.239000. Accessed April 7, 2015.

Stemberger, Martina. *Irène Némirovsky: Phantasmagorien der Fremdheit*. Würzburg, Germany: Königshausen-Neumann, 2006.

Steiman, Lionel. *Franz Werfel: The Faith of an Exile*. Waterloo, Ontario: Wilfrid Laurier University Press, 1985.

"The *Suite* Smell of Success." *Upstart Business Journal*, May 14, 2008. http://www.upstartbizjournals.com. Accessed September 3, 2014.

Suleiman, Susan. *The Némirovsky Question: The Life, Death, and Legacy of a Jewish Writer in Twentieth-Century France*. New Haven: Yale University Press, 2016.

Suleiman, Susan Rubin. "Irène Némirovsky and the 'Jewish Question' in Interwar France." *Yale French Studies* 121 (2012): 8–33.

———. "Némirovsky in Context." Letter to the editor. *New York Times Book Review*, May 28, 2010. https://mobile.nytimes.com/2010/05/30/books/review/Letters-t-NMIROVSKYINC_LETTERS.html. Accessed February 7, 2011.

"Terror among the Exiles." *Telegraph of India*, March 27, 2009. https://www.telegraphindia.com/1090327/jsp/opinion/story_10725203.jsp. Accessed April 7, 2015.

U.S. Department of Justice. "World War I Casualty and Death Tables." http://www.pbs.org/greatwar/resources/casdeath_pop.html. Accessed October 1, 2015.

Walker, Lesley H. *A Mother's Love: Crafting Feminine Virtue in Enlightenment France*. Lewisburg, Penn.: Bucknell University Press, 2008.

Weber, Eugen. *Action Française: Royalism and Reaction in Twentieth-Century France*. Stanford, Calif.: Stanford University Press, 1962.

———. *The Hollow Years: France in the 1930s.* New York: Norton, 1995.

Weiss, Jonathan. *Irène Némirovsky: Her Life and Works.* Palo Alto, Calif.: Stanford University Press, 2006.

Werth, Léon. *Déposition: Journal 1940–1944.* Ed. Lucien Febvre. 1946. Paris: Viviane Hamy, 1992.

Young, Robert. *In Command of France: French Foreign Policy and Military Planning, 1933–1940.* Cambridge, Mass.: Harvard University Press, 1978.

Index